P9-CQR-404

# New Ways to Kill Your Mother

*Writers and Their Families*

COLM TÓIBÍN

SCRIBNER

New York   London   Toronto   Sydney   New Delhi

For Andrew O'Hagan

SCRIBNER
A Division of Simon & Schuster, Inc.
1230 Avenue of the Americas
New York, NY 10020

First Scribner hardcover edition June 2012

SCRIBNER and design are registered trademarks of The Gale Group, Inc.,
used under license by Simon & Schuster, Inc., the publisher of this work.

For information about special discounts for bulk purchases,
please contact Simon & Schuster Special Sales at 1-866-506-1949
or business@simonandschuster.com.

The Simon & Schuster Speakers Bureau can bring authors to your live event.
For more information or to book an event contact the Simon & Schuster Speakers Bureau
at 1-866-248-3049 or visit our website at www.simonspeakers.com.

Manufactured in the United States of America

10  9  8  7  6  5  4  3  2  1

Library of Congress Control Number: 2012011959

ISBN 978-1-4516-6855-1
ISBN 978-1-4516-6857-5 (ebook)

# Contents

Jane Austen, Henry James and the Death of the Mother    1

PART ONE: IRELAND

W. B. Yeats: New Ways to Kill Your Father    33

Willie and George    52

New Ways to Kill Your Mother: Synge and His Family    78

Beckett Meets His Afflicted Mother    111

Brian Moore: Out of Ireland Have I Come, Great Hatred, Little
     Room    134

Sebastian Barry's Fatherland    156

Roddy Doyle and Hugo Hamilton: The Dialect of the Tribe    166

PART TWO: ELSEWHERE

Thomas Mann: New Ways to Spoil Your Children    185

Borges: A Father in His Shadow    212

Hart Crane: Escape from Home    246

Tennessee Williams and the Ghost of Rose    262

John Cheever: New Ways to Make Your Family's Life a
     Misery    276

Baldwin and "the American Confusion"    296

Baldwin and Obama: Men Without Fathers    316

Bibliography    329

Acknowledgements    331

Index    333

# Jane Austen, Henry James
# and the Death of the Mother

In November 1894 Henry James set down in his notebooks a sketch for the novel that became *The Wings of the Dove*, which was published eight years later. He wrote about a possible heroine who was dying but in love with life. "She is equally pathetic in her doom and in her horror of it. If she only could live just a little; just a little more – just a little longer." In his outline James also had in his mind a young man who "wishes he could make her taste of happiness, give her something that it breaks her heart to go without having known. That "something" can only be – of course – the chance to love and be loved." James also noted as a possibility the position of another woman to whom the man was "otherwise attached and committed . . . It appears inevitably, or necessarily, preliminary that his encounter with the tragic girl shall be through the other woman." He also saw the reason why the young man and the woman to whom he was committed could not marry. "They are obliged to wait . . . He has no income and she no fortune, or there is some insurmountable opposition on the part of her father. Her father, her family, have reasons for disliking the young man."

This idea, then, of the dying young woman and the penniless young man on one side and, on the other, of father, family and young woman with no fortune circled in James's fertile mind. There was no moment, it seemed, in which the second young woman would have a mother; it was "her father, her family" that would oppose the marriage; over the next five or six years James would work out the form this opposition would take, and who exactly "her family" would be.

In her book *Novel Relations*, Ruth Perry looked at the makeup of the family in the early years of the novel. "Despite the emphasis," she wrote, "on marriage and motherhood in late eighteenth-century society, mothers in novels of the period are notoriously absent – dead or otherwise missing. Just when motherhood was becoming central to the definition of femininity, when the modern conception of the all-nurturing, tender, soothing, ministering mother was being consolidated in English culture, she was being represented in fiction as a memory rather than as an active present reality."

In nineteenth- and early-twentieth-century fiction, the family is often broken or disturbed or exposed, and the heroine is often alone, or strangely controlled and managed. If the heroine and the narrative itself are seeking completion in her marriage, then the journey there involves either the searching for figures outside the immediate family for support, or the breaking free from members of the family who seek to confine or dictate. In creating the new family upon marriage, the heroine needs to redefine her own family or usurp its power. In attempting to dramatize this, the novelist will use a series of tricks or systems almost naturally available to Jane Austen and the novelists who came after her; they could use shadowy or absent mothers and shining or manipulative aunts. The novel in English over the nineteenth century is filled with parents whose influence must be evaded or erased to be replaced by figures who operate either literally or figuratively as aunts, both kind and mean, both well-intentioned and duplicitous, both rescuing and destroying. The novel is a form ripe for orphans, or for those whose orphanhood will be all the more powerful for being figurative, or open to the suggestion, both sweet and sour, of surrogate parents.

It is easy to attribute the absence of mothers in novels of the eighteenth and nineteenth centuries to the large numbers of women who died in childbirth, as high as 10 per cent in the eighteenth century. The first wives of three of Jane Austen's brothers died in childbirth, for example, leaving motherless children. But this explanation is too easy. If it had suited novelists to fill their books with living mothers – Jane Austen's mother outlived her, for example – then they would have done so. In *Novel Relations* Ruth Perry takes the view that all the motherless heroines in the eighteenth-century novel – and all the play with substitutions – "may derive from a new necessity in an age of intensifying individualism." This necessity involved separating from the mother, or destroying her, and replacing her with a mother-figure of choice. "This mother," Perry writes, "who is also a stranger may thus enable the heroine's independent moral existence."

Thus mothers get in the way in fiction; they take up the space that is better filled by indecision, by hope, by the slow growth of a personality, and by something more interesting and important as the novel itself developed. This was the idea of solitude, the idea that a key scene in a novel occurs when the heroine is alone, with no one to protect her, no one to confide in, no one to advise her, and no possibility of this. Thus her thoughts move inward, offering a drama not between generations, or between opinions, but within a wounded, deceived or conflicted self. The novel traces the mind at work, the mind in silence. The presence of a mother would be a breach of the essential privacy of the emerging self, of the sense of singleness and integrity, of an uncertain moral consciousness, of a pure and floating individuality on which the novel comes to depend. The conspiracy in the novel is thus not between a mother and her daughter, but rather between the protagonist and the reader.

Jane Austen's last three novels have motherless heroines. Austen, however, does not allow this to appear as loss, or does not let this expose the heroine, or take up much of her time.

Rather it increases her sense of self, it allows her personality to appear more intensely in the narrative as though slowly filling space that had been quietly and slyly left for that purpose.

In *Pride and Prejudice* there is a mother, but there are also two aunts, Elizabeth Bennet's Aunt Gardiner and Mr. Darcy's aunt Lady Catherine de Bourgh. It is an aspect of Austen's genius that, while the novel dissolves the power and influence of the mother, neutralizes her in ways both comic and blunt, the two aunts are painted in considerably different shades, one allowed a calm, civilizing subtlety, the other given a histrionic sense of entitlement. But none of the three older women in the book has any actual power, although two of them seek power and influence; power instead is handed directly to the heroine and this power arises from the quality of her own intelligence. It is her own ability to be alone, to move alone, to be seen alone, to come to conclusions alone, that sets her apart.

When Jane Austen's niece herself became an aunt she wrote to her: "Now that you have become an Aunt, you are a person of some consequence & must excite great Interest whatever you do. I have always maintained the importance of aunts as much as possible, & I am sure of your doing the same now." Austen was close to her own nieces and nephews, looked after some of them after their mothers died, and seemed to have been remembered fondly by all of them. She also lived in the hope of an inheritance from her mother's brother Mr. Leigh-Perrot, who was married and lived in Bath. The Leigh-Perrots were childless and not amusing, but they had to be kept sweet. Her uncle's will, which in 1817 left Austen and her siblings a thousand pounds only after their aunt's death, did not help Austen as she herself was ill and died soon afterwards.

In *Pride and Prejudice* the two aunts also represent a changing England. Mrs. Gardiner's husband, who is Mrs. Bennet's brother, lived from trade. He was, we are told, "greatly superior to his sister, as well by nature as education" and it is pointed out that the Netherfield ladies, Mr. Bingley's sisters, superior and snobbish and alert to class difference, "would have had difficulty in believing that a man who lived by trade, and within view of his own warehouses, could have been so well bred and agreeable." His wife "was an amiable, intelligent, elegant woman, and a great favourite with all her . . . nieces. Between the two eldest and herself especially, there subsisted a very particular regard." It is to her house in London that the sisters repair in that hushed interregnum in the book when both Bingley and Darcy have disappeared and with them the prospects for Jane. It is while travelling with her aunt and uncle that Elizabeth renews her relations with Darcy. It is via them that she discovers that Darcy has rescued her sister Lydia. In other words, the Gardiners in *Pride and Prejudice* offer stillness, unforced opportunity, vital information, none of which is available from their mother, or indeed their father. This idea that the sisters have to be removed from the family home for the novel to proceed makes the role of their uncle and aunt essential in the book, but also natural.

Austen feels free, on the other hand, to make Lady Catherine de Bourgh imperious and comic, her wealth and power serving to make her ridiculous rather than impressive. She is an aunt who does not prevail; her presence in the book succeeds in making Darcy her nephew more individual, more himself and less part of any system. His aunt's function is not merely then to amuse us, or to show us an aspect of English manners that Jane Austen thought was foolish, but to allow her nephew, who refuses to obey her, a sort of freedom, a way of standing alone, that will make him worthy of Elizabeth and worthy too of the novel's moral shape. Its suggestion that only those who are prepared to move outside their family's arena of influence, to move out of the sphere of blood and inheritance as the centre of control, towards the autonomous and the personal, will become important in other areas of English life as the nineteenth century proceeds.

Austen understood, however, the strange dynamic of an extended family and how much could be made fluid and uncertain, detached and semi-detached, within its boundaries. Within their family, both Jane Austen and her sister, Cassandra, as Marilyn Butler has pointed out in "Jane Austen and the War of Ideas," "played a key role as travellers between the households [of their brothers] and assiduous correspondents . . . Jane somewhat closer to and more preoccupied with two of her younger brothers – Henry, said to have been her favourite, who lived in London, and the sailor Frank, who reported to her from various war fronts . . . The sisters made good aunts and friends to the next generation."

Since two of her brothers, Frank and Charles, went to sea and were away from home for long periods of time, it is easy to see the intensely tender and constant feelings that Fanny Price in *Mansfield Park* has for her brother William, also away at sea, as being a fundamental part of Austen's emotional world. The novel itself begins by breaking a family, by taking Fanny Price from her own impoverished family and handing her, almost as a changeling, to the care of her two aunts. The fact that she is penniless leaves her unprotected and requires her to be timid and passive.

Since the opening of the novel has all the bearings of a fairy tale, it must have been tempting for Austen to make Lady Bertram, the aunt in whose house Fanny will live, an evil ogre and make Mrs. Norris, the aunt who lives nearby, into the kind and watchful aunt. Or make them both ogres. What she decided to do was to hand all the badness to Mrs. Norris. It is Mrs. Norris who emphasizes Fanny's precarious position as someone who is inside the family enough to be given shelter but outside it enough to be regularly insulted. When Fanny refuses to take part in the play-acting, for example, her aunt Norris emphasizes her isolation and vulnerability: "I shall think her a very obstinate girl, if she does not do what her aunt and cousins wish her – very ungrateful indeed, considering who and what she is."

The reader is thus free to dislike Mrs. Norris for her cruelty and to admire Fanny for her forbearance. Austen's biographer Claire Tomalin sees Mrs. Norris as "one of the great villains of literature"; the critic Tony Tanner as "one of Jane Austen's most impressive characters and indeed one of the most plausibly odious characters in fiction." All this is clear, at times rather too clear. What is not clear is what the reader should feel about the other aunt, Lady Bertram, the mistress of Mansfield Park. Tomalin dislikes her: "Fanny's experience at Mansfield Park is bitter as no other childhood is in Austen's work. Her aunt, Lady Bertram, is virtually an imbecile; she may be a comic character and not ill-tempered, but the effects of her extreme placidity are not comic." Tanner takes a similar view:

Lady Bertram is a travesty of those values [of quietness and repose]. She is utterly inert, unaware, and entirely incapable of volition, effort or independent judgement. She is of course an immensely amusing character; but she also reveals the Mansfield values run to seed. In effect, she never thinks, moves, or cares: amiable enough in that she is not malicious, she is, in her insentient indolence, useless as a guardian of Mansfield Park and positively culpable as a parent. And it is her sofa-bound inertia which permits the ascendancy of Mrs. Norris. Lady Bertram does not represent quietness and repose so much as indifference and collapse.

In his essay on *Mansfield Park*, Lionel Trilling has another reading of Lady Bertram, claiming that she is a self-mocking representation of Jane Austen's wish to "be rich and fat and smooth and dull

. . . to sit on a cushion, to be a creature of habit and an object of ritual deference."

It is possible to argue, on the other hand, that Lady Bertram, rather than being merely a piece of self-mockery, is one of Austen's most subtle, restrained and ingenious creations. This probably requires a different attitude to the novel than that displayed by Tomalin and Tanner, or indeed Trilling. The novel is not a moral fable or a tale from the Bible, or an exploration of the individual's role in society; it is not our job to like or dislike characters in fiction, or make judgements on their worth, or learn from them how to live. We can do that with real people and, if we like, figures from history. They are for moralists to feast on. A novel is a pattern and it is our job to relish and see clearly its textures and its tones, to notice how the textures were woven and the tones put into place. This is not to insist that a character in fiction is merely a verbal construct and bears no relation to the known world. It is rather to suggest that the role of a character in a novel must be judged not as we would judge a person. Instead, we must look for density, for weight and strength within the pattern, for ways in which figures in novels have more than one easy characteristic, one simple affect. A novel is a set of strategies, closer to something in mathematics or quantum physics than something in ethics or sociology. It is a release of certain energies and a dramatization of how these energies might be controlled, given shape.

Lady Bertram in *Mansfield Park* in this context is easy to read; her role in the pattern of the book is obvious. She is not good, she performs no good or kind act that matters; nor is she bad, since, in turn, she performs no bad act that matters. But she is there in the book, in the house, in the family. Fanny has already lost one mother, who effectively has given her away. Aunt Norris plays the role of wicked aunt who appears now and then. Lady Bertram has four children of her own, and with the arrival of Fanny she has a fifth. Since there is something in Austen's imaginative system that tends to resist mothers who have an active energy, Austen has a problem now with Lady Bertram. If she makes her merely unpleasant, Fanny will have to respond to this in scene after scene because Lady Bertram is, unusually, an aunt in residence rather than an aunt who comes and goes. This then will become the story of the book, a simple story of cruelty and resistance to cruelty. If Lady Bertram is actively cruel to Fanny, then how will she treat her own children? If she treats them with kindness and cares for them, then the intensity of their agency will be diluted. If she is cruel to them too, then the singleness of Fanny, her solitude as a force in the book, will not emerge.

It would really make sense to kill Lady Bertram, or to have her not there, allow her to be one of those unmentioned mothers in fiction, an unpalpable absence. But in that case, there will be no real impulse for Fanny to join her household rather than that of Aunt Norris and Fanny will miss daily contact with Edmund, who notices her and then doesn't, thus releasing important dramatic energy in the book.

In patterning the book, in creating its dynamic and its dramatics, Austen has to have Lady Bertram there as a mother and not there all at the same time; she has to give her characteristics that are essentially neutral. She might have been easily amusing or irritating or silly like Mrs. Bennet in *Pride and Prejudice*. Since her husband is away so much, she might have been given a more significant role. The pattern of *Mansfield Park* is essentially the pattern of the family. Even the outsider Henry Crawford comes armed with two sisters. When we look for the pattern of the book, we must therefore examine the dynamic of the family, the strange way power is held and withheld which allows the events of the novel to unfold and, more than anything, lets Fanny Price, so ostensibly dull and powerless and passive, emerge as deeply drawn and deeply powerful within the silence of her own consciousness. The novel gives her a sort of autonomy that she could not have were the pattern to be different; it allows her to move from being an outsider to taking over the narrative and, indeed, taking over generally.

Thus Austen has the ingenious idea of making the sofa, rather than the household, the realm over which Lady Bertram reigns, and making sleep, or half-sleep, her dynamic. She is too sleepy to care. When her husband is leaving for the West Indies, Austen writes: "Lady Bertram did not like at all to have her husband leave her; but she was not disturbed by any alarm for his safety, or solicitude for his comfort, being one of those persons who think nothing can be dangerous, or difficult, or fatiguing to anyone but themselves." While she thinks about her own comfort, she does not dwell too much on the subject. It defines what she does not do rather than any of her actions. She hardly has any actions. Austen writes: "Lady Bertram did not go into public with her daughters. She was too indolent even to accept a mother's gratification in witnessing their success and enjoyment at the expense of any personal trouble . . ." What Lady Bertram does in the book most of the time is not merely ignore others, but effectively ignore herself; she lives a gloriously underexamined life, so placing her in precisely the opposite force field to Fanny, who notices herself with considerable, almost intrusive, care, as though she were a little orphan novelist. Lady Bertram is lazy, has little to say, suffers from mild ill health. Her passivity and general lassitude play comically against her sister's energy. But more than anything, the state of non-being, her presence as outline rather than line, her sheer inertia, her belief in the power of her own placid beauty, allow other forces in the novel – the venality of some of her children, Edmund's sincerity – to happen, or have their effect, not because of their mother or their family or even despite the mother or the family; instead, naturally, organically, each character is given their own autonomy, thus allowing *Mansfield Park* to unfold as complex pattern. Lady Bertram, for example, is a loved figure in the book, but also comic. She is not merely interesting for the reader, she has a surprising way of attracting the other characters. In the centre of the book like a strange and insistent mass stands the consciousness of Fanny Price. She has no vivacity, no wit; she is mainly silent. She repels as much as she attracts. Trilling, for example, dislikes her, and writes: "Nobody, I believe, has ever found it possible to like the heroine of *Mansfield Park*. Fanny Price is overtly virtuous and consciously virtuous." This may be so, if we insist on looking at her from outside as though she were human. What is more important is that the novel is a register of her very essence. More than irritating virtue, this essence contains reason and feeling. She has a way of noticing and registering that has nothing to do with virtue, but everything to do with narrative impetus, holding the reader. It is uncertain how she will live in the book, thus filling the book with momentum.

For this momentum to happen, it is essential that she is taken away from her mother and put in the care of two aunts, neither of whom behaves in a way that is motherly. This gives her presence in the book a sort of density and strength. The idea of aunts in fiction in the nineteenth century is not merely to give the main character strength, however. It arises from a need that is more fundamental and displays the novel form itself as oddly hybrid and insecure and open to change and influence.

The novel is unsure whether it is a story, told by a single teller, or a play enacted by a number of actors. It is both static and theatrical in its systems, a sphere in which a single controlling voice operates, or many competing voices. The value of aunts in the dramatic structure of a novel is that they arrive and then they depart. They break up space and they add spice to things. Thus the arrival in *Pride and Prejudice* of Lady Catherine de Bourgh, Mr. Darcy's aunt, comes with a considerable new energy in the rhythmic tone of the novel as though it were being played out not for a single passive reader but for a large eager audience. It reads as follows:

One morning, about a week after Bingley's engagement with Jane had been formed, as he and the females of the family were sitting together in the dining room, their attention was suddenly drawn to the window, by the sound of a carriage; and they perceived a chaise and four driving up the lawn. It was too early in the morning for visitors, and besides, the equipage did not answer to that of any of their neighbours. The horses were post; and neither the carriage, nor the livery of the servant who preceded it, were familiar to them. As it was certain, however, that somebody was coming, Bingley instantly prevailed on Miss Bennet to avoid the confinement of such an intrusion, and walk away with him into the shrubbery. They both set off, and the conjectures of the remaining three continued, though with little satisfaction, till the door was thrown open, and their visitor entered. It was Lady Catherine de Bourgh.

This idea of aunts arriving and then departing and the movement within the rhythm of the prose bearing signs of all this excitement makes its way through the novels of the nineteenth century. Chapter 7 of Book 1 of George Eliot's *The Mill on the Floss*, for example, is entitled "Enter the Aunts and Uncles," as though the page of the novel were a stage in a theatre. And in how she paints the four sisters, Mrs. Tulliver, Mrs. Glegg, Mrs. Deane and Mrs. Pullet, she moves between the comic and the serious using both dialogue and witty authorial observation; she uses the young Tom and Maggie Tulliver as observers, almost readers, almost audience, of the scene being worked out within the older generation. At stake here in this chapter is the idea of the family as a unit, as a united way of doing things, and how things will move and develop within this sense of tradition will become an important aspect of the novel's pattern. This will be outlined in the simplest and most domestic way as Mrs. Glegg remembers that in her "poor father's time," every member of the family arrived for meals at the same time. Soon when Mrs. Pullet cries about the death of a neighbour, her sister argues with her in the name of family tradition rather than good sense: "'Sophy,' said Mrs. Glegg, unable any longer to contain her spirit of rational remonstrance, 'Sophy, I wonder at you, fretting and injuring your health about people as don't belong to you. Your poor father never did so, nor your aunt Frances neither, nor any o' the family as I ever heared of.'"

And since the novel is made up not of moving characters on the stage wearing colourful costumes and knowing how to project their voices, but of grim black marks on the page, then one of the other purposes of aunts is to allow them dramatic departures or vicious arguments for the amusement of both the younger generation and the reader. The departure of Lady Catherine de Bourgh, for example, is tremendously exciting. "I take no leave of you, Miss Bennet. I send no compliments to your mother. You deserve no such attention. I am most seriously displeased." Or the departure of Mrs. Glegg in *The Mill on the Floss*: "'Well,' said Mrs. Glegg, rising from her chair, 'I don't know whether you think it's a fine thing to sit by and hear me swore at, Mr. Glegg, but I'm not going to stay a minute longer in this house. You can stay behind, and come home with the gig, and I'll walk home.'" Or the row half a century later between Stephen's father and his aunt Dante on Christmas Day in James Joyce's *A Portrait of the Artist as a Young Man*: "Dante shoved her chair violently aside and left the table, upsetting her napkinring which rolled slowly along the carpet and came to rest against the foot of an easychair. Mr. Dedalus rose quickly and followed her towards the door. At the door Dante turned round violently and shouted down the room, her cheeks flushed and quivering with rage . . ."

Thus aunts depart in novels as aunts arrive, to break the peace and lighten the load. Of all the novelists, the one who comes most to mistrust the mother and make use of the aunt is Henry James. In his critical writings, his prefaces and his letters, James wrote very little about Jane Austen. Early on he made clear his admiration for her: "Miss Austen," he wrote, "in her best novels, is interesting to the last page; the tissue of her narrative is always close and firm, and though she is minute and analytical, she is never prolix or redundant." But he also wrote that "Jane Austen, with her light felicity, leaves us hardly more curious of her process, or of the experience that fed it, than the brown thrush who tells his story from the garden bough." He alluded sarcastically to "the body of publishers, editors, illustrators, producers of the present twaddle of magazines, who have found their 'dear,' our dear, everyone's dear, Jane so infinitely to their material purpose." There are many ways of reading this, but it should be noted that James was not, in general, in the habit of praising other novelists; he saw his own work as a deeply self-conscious art, refined into a system, an exquisite tapestry. He did not notice anyone else operating at the same intensity and degree of deliberation as he did. But he took what he needed, as any novelist does, from his colleagues' work, and unlike "the brown thrush who tells his story from the garden bough," he saw no reason to let everyone know.

In his creation of aunts, in any case, thrush or no thrush, James took his bearings from Austen not only in the outlines of what she did, but in the complexity she sought and the dense pattern she managed while breaking up a family for the purposes of her fiction. Both Austen and James made fictional space in which things moved unexpectedly or changed shape, in which there was much ambiguity and duality. If they played with pattern, it was a pattern that left space for what was shimmering and dynamic. Both Austen and James placed at the very centre of their pattern a throbbing consciousness, a striving presence who could filter experience, on whom experience could press in ways that were unpredictable, and fascinating for the reader.

In James's six greatest works there is an absent mother who is replaced by a real aunt or by a set of surrogate aunts. In *Washington Square*, for example, Dr. Sloper's wife has died, leaving Catherine, his daughter, motherless. Her helper and confidante becomes her aunt, who is conspiratorial, mischievous, oddly kind and somewhat foolish, and always on the verge of being banished by Dr. Sloper. In *The Portrait of a Lady* Isabel Archer is also motherless, indeed her father is dead too, and she is found as an unprotected orphan in Albany by her aunt Mrs. Touchett, who is eccentric, wilful, bossy, interesting, both kind and brittle. Mrs. Touchett takes over Isabel's life, takes her to England and Italy, introduces her to a new world of possibility; the aunt is effectively the agent who causes the action of the novel to take place.

This idea of James killing off mothers and replacing them with aunts could be easily misunderstood. He was close to his own mother, as he was also to his aunt Kate, who lived with the family for most of James's upbringing, and travelled with them when they crossed and recrossed the Atlantic. But he also sought to get away from his mother, and managed to do so by settling in Europe. He was devoted to his mother and he arranged not to see her much, thus making the devotion all the more heartfelt as time went on. He wrote to her and about her with considerable filial tenderness. His response to her death was one of genuine shock and grief.

His connection to his mother, both close and tenuous, may be one of the reasons why he sought to erase so many mothers from his best work. It was an area that he did not want to explore; it was complicated and raw, too complicated and raw to be easily shaped into narrative. And his replacing her with aunts or surrogate aunts may have had something to do the constant presence of his own aunt Kate in the household, and we may be led to this view because James tended to use the hidden or secret shape of his own life, of his own fears, and find metaphors for them in his fiction. Thus killing off your mother and replacing her with your aunt might have satisfied some hungry need James had, which he kept locked in a cupboard in the house of fiction to be produced on special occasions.

But this is too crude a reading, just as it is too easy to explore Jane Austen's own life as an aunt, or her need to assert herself in her fiction as someone who had no mother worth speaking about, and offer these as reasons why she did not have mothers in her last three books. There is another way of reading James's motives or reasons for sending mothers into eternity while his characters lived in finite time. It simply suited the shape of the story he was trying to tell; it was impelled by the novel rather than the novelist. In other words, it was a technical problem that the novel had, rather than a psychological problem of his own that James needed to address. In his fiction, he needed mothers to be absent because having them present would undermine his entire enterprise. The main protagonists of his best books enact a drama of self-reliance, self-invention; they live alone and unnurtured in their minds. James could make their aunts silly, foolish, capricious and eccentric, and thus make their arrival and departure interesting and delicious for the reader, but he could not bring himself to create a very foolish or indolent mother as Austen had done in *Pride and Prejudice* and *Mansfield Park*. This was not because he didn't have the heart or the urge – he did, after all, create bad and capricious mothers in works such as *What Maisie Knew* and *The Spoils of Poynton* – but because such an approach would not be subtle, would be too easily comic, would destroy the level of moral seriousness that he sought to conjure up in how he displayed his characters and let them respond to each other.

Dr. Sloper's loss of his wife and second child in *Washington Square* is seen not only as personal but as professional. "For a man whose trade was to keep people alive, he had certainly done poorly in his own family," James writes. When Catherine, his only living child, is ten, Dr. Sloper "invited his sister, Mrs. Penniman, to come and stay with him." Mrs. Penniman, whose first name is Lavinia, "had married a poor clergyman, of a sickly constitution and a flowery style of eloquence, and then, at the age of thirty-three, had been left a widow, without children, without fortune – with nothing but the memory of Mr. Penniman's flowers of speech, a certain vague aroma of which hovered about her own conversation." She is interested in melodrama and romance, she is a schemer, she has, James writes, "a taste for light literature, and a certain foolish indirectness and obliquity of character. She was romantic, she was sentimental, she had a passion for little secrets and mysteries."

This allows her to scheme and meddle, it allows her to amuse the reader, but it allows her also to stand in great opposition to Catherine Sloper, despite her efforts to be helpful and supportive. Her presence in the book allows Catherine to be more alone, allows her to become herself with greater force and conviction, allows the reader to see Catherine more clearly, enter her spirit more intensely. Catherine knows how to feel, and the novel is an exploration and a dramatization of this knowledge and these feelings. As the short novel proceeds, what Catherine feels becomes more solid and more complex; she becomes almost heroic in her steadfast solitude, her single-mindedness, her stubbornness. James has taken not only the figure of Fanny Price, the young girl as dull and silent orphan from *Mansfield Park*, but also the orphan from folk tales, and he has given her a scheming aunt, a loathsome father and a pent-up sexuality. He has also offered her silence, the silence that only the novel can exploit with exact plenitude as it takes over her yearning spirit and allows her motives a painful complexity. Part of Catherine's strange nobility comes from the fact that she is alone in the world, her mother is absent, her aunt is a fool.

In *The Portrait of a Lady*, written soon afterwards, Mrs. Touchett, Isabel's aunt,

was a plain-faced old woman, without graces and without any great elegance, but with an enormous respect for her own motives . . . She was not fond of the English style of life, and had three or four reasons for it to which she currently alluded; they bore upon minor points of that ancient order, but for Mrs. Touchett they amply justified non-residence. She detested bread sauce, which, as she said, looked like a poultice and tasted like soap; she objected to the consumption of beer by her maid-servants; and she affirmed that the British laundress . . . was not a mistress of her art.

Thus in his introduction to both Mrs. Touchett and Mrs. Penniman, James can use a style that one could describe as self-amused. The sentences chosen to describe both aunts, as indeed the very names chosen for these personages, must have been enjoyable to compose. They set a tone, but oddly enough, it is not a tone for the novel itself, which will have a different tone and texture. Rather, they alert the reader that the heroine who will suffer in the book will be alone in her suffering, it will be done in silence, with no terms for it that belong to any woman of the previous generation. These are novels that project the individual as alone in the world, her singleness a metaphor perhaps for how the world is moving and developing, and with echoes of the space in which capital must be acquired and how it must grow; but these non-fictional issues are side-shows, the individual is alone in these novels more than anything else as a way of allowing the novels themselves to breathe and thrive, to live dynamically. It is for this that the young women Catherine Sloper and Isabel Archer will have to be removed from the control and the cocoon of family. What they do, what they decide, how they live, will have a stark drama; nothing will be inevitable or part of a communal system of feeling, something passed on to generations. The idea of generation in these novels is not something organic and biological; generation occurs as energy in the individual, self-made conscience, it happens there alone.

*The Portrait of a Lady* exudes more energy than *Washington Square* not only because its heroine fills a larger space spiritually and intellectually but for two other reasons. The first is that Isabel's solitude is not only denser and richer, but it is also given more dramatic weight. In the Preface he wrote more than twenty years later James analyzed what he had done with Isabel Archer's "inward life," when he referred to that scene where, by allowing her mind to circle and re-circle, he brought Isabel and the reader to a realization of what has been hidden from both up to then. "And I cannot think," James wrote,

of a more consistent application of that ideal [of making the inward life of a character as dramatic as any set of external events] unless it be in the long statement, just beyond the middle of the book, of my young woman's extraordinary meditative vigil on the occasion that was to become for her such a landmark. Reduced to its essence, it is but a vigil of searching criticism; but it throws the action further forward than twenty "incidents" might have done. It was designed to have all the vivacity of incident and all the economy of picture. She sits up, by her dying fire, far into the night . . . it all goes on without her being approached by another person and without her leaving her chair. It is obviously the best thing in the book . . .

The other scene from the book that James mentions in the Preface as also a key to the book's dynamic is the scene in which

Isabel, coming into the drawing-room at Gardencourt, coming in from a wet walk or whatever, that rainy afternoon, finds Madame Merle in possession of the place, Madame Merle seated, all absorbed but all serene, at the piano, and deeply recognises, in the striking of such an hour, in the presence there, among the gathering shades of this personage, of whom a moment before she had never so much as heard, a turning-point in her life.

Madame Merle is presented to both Isabel and the reader as a surrogate aunt for Isabel, who will take the place of Mrs. Touchett or augment her effort to direct Isabel towards her destiny. Isabel will be free, of course, to resist such direction, being less brittle and selfish than Mrs. Touchett and less worldly and sociable than Madame Merle. What James then does is allow the character of Madame Merle to shift in the book, or move from being an aunt to being a rival. He sexualizes an aunt, and this act gives *The Portrait of a Lady* its power. He radically destabilizes the category of aunt, moves Madame Merle from being someone who protects Isabel, who stands in for her mother without having a mother's control, to being someone who seeks to damage her, defeat her. He makes Isabel realize this by herself, through her own powers, thus making her solitude a sharp weapon, a tactic almost, as much as a vulnerable condition.

But James also wishes to dramatize, to take what happens in the secret chambers of the self, the mind at work in silence as registered by the novelist in sentences, and move this into dialogue, open drama. The scene where Madame Merle confronts Isabel, asking why Lord Warburton has not continued his interest in Pansy, the daughter of Isabel's husband, is masterly in its stagecraft, its creation of dramatic illusion, its understanding of the sheer power in a novel of playing it as though there were two actresses on the page, rather than a silent novelist communicating with a silent reader. When Madame Merle overplays her hand by asking Isabel to "let us have him," to let her and Osmond and Pansy have Lord Warburton, "Madame Merle had proceeded very deliberately," James writes:

watching her companion and apparently thinking she could proceed safely. As she went on Isabel grew pale; she clasped her hands more tightly in her lap. It was not that her visitor had at last thought it was the right time to be insolent; for this was not what was most apparent. It was a worse horror than that. "Who are you – what are you?" Isabel murmured. "What have you to do with my husband?" It was strange that for the moment she drew as near to him as if she had loved him. "Ah then, you take it heroically! I'm very sorry. Don't think, however, that I shall do so." "What have you to do with me?" Isabel went on. Madame Merle slowly got up, stroking her muff, but not removing her eyes from Isabel's face. "Everything!" she answered.

In that moment a transformation of an exquisite kind takes place in the book as the older woman removes her guise as aunt and puts on the mask of rival. There is another moment worthy of attention when shapes change, when figures who played one role move into another, thus adding to the texture of the book. It is in the very last chapter after the death of Ralph Touchett when Isabel embraces her aunt:

She went to her aunt and put her arm around her; and Mrs. Touchett, who as a general thing neither invited nor enjoyed caresses, submitted for a moment to this one, rising, as might be, to take it. But she was stiff and dry-eyed; her acute white face was terrible. "Dear Aunt Lydia," Isabel murmured. "Go and thank God you've no child," said Mrs. Touchett, disengaging herself.

Thus it emerges that Mrs. Touchett, as well as being an intrepid and amusing aunt, has all the time been a mother, watching over Ralph as he weakens as the book proceeds. Like Madame Merle, her role in a novel that is itself filled with duplicity is dual; the fact that she does not simply play one role, or that the simplicity of her role is so starkly undermined in that scene with Isabel, by allowing the novel to layer and offer density to its own procedures, gives it a powerfully protean dynamic.

In James's novel *The Ambassadors*, written more than twenty years later, Lambert Strether appears in the guise of uncle, as, initially, Marie de Vionnet appears as aunt. Thus Chad can play the role of nephew to both and can seem to have an interest in Madame de Vionnet's daughter. Once again, as the novel develops, James plays with absence. Chad's father is dead; his mother is alive, but does not appear in the book except as an energy that pulls him towards her. In the empty space left by absent parents, then, it is clear what must happen. The surrogate uncle will fall for the surrogate aunt. And the two young people will find each other attractive. And the novel will, once more, be the story of the further exclusion of the mother, her annihilation all the more dramatic and satisfying because she is so needy.

James has other plans, however, and he plays these out in a recognition scene of exquisite subtlety as Strether, having made a random trip outside Paris, observes two figures in a boat, slowly sees that they have spotted him too; they are not Chad and Madame de Vionnet's daughter, however, but Chad and the Madame herself. In the way they seek to avoid being seen, everything becomes apparent. "This little effect," James writes,

was sudden and rapid, so rapid that Strether's sense of it was separate only for an instant from a sharp start of his own. He too had within the minute taken in something, taken in that he knew the lady whose parasol, shifting as if to hide her face, made so fine a pink point in the shining scene. It was too prodigious, a chance in a million, but, if he knew the lady, the gentleman, who still presented his back and kept off, the gentleman, the coatless hero of the idyll, who had responded to her start, was, to match the marvel, none other than Chad.

Thus once more James has sexualized an aunt. It is as though Henry Crawford came to Mansfield Park in search of Lady Bertram rather than Fanny; or Mr. Darcy were found in the countryside in his shirtsleeves with none other than Mrs. Bennet, or Aunt Gardiner; or Mr. Bingley were found in a carriage with Lady Catherine de Bourgh. In other words, James took what was necessary for a novel in his time to have power and weight – the replacement of the mother by the aunt – and then saw what was possible, the making of the aunt not simply an enabling figure, or a cruel comic figure, or a passive figure, but a highly sexualized woman, and so, within the dynamic of the novel, a figure capable of moving at will from one role to another, causing havoc within the narrative systems created for her.

In both *The Turn of the Screw* and *The Golden Bowl*, it is as though the mother never existed, as though the characters came into being by some method specially created by the novelist rather than by nature. She is not an absence; she was never present. She is unthinkable. Instead, a surrogate aunt emerges, who is deeply neurotic in the former book, and oddly nosy and wise in the latter. The children Flora and Miles thus inhabit that rich space made for Victorian fictional characters; they are orphaned, and nothing can happen to them until the aunt figure, in the guise of the governess, arrives, and then everything can happen. In *The Golden Bowl*, just as Charlotte Stant appears ready to become Maggie Verver's potential stepmother, by marrying Adam Verver, Maggie's father, she also becomes Maggie's rival for the Prince, who is Maggie's husband. As every other force in the book remains stable, solid, Charlotte is the element who is shape-changing, untrustworthy, duplicitous. Those around her can be released from being contaminated by Charlotte by the arrival of a surrogate aunt in the guise of Fanny Assingham, who will treat the story of the book as story, in the same way as a reader will, but will also be the figure who will smash the golden bowl.

In *The Wings of the Dove*, Kate Croy goes to her rich aunt Maud on her mother's death, her mother having left her more or less penniless, and her aunt Maud makes her an offer that is outlined in the opening of the book. It is the offer that is at the very basis of the novel from Austen to James. Aunt Maud wishes her niece to be an orphan and wishes to control her life, or manipulate her future. She wants her niece to go and see her father. Kate tells him: "The condition Aunt Maud makes is that I shall have absolutely nothing to do with you; never see you, nor speak nor write to you, never go near you nor make you a sign, nor hold any sort of communication with you. What she requires is that you shall cease to exist for me."

Having given up her father, Kate is now in the hands of her aunt, and it is these hands that slowly mould her and come subtly close to corrupting her. It is her aunt's will that causes her to behave as she does. Her aunt watches over her possessively, as Aunt Peniston does Lily Bart in Edith Wharton's *The House of Mirth*, published three years later. In neither book is the younger woman loved or offered unconditional protection by the older woman; in both books the aunt is manipulative and difficult rather than hospitable to the orphaned niece, or comforting, or understanding. In Wharton's book Lily Bart is brought to ruin; in *The Wings of the Dove* Kate Croy is allowed to ruin herself in a much more ambiguous and spiritual way; in both books, the brittle presence of the aunt hovers over the action, darting in and out of the narrative like a large needy reptile.

Into the action arrives the young heiress Milly Theale, whose history, we are told, was a New York history, confused as yet, but multitudinous, of the loss of parents, brothers, sisters, almost every human appendage, all on a scale and with a sweep that had required the greater stage; it was a New York legend of affecting, of romantic isolation, and, beyond everything, it was by most accounts, in respect of the mass of money so piled on the girl's back, a set of New York possibilities. She was alone, she was stricken, she was rich, and in particular was strange – a combination in itself of a nature to engage Mrs. Stringham's attention.

Mrs. Stringham is, of course, childless, old enough to be Milly's aunt, and she becomes Milly's surrogate aunt to match Kate's aunt in the novel about two women, both orphans, both in the care of their aunts, both moving slowly towards destruction, one of the body, one of the moral spirit.

This idea of the family as anathema to the novel in the nineteenth century, or the novel as an enactment of the destruction of the family and the rise of the stylish conscience, or the individual spirit, comes in more guises than the replacement of mothers by aunts. As Lionel Trilling has pointed out: "Of all the fathers of Jane Austen novels, Sir Thomas [Bertram] is the only one to whom admiration is given." This idea of the annihilation of the communal and its replacement with the person, and the novel being one of the agents of this, as much as a result of it, comes throughout the century, however, in the guise of mothers fading and aunts arriving. As Rupert Christiansen has pointed out in *The Complete Book of Aunts*, it occurs in the novels between Austen and James as much as it does in their work. It occurs in the novels of Dickens (*David Copperfield* and *Little Dorrit*) and Charlotte Brontë (*Jane Eyre*), of Thackeray (*Vanity Fair*) and Trollope (*He Knew He Was Right*).

But as the century went on, novelists had to contemplate the afterlives of Elizabeth and Darcy, Fanny Price and Edmund Bertram, had to deal with the fact that these novels made families out of the very act of breaking them. It was clear that since something fundamental had been done already in the novel to the idea of parents, something would also have to be done to the very idea of marriage itself, since marriage was a dilution of the autonomy of the individual protagonist. There is a line that can be drawn between Trollope and George Eliot and Henry James in which all three dramatize precisely the same scene, each of them alert to its implications. Each of them is alert to the power of the lone, unattached male figure in the novel. This male figure is not openly looking for a wife, and this is what makes him dangerous, more dangerous than any aunt has been. He can have an uneasy sexual presence with a way of noticing and listening. He can have the power of conscience, and the pure strength of someone who does not have obvious desires. He can represent the novelist in the novel, but is also from the future, from a world in which the making of marriages is no longer the main subject for a novelist. Once more, it is his solitude that gives him power, as Darcy in *Pride and Prejudice* derives his power from his solitude as much as his fortune, until he marries Elizabeth.

There is a chapter in Trollope's novel *Phineas Finn*, published in 1869, called "Lady Laura Kennedy's Headache," when Laura Kennedy tells Phineas that her marriage has been a mistake. In doing so, she uses his first name, not having done so before, and becomes oddly intimate with him while making clear, as she says, that "I have blundered as fools blunder, thinking that I was clever enough to pick my footsteps aright without asking counsel from any one. I have blundered and stumbled and fallen, and now I am so bruised that I am not able to stand upon my feet."

As they talk she compares Phineas, who is young, sympathetic, handsome, free, to her dry, bullying husband. As she does so, her husband approaches, and bullies her further, doing so in the presence of Phineas, who is now in possession of very dark knowledge indeed.

In George Eliot's *Daniel Deronda*, published in 1876, Deronda himself comes into possession of precisely the same knowledge when Gwendolen takes him into her confidence. She, like Lady Laura Kennedy, has married a bully. As in *Phineas Finn*, the reader learns how dangerous the Phineas or Daniel figure is, how much the bullying husband will resent him and how much the wife, locked in a nightmare marriage, will depend on him not only in her dreams but in the construction of her own narrative. Phineas and Daniel operate irresponsibly in this aspect of the novel, they are like cells who do not duplicate, or atoms whose power cannot be penetrated or dissolved. They stand outside a marriage as a force even more destructive than the husband himself, someone outside the family, utterly attractive, stealing power for themselves. A woman talking about her husband to another man offers an electric charge to the novel, a charge reflected in the very response of Gwendolen to her own confession:

She broke off, and with agitated lips looked at Deronda, but the expression on his face pierced her with an entirely new feeling. He was under the baffling difficulty of discerning, that what he had been urging on her was thrown into the pallid distance of mere thought before the outburst of her habitual emotion. It was as if he saw her drowning while his limbs were bound. The pained compassion which was spread over his features as he watched her, affected her with a compunction unlike any she had felt before . . .

In the meantime Grandcourt, the tyrant husband, watched his wife and Daniel: "No movement of Gwendolen in relation to Daniel escaped him." In a later scene, when Gwendolen once more appeals to Deronda to understand what is happening in her marriage and he tells her, "My only regret is, that I can be of so little use to you," the writing takes on a force, filled with shimmering movement and dramatic excitement. "Words," she writes,

seemed to have no more rescue in them than if he had been beholding a vessel in peril of wreck – the poor ship with its many-lived anguish beaten by the inescapable storm. How could he grasp the long-growing process of this young creature's wretchedness? – how arrest and change it with a sentence? He was afraid of his own voice. The words that rushed into his mind seemed in their feebleness nothing better than despair made audible, or than that insensibility to another's hardship which applies precept to soothe pain. He felt himself holding a crowd of words imprisoned within his lips, as if the letting them escape would be a violation of awe before the mysteries of our human lot. The thought that urged itself foremost was – "Confess everything to your husband; leave nothing concealed" – the words carried in his mind a vision of reasons which would have needed much fuller expression for Gwendolen to apprehend them, but before he had begun to utter those brief sentences, the door opened and the husband entered.

Henry James, by the time he began *The Portrait of a Lady* in 1879, had followed the serialization of *Daniel Deronda*. He read the book carefully and disapproved of it and then took what he needed from it. In Ralph Touchett he created another male whose role was both playful and pivotal, whose skepticism and illness undermined the very idea of attachment. He operates as a sort of surrogate novelist in the book, conspiring with his father to leave Isabel a fortune so that he can amuse himself watching what she might do with freedom. When Isabel marries Osmond, Ralph becomes the one who guesses how unhappy she is, and how bullying and cold her husband. As he lies dying, once more the unhappy wife finds in a single, unattached figure a saviour, someone who will help her break the glass of her marriage. "I believe I ruined you," he said, as she replies starkly: "He married me for the money" and then later in the scene: "Oh yes, I've been punished."

Soon afterwards Ralph dies, and the family is broken. When his mother, Mrs. Touchett, hears that Madame Merle has gone back to America, she offers one of the truest and funniest lines of the book: "To America? She must have done something very bad." And Isabel returns to her husband, and there is a sense at the end of the book that she has not returned to be his wife, part of his family, but with a new power she has found, a resource that will allow her to resist him, repel him, move in the world alone and free not only of the family she inherited and came into, but the one she chose and sought to make.

PART ONE

*Ireland*

# W. B. Yeats: New Ways to Kill Your Father

For a number of sibling artists who flourished in the last quarter of the nineteenth century and the first quarter of the twentieth century – Heinrich Mann and Thomas Mann; Henry James and William James; Virginia Woolf and Vanessa Bell; W. B. Yeats and Jack Yeats – the death of the father, an overwhelming presence while alive, or the gradual and often dramatic enactment of a metaphorical killing, allowed the children a strange new freedom, the right to become themselves, and then do battle with each other over politics and style.

In the case of the Manns and Virginia Woolf and Vanessa Bell, the literal death of their father when they were young and unformed allowed them to move to new quarters, both physically and emotionally, and removed a burden whose shadow alone would continue to haunt them. In the case of the James brothers and the Yeats brothers, the burden remained a living reality. In his book *Yeats: The Man and the Masks*, Richard Ellmann quotes Ivan Karamazov: "Who doesn't desire his father's death?" Ellmann writes:

From the Urals to Donegal the theme recurs, in Turgenev, in Samuel Butler, in Gosse. It is especially prominent in Ireland. George Moore, in his *Confessions of a Young Man*, blatantly proclaims his sense of liberation and relief when his father died. Synge makes an attempted parricide the theme of his *Playboy of the Western World*. James Joyce describes in *Ulysses* how Stephen Dedalus, disowning his own parent, searches for another father . . . Yeats, after handling the subject in an unpublished play written in 1884, returns to it in 1892 in a poem "The

33

Death of Cuchulain," turns the same story into a play in 1903, makes two translations of *Oedipus Rex*, the first in 1912, the second in 1927, and writes another play involving parricide, *Purgatory*, shortly before his death.

1

In the autumn of 1828, when Henry James Senior, the father of the novelist, briefly attended Union College in Schenectady, New York, he entered fully into student life, drinking in taverns and having expensive suits made by the local tailor. He charged it all to his father, William, who was so wealthy that he owned the very land on which the campus of Union College was built. William James, who had been born in Bailieborough in County Cavan, was also one of the two trustees of the college.

Henry James Senior's departure from Union College, not long after his arrival, was the beginning of a lifelong journey in search of freedom of thought, eternal truth and interesting companions who were good listeners. James, like John Butler Yeats, the father of W. B. Yeats, was a great talker. There are a number of resemblances between the two men. Each of them, for example, married the sister of a classmate to whom he was close. Both of them suffered from, and also enjoyed, a lifelong indolence and restlessness; they dominated their households but failed, or seemed to fail, in the larger world; they sought self-realization through art and religion despite family traditions of commerce and industry.

Both men created households where artists and writers visited and where becoming an artist was a natural development. Both men believed that the self was protean and they opposed both the settled life and the settled mind. Thus neither Henry James the novelist nor William Butler Yeats benefited from, nor had his mind destroyed by, a university education. Their fathers, believing themselves to be formidable institutions of higher learning in their own right, had no interest in exposing their sons to any competition. Both fathers were ambitious but almost incapable of bringing a large project to fruition. Talking for both took the place of doing, but both men were also capable of writing sentences of startling beauty. Both men loved New York, not for its intellectual life but for its crowded street-life, which they observed with fascination. Henry James Senior believed (or, to amuse a listener, claimed to believe) that the companionship of the crowded horsecar was the nearest thing to heaven on earth he had ever known. Their friends viewed both men as supremely delightful fellows; their company was much sought after. They both believed passionately in the future, seeing their children as fascinating manifestations of its power and possibility, at times much to their children's frustration. They were both capable of real originality. On 4 June 1917, for example, before his son wrote his poem "The Second Coming," John Butler Yeats wrote to him: "The millennium will come, and come it will, when Science and applied Science have released us from the burthens of industrial and other necessity. At present man would instantly deteriorate and sink to the condition of brutes if taken from under the yoke and discipline of toil and care." In a similar vein, Henry James Senior in 1879, almost two decades before his son wrote *The Turn of the Screw*, wrote the following account of a terror that came upon him on an ordinary evening in a rented house in Windsor Park:

To all appearances it was a perfectly insane and abject terror, without ostensible cause, and only to be accounted for, to my perplexed imagination, by some damned shape squatting invisible to me within the precincts of the room, and raying out from his fetid personality influences fatal to life. The thing had not lasted ten seconds before I felt myself a wreck, that is, reduced from a state of firm, vigorous, joyful manhood to one of almost helpless infancy.

Henry James Senior had five children and John Butler Yeats six, although two of the Yeats children died in infancy. Both men had a daughter in possession of a rich and sharp and brittle intelligence, so brittle indeed that it would somehow prevent both Lily Yeats and Alice James from separating from their families; both women had a magnificent and acid epistolary style. Both fathers cared, it seemed, more about their two elder children than the rest of their brood: William and Henry James and W. B. and Lily Yeats were treated differently than their younger siblings. John Butler Yeats and Henry James Senior each fathered two genius sons, four men – Henry and William James, W. B. and Jack Yeats – who specialized, unlike their fathers, perhaps almost in spite of their fathers, in finishing nearly everything they started. Three of them developed a complex, daring and extraordinary late style. All four boys studied art; William James had serious ambitions to be a painter. Two of them – W. B. Yeats and William James – began by dabbling in magic and mystical religion and went on to make it an important aspect of their life's work. While all four men were greatly influenced by their respective fathers – sometimes the influence was negative – they had hardly anything to say about their respective mothers. Both fathers employed the Atlantic Ocean as a weapon in their arsenal, John Butler Yeats using it as a way of getting away from his family in old age; Henry James Senior using it as a way of further unsettling his unsettled children.

Although Henry James the novelist saw a great deal of Lady Gregory in London in the 1880s and 1890s, he was not a friend of W. B. Yeats. By the time Yeats began to flourish in London, James had withdrawn to Rye. James, however, attended a performance of Yeats's play *The Hour-Glass* in Kensington in May 1903, and in 1915 he contacted Yeats on behalf of Edith Wharton, asking for a poem for a fund-raising anthology for the war effort. John Butler Yeats had strong views on the question of Henry James. In July 1916 he wrote to his son: "I have just finished a long novel by Henry James. Much of it made me think of the priest condemned for a long space to confess nuns. James has watched life from a distance." When James's unfinished third volume of autobiography was published posthumously, John Butler Yeats wrote to a friend: "Some believe that this war is a blessing disguised. It is enough for me that it stopped Henry James writing a continuation of 'The Middle Years.'" Two years earlier, he wrote to his son the poet: "Thinking about H James, I wonder why he is so obscure and why one's attention goes to sleep or wanders off when trying to make him out . . . In James, it is his cunning to make suspense dull, tiresome, holding you in spite of yourself."

When an exasperated John Quinn, the New York lawyer and art collector, wished to describe John Butler Yeats's endless and expensive stay in New York, he used James as his literary model. "The whole damn thing," Quinn wrote, "would make a perfect Henry James novel, and how he would get under your skin!" Quinn made himself the Ambassador and John Butler Yeats the Lama:

And so the book comes to a triumphant close, with the victory of the Lama over his family, over the Ambassador, over the Doctor, over the nurse, and over his friends, it all being a triumphant vindication of the philosophy of the ego, of the victory of the man who regards only himself, of the man who does not care for others when they cease to amuse him, the artist's ego, the ego parading in the poet's singing robes, and – to use a vulgarism which Henry James would, I am sure, hugely enjoy – the egotist in his singing robes, crowned with laurel, the consummate artist, the playboy of West 29th Street, the youth of eighty without a care, with never a thought of his family or his friends, with eternal self-indulgence, with an appetite for food and drink at the age of eighty that is the envy of his younger friends and the despair of the Ambassador; this young man who has enjoyed fifty years of play and talk and health and high spirits and wine and drink and cigars, the man who enjoys the evasions of the artist – he "gets away with it," as Henry James would say.

In 1884, two years after the death of Henry James Senior, William, his eldest son, edited a selection of his writings. This publication caused Henry James the novelist to feel "really that poor Father, struggling so alone all his life, and so destitute of every worldly or literary ambition, was yet a great writer." Henry James was thirty-nine when his father died and already, having published *The Portrait of a Lady*, one of the most famous novelists of the age. He could afford to be generous. His father's writings centred on religious questions and did not stray into the territory of fiction.

2

When W. B. Yeats was thirty-nine, in 1904, he could look forward to eighteen more years of his father's life; John Butler Yeats was said to be one of the few fathers who had lived long enough to be influenced by his son. He moved to New York at the end of 1907 and spent the last fourteen years of his life in the city. His letters to W. B. Yeats have been assembled by William M. Murphy and painstakingly typed and lie at peace in the library of Union College, Schenectady, where I read them in the summer of 2004, across the square from the dining hall where a portrait of William James of Albany hangs. In 1922 when John Butler Yeats died, John Quinn suggested that a new selection of his letters should be published. He wrote to W. B. Yeats: "I feel very strongly that instead of making extracts from his letters, his letters should be published in full as were the letters of Henry James."

These letters from father to son, from New York to Dublin, from the great unfinisher to the connoisseur of completion, are among the greatest ever written. They centre on art and on life in equal measure. They are mostly good-humoured, but their author can be angry when roused. Both Yeats and Henry James wrote autobiographies that included careful self-positioning and some invention, and that caused difficulty to family and friends; but James wrote his books when both his father and brother were dead. "Four Years," Yeats's essay in autobiography, was produced while his father was still alive. His father now felt free to attack his son's work. He wrote:

Had you stayed with me and not left me for Lady Gregory and her friends and associations you would have loved and adored concrete life for which as I know you have a real affection. What would have resulted? Realistic and poetical plays, and poetry in closest and most intimate union with the positive realities and complexities of life. And that is the world that awaits, so far in vain, its poet.

In families such as the Yeatses and the Jameses, where discussion of art and style was part of emotional life and writing was held in high esteem, attacks on each other's tone in poetry and prose could be used as a way to mask other attacks, or make the attacks more fierce. Literary criticism became the coinage in which old family feuds were paid and repaid. Thus in 1905, having read *The Golden Bowl*, William James could write to his brother, who was sixty-two years old: "But why won't you, just to please Brother, sit down and write a new book, with no twilight or mustiness in the plot, with great vigour and decisiveness in the action, no fencing in the dialogue, no psychological commentaries, and absolute straightness in the style?" So too in June 1921, when his son was in his mid-fifties, John Butler Yeats wrote:

Never are you happier and never more felicitous in words than when in your conversation you describe life and comment on it. But when you write poetry you as it were put on your dress coat and shut yourself in and forget what is vulgar to a man in a dress coat. It is my belief that some day you will write a play of real life in which poetry will be the inspiration, as propaganda is of G. B. Shaw's plays. The best thing in life is the game of life and some day a poet will find this out. I hope you will be that poet. It is easier to write poetry that is far away from life, but it is infinitely more exciting to write the poetry of life.

William James had begun as a painter and become a psychologist, but he was also a deeply self-conscious prose stylist. His style, he wrote to his brother in 1907, was "to say a thing in one sentence as straight and explicit as it can be made, and then to drop it for ever," as opposed to Henry's, which was, William wrote, "to avoid naming it straight, but by dint of breathing and sighing around and around it, to arouse in the reader who may have had a similar perception already (Heaven help him if he hasn't!) the illusion of a solid object."

The failure of Henry James Senior in life was compounded after his death by the failure of the collection of his writings. In 1887, when it was clear that sales had reflected critical reception, Henry, who had written to one reviewer telling him that his attack on the book had been contemptible and barbarous, wrote to William: "What you tell me of poor Father's book would make me weep if it weren't somehow outside and beyond weeping." Thus the two successful authors, William and Henry James, each in his prime, had managed to kill their father rather fatally, as it were, by letting his work be published in book form.

3

During his time in New York, John Butler Yeats was worried over and advised and bankrolled by his son the poet, who wrote about him and spoke about him as though he were an errant adolescent, a "youth of eighty without a care," as John Quinn put it. Slowly, over the years, father and son had exchanged roles. As a painter, John Butler Yeats could not compete with his elder son nor be overshadowed by him. But from the beginning of his exile in New York, John Butler Yeats also began to write stories and poems and a play, and in his letters he spoke of them to his son, as a starter to an older and more experienced writer. It is as if Senator Mann, having read his son's *Buddenbrooks*, began to write his own faltering fiction, or Sir Leslie Stephen, having seen paintings by his daughter Vanessa Bell, began to dabble in drawings. In the annals of letters between father and son, there is no starker enactment of a slow and humiliating murder than in the letters about writing between John Butler Yeats and his son. The old man is an infant, innocent in his pride and hope, the son distant, godlike and all-powerful, ready to ignore and criticize and quietly destroy. The son is cold and ruthless; the old man desperate to be murdered. It is as though Oedipus and Herod and some third force out of Freud's dark laboratory had joined forces.

At the turn of the century, John Butler Yeats incurred the wrath of the gods by praising his son Jack's play in a letter to his playwright son. He wrote: "I am greatly disappointed to learn from Cottie [Jack's wife] that you did not seem to care much for Jack's 'Flaunty.' I do think you are quite wrong." A few months later he wrote again: "Did I tell you about Jack's play written for the puppet theatre. It is the prettiest and most poetical little play I ever read . . . You and Moore and Pinero and Arthur Jones had better take lessons from Jack. I assure you the play haunts me. He must have a real gift for construction." In 1901 and 1902, as new plays by W. B. Yeats were performed, his father became one of his critics. "I cannot tell you how much I enjoyed your play," he wrote in 1902, "but I maintain that the end won't do." In 1913, having seen a production of *The Countess Cathleen* in New York, he wrote: "I think the play should have a prologue. It would help the illusion and give the necessary atmosphere. All at once we are expected without any warning to enter the world of miracle and hobgoblin, and it is too much."

Some of John Butler Yeats's letters to his son about his own writings date from the early years of the century. In 1902, he wrote:

I am finishing my story and am longing to read it to you. I shall be disappointed if you do not like it. So far no one except Susan Mitchell and Norman have heard it and they are very enthusiastic. G. Moore heard the first part some time ago and commended it much, although it is not the sort of story he would naturally like.

In March he wrote again: "If I get my story finished I think you will be pleased. I read the first part to Moore and Magee and their commendations have induced me to go on with it."

In 1908, in New York, John Butler Yeats wrote two short stories and sent them to his son. "I don't know what you will think about them," he wrote. A month later, when he had received no reply, he wrote: "I fear your not writing means that you don't care for my stories (possibly condemned unread). At any rate I should be much obliged if you would put them into a large envelope and send them back." The offhand reply that came nearly a year later did not help. It was dated 10 October 1909 and written from Coole. It ended: "I have found your two stories – they were among papers of Lady Gregory's. I must have lent them to her and asked her to read them. I send them to you. The one without a name is much the best, I think."

On 11 November, John Butler Yeats wrote unhappily once more about his stories, still not in fact returned. He was unclear, it seems, which one W. B. Yeats had liked:

You don't give me any clue as to which story of mine you read. There were two. I am very sorry that I sent them, but I shall now be much obliged to you if you will send them back to me as soon as possible. I want them. Of one of the stories, "The Ghost Wife," I have no other copy.

The one-sided argument between them over the stories continued. The following year he announced to his son: "I have my four stories in the hands of a literary agent, one a modern story, very crisp."

In 1909 John Butler Yeats began to correspond with his son about a play he was discussing with many people in New York, but not actually writing. One of those to whom he spoke was a producer called Percy MacKaye. On 24 March he wrote: "I enclose a little paragraph from 'The Sun' to show you that Percy MacKaye, who is so enthusiastic about my play, is a person of some position." Three weeks later, he wrote that the same Percy MacKaye had told him that "he felt sure if I submitted its scenario he could get a commission to write it. He spoke of the matter to me not once but a dozen times . . . He was most enthusiastic, imploring me to finish it, saying he would himself show it to every manager in New York."

Four years later, John Butler Yeats, full of hope, was still writing to his son about the play, but it remained in the realm of the imagination. "My heart is set on a play," he wrote in February 1913,

a psychological comedy. There are several thrills in it, where people will weep happy tears, and it will be all as a clever girl puts it "well woven." And as you may remember, Synge paid me one of his few compliments. He said I could write dialogue. The play has Unity and will go with a rush. Percy MacKaye told me he felt sure he could get me a commission to write it, if I would provide him with a written sketch of it.

It is likely that John Butler Yeats, in mentioning praise from Synge, was conscious of Synge's attitude towards the plays of W. B. Yeats and Lady Gregory, his fellow directors at the Abbey Theatre. Synge was, to say the least, grudging in his praise.

In 1916, now seventy-seven, J. B. Yeats continued to remind his son about the play he had still not written. On 6 January he wrote: "You know I have a play in my head and mean someday to write it . . . And you know Synge praised my dialogue. And I bet if it is written it will be a success. Just you wait and see." Nine days later he returned to the subject. "I am thinking more and more about my play. I think it will surprise you, but at present I am busy on my own portrait." The self-portrait was still not finished at the time of his death six years later.

Instead of finishing the play, W. B. Yeats's father wrote some poems which he sent to his son at the end of January 1916 with a letter of self-recommendation. "I send you some impromptu verses . . . I think they contain the rudiments of art and are spirited and have a beginning, a middle and an end and that's saying a good deal." When his son had not replied, he wrote again:

I send you a great many letters. I begin to think I am a born writer. Did you get my "poem"? I thought it had spirit and a sort of flowing inspiration. Flowing in its small way at full tide. When I was in College I once wrote some verses and showed them to a clever friend, the present Sir John Edge of the India council, and he pronounced them to be superior to anything by E. Dowden, who was then writing poetry for the College magazine. Perhaps had I followed up my "success," you would not be the first poet of my name. Ahem.

Two days later, John Butler Yeats wrote again: "I think I am entitled to call myself 'an inheritor of unfulfilled renown.' I told [Padraic] Colum and his wife the whole plot of my play. I never saw people more delighted or more eager that it should be written. Percy

MacKaye if he begged me once begged me twenty times to write it." Less than a fortnight later, he sent another letter about the play he was going to write:

As soon as my lecture [on 4 April] is over and past, I mean to get to work on my play. It is Destiny and must be fulfilled. All the details are in my mind, and I will make it drama. The characters, the dialogue, all shall be drama – with a breadth of treatment that will carry across the footlights. The hero is a poet whose idea is revolt against the sovereignty of any woman, he being in himself exceptionally susceptible to women – the heroine very much in love with the hero – her love a woman's, that is more of soul than of passion.

For the third time, Yeats the father mentioned Synge: "And remember Synge said I could write dialogue," he wrote, and then went on: "The whole play will be a novelty. I am confident. I have the idea, and I think that execution will be granted unto me. The play a success, I shall sing my 'nunc dimittis.'" His references to his writing and his sending his poems were met with silence from the other side of the Atlantic. On 19 March 1916 he wrote: "You say nothing about my 'poetry.' I did hope for a compliment on the 'spirit and go of my lines.'" In a postscript he added: "At any rate let me know if you got my verses."

By the end of May he had written more of the play:

I tell you it is good – not a tragedy or a satire or in any way profound, but a lively comedy. A psychological comedy, each character with its outlines distinct, with happy laughter and happier tears. I have not the slightest doubt that some day it will be acted. It is all in my head to the last line, and half or more of it is written, and it has its own melody and is a dream throughout.

The play was finished by October 1916. On 25 October he wrote to his son:

I have revised my play and as soon as possible will have it typed. And you will hear with consternation [my] mak[ing] the ghost express the state of his mind in rhymed verse, and by my soul, I think it is poetry – and it is modest poetry, like the poor ghost who sees it, and whose only wish is that he may be released from ghostdom and permitted to go down into Hell where his sweetheart waits.

Once the play was typed, its author was euphoric and foolish enough to write the following to his son, who had, by this time, written eleven plays:

As soon as I can manage it, I will send you my play. It is a Psychological Comedy and goes with speed and substance. I am convinced that when you have read it you will write to consult me as to your next play, showing it to me in its prose form. I think I shall be able to help you. I remember of old how quick you were to take a hint. You are receptive as well as creative.

Eleven days later, W. B. Yeats's father had more good news about his play. "Yesterday for the first time," he wrote, "I read my play to a group of friends, and I assure [you] I had a most successful first night. Also be it noted that they praised my poetry, which is I assure you in excellent rhyme." Eight days later he wrote again:

A few nights ago at Sloan's I read my little play to a small company. They were not literary, but just ordinary theatre-goers, and they were enthusiastic. It caught their fancies and I was given a very successful "first night." Among them was a literary man who admired my poetry. For there is a ghost who tells his story in rhymes which are as old as your castle. Age in a castle is admirable, but in Rhymes may be another matter.

In January of the following year, John Butler Yeats returned to the matter of his own value as a teacher of playwriting to his son. "I sometimes wish," he wrote, "that it had been possible for you to have consulted with me about your plays. I think I have a play-writing instinct, and that my play . . . proves it. And if it is simple it is without pretences, unaffected and easy, and yet fresh and new as a morning in June."

Later that year, John Butler Yeats wrote another story and a letter to his son displaying his confidence in it. "I have just completed what I think is a very pretty story, a tale of magic that will be said or sung I think many times by many people. You see how confident I am." A week later, he wrote again: "I have just written what I do not hesitate to call a lovely story which Spenser would not have been ashamed to have contrived. I never saw greater enthusiasm than Colum's when I read it to him. I am sure it will sell. There are several other stories which I have written. There is money in these." Two weeks later the euphoria about his stories remained: "Yesterday, I was at Quinn's and read to him two stories just finished, one from the land of phantasy, 'The Wizard's Daughter,' the other out of real life. He did not [know] which to prefer but was enthusiastic about both. Colum heard the wizard one and wanted then and there to carry it off to a magazine." The following day, John Butler Yeats decided to deliver the stories to a magazine himself. "Yesterday," he wrote to his son, "I left at Harper's my two stories, and I am very hopeful."

Despite his work on the stories, his interest in plays did not fade. On 5 November 1917 he wrote to his son: "It is my belief that if all of these years you had seen more of me you would have written quantities of plays." On 25 January he referred once more to his own play:

You will remember that I have for a long time been meditatively at work on a play. It is now finished and typed (it cost 6 dollars) . . . I am certain you will like it and perhaps be moved to re-write some lyrics I have written. They had to be written, but are of course quite amateurish. I think when you have read the play you will be inspired, yes inspired, to write real lyrics. I am certain there is money in the play, and that it will hold the boards, and perhaps return to them many times.

Two weeks later, the play had been sent. "I hope by this time," he wrote, "you have seen my play sent in a reg. Letter by John Quinn to Lilly [*sic*] and Lolly [Yeats]." Twelve days later, on 21 February 1918, he wrote again on the matter: "I am waiting to hear what you think of my play. If I find you like it I will be moved to write another scene (about which I have thought a great deal)." Still there was silence from the other side of the ocean. "Why don't you tell me about my play?" he wrote in June. "You need not be afraid to praise [it] . . . I feel quite sure that someday [it] will be acted and be a success."

4

Four days later, from Ballinamantane House in County Galway, where he was staying while Ballylee was being restored, W. B. Yeats, now fifty-two, wrote to his father, who was seventy-eight. "My dear Father," his letter began,

I have never written to you about your play. You choose a very diffi-cult subject and the most difficult of all forms, and as was to be foreseen, it is the least good of all your writings. I have been reading plays for the Abbey Theatre for years now, and so know the matter practically. A play looks easy, but is full of problems, which are almost a part of Mathematics – French dramatists display this structure and 17th century English dramatists disguise it, but it is always there. In some strange way, which I have never understood, a play does not even read well if it has not this mathematics. You are a most accom-plished critic – and I believe your autobiography will be very good, and this is enough for one man. It takes a lifetime to master dramatic form.

In March 1918 John Quinn received a letter from W. B. Yeats in which the poet arranged a matter that had been previously discussed by them: in exchange for Quinn's financial support for Yeats's improvident father in New York, Yeats would send Quinn manuscripts. Yeats went on:

Do you know is he going on with his autobiography? If he would finish that I might be able to get a very good price for that indeed from Macmillan, and would illustrate it with reproductions of pictures by himself, by Potter, by Nettleship etc. I hear with some alarm that he is writing a play, in which, as it is the most highly technical of all literary forms, he will most certainly not succeed while he certainly can succeed in the autobiography, and may do one of the finest that there is.

John Butler Yeats was not greatly disturbed by his son's view on his playwriting. On 8 July 1918 he wrote to him:

Your opinion of my play does not alter my opinion. I am quite sure that it will ultimately reach the boards and the public, although doubtless it will need alterations. But these will be superficial. The germ idea will remain. I have no doubt you are overanxious, the play being by your father. That is only natural. Percy MacKaye, a man of some expression, was of all my critics the one that gave me the most encouragement. He did not see the actual play, but I told him all about it.

Having invoked the spirit of Percy MacKaye, who had not read the play, Yeats the father clearly saw no difficulty in invoking the spirit once more of Synge, now dead almost ten years. "When I told Synge that you had discouraged my writing the play, and that you spoke a good deal about Rules etc he said 'Ask him if he himself obeys the rules.' Synge praised my dialogue. 'You at any rate can write dialogue' were his exact words and as you know praise from Synge was rather a rarity."

The significance of the phrase "You at any rate can write dialogue" would not have been lost on Yeats the son. It suggested that there were others who could not write dialogue and it implied that among them may have been W. B. Yeats himself. His father went on:

In my play there is phantasy. The old man made young is a creature of phantasy, and being good phantasy and consistent with itself is quite credible. I think he is a dear old man, and my heroine is right to love him even when he falls into sinfulness. The Colonel is the germ of my play, and the public won't miss it. I laugh to scorn all the croakers. But I must be careful, for you yourself are my only croaker.

It would be very easy to misinterpret John Butler Yeats's letters to his son about his own writings, to see them as merely foolish or boastful. They represent, it should be said, a tiny fraction of his concerns. He was mainly interested in the vocation of the poet, and he wrote with very great range, originality and energy on that subject; he was also fascinated by the meaning of life and was an astute observer of America. But unlike Henry James Senior, who was reduced by a crisis to a state of helpless infancy, John Butler Yeats did not need a crisis; he sought that state as an aspect of freedom, a way of living easily and hopefully and unsuspiciously in the world. He expressed this view often in his correspondence, most eloquently, perhaps, in a letter to W. B. Yeats written on 27 February 1916, where he pitted his own humility and his intense optimism against his son's grand majestic spirit:

I think there is always with me a residuum, a something at the bottom of the cup of my sorrows, and that something is a conviction, an intuition inseparable from life – that nothing is ever really lost, and that if we could see our world and all that takes place on its surface, and see it from a distance and as if from the centre of the sun, we should find it to be a fine piece of machinery working to certain ends with an absolute precision. I had in my only philosophy a faith founded like that of

Socrates upon the basis of my conscious ignorance – it is a sort of sub-lime optimism, and I am very satisfied with my ignorance as my betters are with their knowledge – and I call it sublime because it soars to such heights, and these logical people cannot reach it with their arrows, and I believe if the truth were known and confessed that this doctrine of a conscious ignorance is, at this present moment, the abiding solace and hope of all my fellow mortals. Grand majestic spirits will spurn it, but passive, inactive beings like myself, and all of us when the time comes that energy can no longer help and pride is humbled, will return to it as a last hope, and indeed the only one left – and so true it is to my mind that I feel I am writing only platitudes; moreover, I think it is only a doctrine for poets.

# Willie and George

In 1979, in a preface to a new edition of *Yeats: The Man and the Masks*, Richard Ellmann wrote about 46 Palmerston Road in Rathmines in Dublin, where George Yeats lived between her husband's death in 1939 and her own death almost thirty years later. Mrs. Yeats lived, Ellmann wrote, among the dead poet's papers. "There in the bookcases was his working library, often heavily annotated, and in cabinets and file cases were all his manuscripts, arranged with care . . . She was very good at turning up at once some early draft of a poem or play or prose work, or a letter Yeats had received or written." When Ellmann came to Dublin in 1946 to work on his book, "she produced an old suitcase and filled it with manuscripts that I wanted to examine. At the beginning she was anxious about one of them, the unpublished first draft of Yeats's autobiography, and asked me to return it speedily . . . I was able to allay her disquiet by returning the manuscript on time." She had, Ellmann wrote, provided Yeats with "a tranquil house, she understood his poems, and she liked him as a man." Now she oversaw the poet's legacy with canniness and care.

When John MacBride, Maud Gonne's estranged husband, was executed after the 1916 Rising in Dublin, Yeats talked once more of marriage to Maud, and then became involved with her daughter Iseult, to whom he also proposed. Joseph Hone writes about this in his authorized biography of the poet, published in 1942. After Iseult finally rejected him in the summer of 1917, he decided to propose to a young Englishwoman, George Hyde-Lees. He wrote to Lady Gregory: "I certainly feel very tired & have a great longing for order, for routine & shall be content if I find a friendly serviceable woman. I merely know... that I think this girl both friendly, serviceable & very able."

She also had money. He wrote to his father: "She is a great student of my subjects and has enough money to put us above anxiety and not too much money. Her means are a little more than my earnings and will increase later, but our two incomes together will keep us in comfort." They were married in October 1917. He was fifty-two; his new wife, soon to call herself George, was twenty-five. Ezra Pound, best man at the wedding, wrote to John Quinn in New York to say that he had known George Hyde-Lees as long as he had known his wife, who had been her best friend; he found her sensible and thought she would "perhaps dust a few cobwebs out of his belfry. At any rate she won't be a flaming nuissance [*sic*] to him and his friends."

Yeats wrote about their honeymoon in the introduction to *A Vision*:

On the afternoon of 24 October 1917, four days after my marriage, my wife surprised me by attempting automatic writing. What came in disjointed sentences, in almost illegible writing, was so exciting, sometimes so profound, that I persuaded her to give an hour or two day after day to the unknown writer . . . When the automatic writing began we were in a hotel on the edge of the Ashdown Forest, but soon returned to Ireland and spent much of 1918 at Glendalough, at Rosses Point, at Coole Park, at a house near it, at Thoor Ballylee, always more or less solitary, my wife bored and fatigued by her almost daily task and I thinking and talking of little else.

The first volume of Roy Foster's biography of Yeats, taking us up to 1914, showed that while no statement or public position by Yeats could be taken at face value, this did not mean that he was a chameleon or in a permanent state of vagueness. He was, it seemed, a chameleon when it suited his imaginative purpose or while he was on the Irish Sea. Once arrived, he could be full of firm and combative conviction. In writing about his life Foster manages an alertness to Yeats's political skills and certainties and his sense of command, and, at the same time, offers a nuanced reading of Yeats's protean enthusiasms and loyalties.

The slow release of Yeats's papers and letters over the past sixty years has helped to establish this sense of a Yeatsian self in constant re-creation. Ann Saddlemyer's biography of George Yeats offers a more taxing version of the life of Mrs. Yeats than Brenda Maddox's *George's Ghosts* (1999), but it does not solve the mysteries surrounding the relationship between Yeats's marriage and his work: it makes them instead more fascinating and more open to different readings and interpretations.

George Hyde-Lees's interest in the occult, which began a number of years before she met Yeats, was part of the spirit of the age. In 1891, the year before George's birth, Alice James confided to her diary: "I suppose the thing 'medium' has done has been more to degrade spiritual conception than the grossest form of materialism or idolatry: was there ever anything transmitted but the pettiest, meanest, coarsest facts and details: anything rising above the squalid intestines of human affairs?" Despite her objections, the James family continued to believe in transactions with the spirit world. When, in 1905, during a séance in Boston, a medium spoke in the presence of Mrs. William James of a communication from a "Mary" to Henry, the message was dutifully passed on to Henry James in England, who wrote that it was his "dear Mother's unextinguished consciousness breaking through the interposing vastness of the universe and pouncing upon the first occasion helpfully to get at me." Both James in his stories and Thomas Mann in *The Magic Mountain* (1924) understood the power that ghosts and séance scenes held in the imaginations of their readers. During the First World War, as Maddox says, "grieving millions turned to the spiritualist movement, searching for messages from their lost men." Arthur Conan Doyle wrote: "I seemed suddenly to see that it was really something tremendous, a breakdown of walls between two worlds, a direct undeniable message from beyond, a call of hope and of guidance to the human race at the time of its deepest affliction."

Both Yeats in the 1880s and his future wife thirty years later would use the occult movement in London as a way of educating themselves outside the confines of a university. Yeats described his early involvement with men "who had no scholarship, and they spoke and wrote badly, but they discussed great problems ardently and simply and unconventionally as men, perhaps, discussed great problems in the medieval universities." In 1911, when she was nineteen, George Hyde-Lees's stepfather gave her a copy of William James's *Pragmatism*, which asserted that "the true is the name of whatever proves itself to be good in the way of belief." She continued to admire William James's writing throughout her life. By 1912 she was attending lectures on early religion and mysticism and reading widely on medieval and Eastern religion. She applied for a reading ticket for the British Museum, expressing her interest in reading "all available literature on the religious history of the first three centuries." By the summer of 1913 she was including the study of the supernormal in her reading; her attendance at séances in London may have begun as early as the previous year. Soon she became interested in astrology. Her study was as serious and systematic as circumstances would allow, helped by an ambitious mother and a private income, and a knowledge of Italian and Latin. She was a regular visitor to her friend Dorothy Shakespear at her London flat after she married Ezra Pound in 1914; her relationship with the Pounds increased the breadth of her reading as well as offering her, and indeed her mother, an example of how someone with her unusual mixture of cleverness, earnestness and independence of mind might marry.

In this world of esoteric reading, leisured mysticism, visiting lecturers and poets making it new, Yeats had iconic status.

George's mother knew him: her second husband's sister was Olivia Shakespear, Dorothy's mother, with whom Yeats had had an affair and remained on good terms. George met Yeats in 1911. She remembered vividly that she saw him and recognized him one morning in the British Museum, and later that same day while he was taking tea with her mother at Olivia Shakespear's she was introduced to him. He was three years older than her mother and the same age as her father, who had been dead for two years, would have been. Over the next while, as George's mother and her circle sojourned outside London, they were joined by the poet on a number of occasions. In February 1912 Yeats wrote to Lady Gregory: "I am at Margate with a Mr. and Mrs. Tucker (she was a Mrs. Hyde-Lees who I have known vaguely for years). I got rather out of sorts, digestion wrong & so on & wanted to do nothing for a day or two . . . This is a dismal place & it rains all day but it is very quiet & a good change & I am with pleasant people & out of the Dublin atmosphere."

Yeats was responsible for the induction with great ceremony and solemnity of George Hyde-Lees into the Hermetic Order of the Golden Dawn, a sort of Masonic Lodge for those interested in the occult, in July 1914. Here once again her dutiful, serious-minded, studious self emerged as she made her way through the Order's elaborate stages, arriving at the same level as Yeats by 1917. In these years, as the war intensified, she worked as a part-time volunteer orderly and nurse in London while continuing her reading and visits to the British Museum. At the end of February 1917 she and Yeats went together to a séance; it seems that the following month he discussed with her the possibility of marriage. He did not then formally propose, but instead left her waiting while he dallied with Maud Gonne and her daughter.

When he did propose, six months later, she accepted him. He described himself as "a Sinbad who after many misadventures has at last found port," but in the days that followed explained his plans for a continuing familiarity not only with Maud Gonne but with her daughter, Iseult. He made this clear to his betrothed and, in turn, to her mother. Her mother wrote in alarm to Lady Gregory, the person who she knew could most influence Yeats, and one of the few who was already aware of the engagement: "I now find this engagement is based on a series of misconceptions so incredible that only the context can prove them to be misconceptions." Her daughter, she wrote, believed that the poet had wanted to marry her for some time, but the mother's own impression now was that, instead, "the idea occurred to him that as he wanted to marry, she might do." George, she wrote,

is under the glamour of a great man thirty years older than herself & with a talent for love-making. But she has a strong and vivid character and I can honestly assure you that nothing could be worse for her than to be married in this manner . . . If Georgie had an inkling of the real state of affairs she would never consent to see him again; if she realized it after her marriage she would leave him at once.

Having interrogated the poet, who had come to Coole, Lady Gregory, in a letter that is now lost, seems to have tried to reassure the mother. She wrote also to George, expressing the hope that she would come to Galway soon before the floods rose above Ballylee, the ruined castle that Yeats had bought a year earlier. George, in the meantime, had been brought by Yeats to meet Maud Gonne and Iseult. Maud wrote to Yeats:

I find her graceful & beautiful, & in her bright picturesque dresses, she will give life and added beauty to the grey walls of Ballylee. I think she has an intense spiritual life of her own & on this side you must be careful not to disappoint her . . . Iseult likes her very much, and Iseult is difficult & does not take to many people.

Despite this, she told others that she believed the marriage to be "prosaic." Arthur Symons wrote to John Quinn: "I wish you had heard Maude [*sic*] laugh at Yeats's marriage – a good woman of 25 – rich of course – who has to look after him; who might either become his slave or run away from him after a certain length of time."

Thus in October 1917 George Hyde-Lees found herself on her honeymoon with W. B. Yeats, who was suffering from nervous stomach disorders. They went first to his flat in London and then to a hotel, where he received a note from Iseult wishing him well. Later, George told an interviewer that she felt him "drifting away from her." He wrote to Iseult making clear his belief that he had made a mistake. Both he and George were miserable. Yeats began work on the poem about Iseult Gonne that eventually became "Owen Aherne and His Dancers," using a notebook that Maud Gonne had given him:

> I can exchange opinion with any
> neighbouring mind
> I have as healthy flesh & blood as any
> rhymer's had,
> But oh my heart could bear no more when the upland caught the wind;
> I ran, I ran from my love's side because my
> heart went mad.

"What followed," Saddlemyer writes,

> has been described several times by George herself . . . Fully aware of the reason for his unhappiness, first she contemplated leaving him. But then, reluctant to surrender what had been for so many years her destination, she considered arousing his interest through their joint fascination with the occult. She decided to "make an attempt to fake automatic writing" and then confess to her deception once her distracted husband was calmer.

George made this admission that she faked it in the early 1950s to Virginia Moore, who was researching her book *The Unicorn*:

*William Butler Yeats' Search for Reality.* Yeats remembered the first words as: "With the bird all is well at heart. Your action was right for both but in London you mistook its meaning." George remembered writing: "What you have done is right for both the cat and the hare." Yeats would have understood that she was the cat and Iseult the hare or the bird. George's hand continued to move and wrote, according to Yeats: "You will neither regret nor repine."

"The word 'fake' would continue to haunt George, even though it was a phrase she herself employed in speaking with Virginia Moore and Ellmann," Saddlemyer writes. In 1961, when Norman Jeffares was writing his introduction to Yeats's *Selected Poems,* she wrote to him: "I dislike your use of the word 'Fake' . . . I told you this before & you had a happier phrasing in your book. However, I cannot ask you to alter this. The word 'Fake' will go down to posterity."

The words she wrote, in any case, worked wonders. Within days, Yeats described his new happiness to Lady Gregory: "The strange thing was that within half an hour after writing of this message my rheumatic pains & my neuralgia & my fatigue had gone & I was very happy. From being more miserable than I ever remember being since Maud Gonne's marriage I became extremely happy. That sense of happiness has lasted ever since."

It is easy to understand George's objection to the word "fake," despite her own use of it. By the time she spoke of these events to young and eager scholars, séances and the occult and automatic writing had gone well out of vogue. Also, the memory of what it was like in that hotel room on her honeymoon with the great poet must have been raw beyond explanation, easier to dismiss casually than explain carefully. Using the word "fake" herself was defensive; seeing someone else using it made it different.

Before she married him, she knew Yeats's work, attended his lectures and bought his books; she knew of his love for Maud

Gonne and his affair with her stepfather's sister. She knew also of his love for Iseult Gonne and may even have known of her mother's letter to Lady Gregory. She realized now not only that the famous poet did not love her and had married her on a whim, but that the idea of the poet, which would have fascinated her, was far removed from the grumpy, sickly, indifferent and miserable man with whom she was now confined in a small space.

In her panic that day, as she began to write in the room, neither her motive nor the language that came to her can be accurately described, however, as fake. What happened was that her needs and her reading converged as she began to eroticize the occult and its attendant forces, just as Maud Gonne had done with Irish nationalism. She was working with desperate longings under pressure; she was producing sentences that made those apparent, followed by words that came at will, easily, from her conscious and her unconscious selves, brought closer to each other by a fear and pain that offered her an unusual receptivity. It seemed that she both believed and didn't believe in what she was doing. She was moving deliberately and sleepwalking at the same time. Ellmann's interview notes with her from 1946 read: "Had it not been for the emotional involvement, she thinks nothing would have come of it – but as it was she felt her hand grasped and driven irresistibly."

Yeats was tireless and unembarrassed in his questioning of the spirit, asking many questions, for example, about former loves. And she, in turn, allowed the automatic writing at times to make clear her own sexual needs. In this strange time between the prevailing influence of Madame Blavatsky and that of Sigmund Freud, they both remained ambivalent about the power of a medium to control the autonomous power of the unconscious mind. In 1913 Yeats wrote: "Because mediumship is dramatisation, even host mediums cheat at times either deliberately or because some part of the body has freed itself from control of the waking will, and almost always truth and lies are mixed together." George's problem was that she was now, on a daily basis, embodying this dramatization, in all its ambiguities and complexities. She was both cheating and allowing some part of herself to be freed from conscious control.

She was moving in dangerous territory, having been enough in occult circles to know how much opprobrium was heaped on the quack and the fake. Her husband needed her to keep working, especially once the medium said, in a beautiful phrase, that he had come "to give you metaphors for poetry"; she needed him, in turn, to stop talking in public about it, and she used the medium to warn him to be silent. She told Ellmann that her only serious quarrel with him in all the years of their marriage concerned his wish to publish a description of her automatic writing in the second edition of *A Vision*.

The medium gave him, as promised, metaphors for poetry. The experience, and her wish to keep it hidden, also gave him one of his narrative poems, "The Gift of Harun Al-Rashid," in which the woman in her sleep offers the scholar hidden knowledge:

> *Or was it she that spoke or some great Djinn?*
> *I say that a Djinn spoke. A live-long hour*
> *She seemed the learned man and I the child.*

The narrator has cause to wonder, as George must have done in those early months of their marriage, if the sleeping wisdom that she offers is the sole basis for his love:

> *What if she lose her ignorance and so*
> *Dream that I love her only for the voice,*
> *That every gift and every word of praise*
> *Is but a payment for that midnight voice*
> *That is to age what milk is to a child?*

His reply to that question must have been of considerable interest:

> All, all those gyres and cubes and midnight things
> Are but a new expression of her body
> Drunk with the bitter sweetness of her youth.
> And now my utmost mystery is out.
> A woman's beauty is a storm-tossed banner.

When George went with her husband to Ireland soon after her marriage, every move she made was studied intensely by the five women who were most involved with the poet. They were his unmarried sisters Lily and Lolly; Maud Gonne and Iseult; and Lady Gregory. The fact that George managed never to quarrel with any of them while maintaining her distance from each says a great deal about her patience and her temperament.

Lily and Lolly wrote to their father in New York describing their new sister-in-law. "You feel that she has plenty of personality but that her disposition is so amiable that she does not often assert herself," Lolly wrote, "not from inertness but because she is happiest in agreement with people around her." When they went to the Abbey Theatre, Lily noticed that "when the lights went down George used to sit forward and look round me at him, smile to herself and sit back again." When George's daughter, Anne, was born in 1919 and son, Michael, in 1921, the sisters became enthusiastic babysitters and general chroniclers of their brother's household. "I think George enjoys the thrill she gets when she gives her name in shops," Lolly wrote. "Mrs. W. B. Yeats." Lily thought her sister-in-law "delightfully sane, just think of all the pests of women that are going about who suffer from nerves and think it soul – and so does some unlucky man till he marries them – Willy is in luck."

In London soon after her marriage, George set about befriending Iseult Gonne, inviting her to stay the night, giving her a dress for Christmas and generally taking the harm out of her. The following year, when her mother was imprisoned for sedition, Iseult stayed at Yeats's old flat in London and was sent money by George, who wrote worried motherly letters to Ezra Pound (who would soon have an affair with Iseult) about the need for her to find a job, doubting if she would consent to doing "machine work." When Iseult began to share a flat with the highly unsuitable mistress of Wyndham Lewis, both Yeats and George arrived from Dublin and swooped on the place, as though they were her parents, removing Iseult, Josephine her maid, her cat, her birds and her furniture to more decent quarters. George was less than two years older than she.

Taking the harm out of Maud Gonne would prove more difficult. In October 1918, while Maud Gonne remained in prison, Yeats and George rented her house, 73 St. Stephen's Green in Dublin. "Should you be released," Yeats wrote to her, "and allowed to live in Ireland we will move out, which strangers would not." The following month, while pregnant with her first child, George caught the influenza virus that was raging through Europe. Yeats feared that she was dying. Maud Gonne, too, had been ill in Holloway Prison, and, after much agitation, was released to a nursing home in London. From there she fled to Yeats's old flat, where Iseult was living. She wrote to Yeats: "My home in Dublin is the best place for all of us, with Josephine to cook for us. Please try & arrange that." Ezra Pound wrote to John Quinn: "I hope no one will be ass enough to let her get to Ireland . . . It is a great pity, with all her charm, that the mind twists everything that goes into it, on this particular subject" – he meant politics, adding in brackets: "Just like Yeats on his ghosts." On 24 November, Saddlemyer writes, "disguised as an emaciated Red Cross nurse (perhaps in the very uniform George had cast off on her marriage), Maud slipped through the immigration line and arrived at the door of 73 St. Stephen's Green, demanding shelter." She was accompanied by her two children and had much menagerie.

Yeats refused to let her in, and even when a doctor arrived and informed Maud Gonne that her continued presence might endanger George's life, "still the lunatic refused to go," as Lily Yeats wrote to John Quinn. Yeats "had a scene with her and turned her out." She wrote him venomous letters and denounced him to her fellow nationalists. "Later she would complain," Saddlemyer writes, "that although married to a rich wife, he took advantage of her in prison by offering such a low rent, and she never forgot that George's pet hares ate all the greenery in her garden." In spite of this, once the Yeatses moved out, cordial but distant relations were established, and Yeats began to attend Maud's "at homes" on Tuesdays at number 73. The following summer, as George stayed with her baby daughter in Galway and Ireland prepared for guerrilla war, one of her mediums warned her husband "not to be drawn into anything . . . you may be tempted to join in political schemes if there is trouble and you must not." The figure of Maud in the automatic writing was the "Bird with white & black head & wings." She was "dangerous . . . Nothing must be said unless *she* speaks of it – then simply say you are destroying the souls of hundreds of young men. That method is most wicked in this country – wholesale slaughter because a few are cruel . . . I am not sure of her." A few years later Yeats wrote to George that Maud Gonne "had to choose (perhaps all women must) between broomstick and distaff and she has chosen broomstick."

Of the women who were closest to Yeats, Lady Gregory was the one he saw most of after his marriage. George, Yeats's father noted when he met her in New York, was "the only woman I have ever met who is not scared of Lady Gregory. I fancy Lady Gregory is extra civil to her – naturally." She was, he wrote, "too intelligent" not to see Lady Gregory's "great merit, but yet alive to the necessities of self-defence." The two women had much in common: notably steadfastness, conscientiousness, and a belief in Yeats's genius. "They were shrewd judges of character," Saddlemyer writes, "and generous in the service of others; although good listeners, neither suffered fools or deceivers gladly."

Later, when the Yeatses had a house in Dublin, Lady Gregory stayed with them on her visits to the city. She attended Yeats's "Mondays" in the house. "It is supposed to be for men only," she wrote, "and might be better so." Unlike Mrs. Oliver St. John Gogarty, however, who presided at her husband's evenings, George Yeats "always discreetly withdrew, reappearing only to serve refreshments." When Lady Gregory came to stay, George gave up her room for her, ran messages and answered the telephone for her, all the while maintaining civil and often warm relations with her. In 1927 she wrote to a friend: "Lady G was here for one whole month . . . only left yesterday and I have been sitting in the smallest possible nutshell in order to preserve a moderate outward sanity." Even though she blamed Gregory for the controversy over the Abbey Theatre's rejection of Sean O'Casey's *The Silver Tassie*, calling her "an obstinate old woman," she kept her resentments to a few correspondents, including Dorothy Pound:

Christ how she repeats herself now . . . she'll tell you the same saga quite literally three times in less than an hour, and repeat it again the next day, and the day after that too. Burn when read . . . She wants W to go down to Coole for most of September, and I hope he will – he doesn't seem to mind the reiterations. Personally they send me nearer lunacy than anything I ever met.

Houses and flats and rooms had the same power for Yeats as phases of the moon. It is not a coincidence that a short time after his marriage he moved Iseult into his flat in London and then rented Maud Gonne's house in Dublin. By allowing Iseult to inhabit his London rooms and by his own moving daily in the house her mother bought, and then by refusing them entry to 73 St. Stephen's Green, he was enacting and exorcizing these two women's haunting of him. He was also behaving sensibly. Yeats was good at making sure that even sensible behaviour had an undertow of symbolic resonance.

Thus he bought the derelict Norman keep at Ballylee in 1917, to assist him in his dreaming, telling Lady Gregory that its decoration would "depend on my wife if I marry." In June he wrote to a friend: "I am 51 myself and do not like it at all and keep thinking of all the follies I have committed not to have someone to talk to after nightfall and to bring me gossip of the neighbours. Especially now that I am going to own a castle and a whole acre of land." Once married, George joined the dream and began to plan the renovation of the tower at Ballylee. "Among the duties she took over," Maddox writes, "was the correspondence with Rafferty, the builder who was renovating Thoor Ballylee. She did more. She paid, from her own bank account, the bills for the tower she had never seen in the country she had never visited."

George's work on planning its restoration became, like her automatic writing, her contribution to the store of myth and symbol that would continue to nourish Yeats's work. Nonetheless, both Yeats and Lady Gregory were concerned that George should not see the tower at its most inhospitable in winter, when it flooded and the walls were wet with damp. When they spent part of the summer of 1919 there, Yeats drew an idyllic picture for his father. "It may well be," William Murphy later wrote in his biography of Yeats's father, "that one of the happiest days of his life was 16 July 1919. Fishing in the stream by the tower, with George sewing and 'Anne lying wide awake in her 17th-century cradle,' he saw an otter chasing a trout." His tower, Yeats wrote to John Quinn, was "a place to influence lawless youth, with its severity and antiquity. If I had had this tower when Joyce began I might have been of use, have got him to meet those who might have helped him." Joyce, however, might have been more interested in the fact that conditions in the tower were so primitive. The nearest shop was four and a half miles away. It had no electricity or plumbing. "Water for washing," Maddox writes,

> had to be fetched from the river in a large galvanised water carrier on wheels, while drinking water came from another source farther away. Family life took place mainly in the cottage (where the single earth-closet was located); peat fires or oil stoves had to be kept lit to reduce the dampness seeping from the walls. The roof and top floors of the tower were unfinished, and there was no possibility of sleeping there.

The tower at Ballylee belonged firmly in the category of writers' second houses, offering shelter to areas of imaginative energy rather than the growing family; it was dreamed into being, and then reworked and reconstructed in the way a poem was made. Both George and Yeats entered into the spirit of it wholeheartedly, pouring money into it, including much of the proceeds of Yeats's American tour in 1920, and mentioning it constantly as the place to which they most longed to go. It was also their main connection to Ireland as the Black and Tan War raged. Lady Gregory must have taken a sly pleasure in writing from Coole in December 1920: "Your Oxford life sounds very peaceful – All chaos here still . . . The Black & Tans visited Ballylee, opened the door with a key & went in & there were rumours they were going to settle there." This caused Pound to report to Quinn: "George just in to say that the Blackantans have tanned Ballylee." No damage was done, however, and, as their second child was born, the Yeatses continued to plan a return to the tower, Yeats writing to Lady Gregory that his wife talked "constantly of the trees and of her garden and of the river."

In April 1921 they returned after an eighteen-month absence and were able to sleep for the first time in the tower itself, in the large bedroom above the ground floor. Yeats wrote to Quinn: "It is a great pleasure to live in a place where George makes at every moment a 14th-century picture. And out of doors, with the haw- thorn all in blossom all along the river banks, everything is so beautiful that to go elsewhere is to leave beauty behind." Yeats wrote at a desk by the window, where he could watch the stares, or starlings, flying in and out of their nest, and, as the Civil War broke out in April 1922, this gave him the final line of each stanza in "The Stare's Nest by My Window":

> *A barricade of stone or of wood;*
> *Some fourteen days of civil war;*
> *Last night they trundled down the road*
> *That dead young soldier in his blood:*
> *Come build in the empty house of the stare.*

While they had sat out the Black and Tan War in Oxford, now they would witness first-hand the Civil War – which was danger- ous for Yeats as a supporter of the Free State. In August, when the bridge at Ballylee was blown up, George wrote to Ottoline Morrell:

& when the fuses were lit & all the men ran off as hard as they could pelt, one man stayed behind to say: "In a few minutes now. There will be two explosions. Good night! Thank you." As though he was thank- ing us for the bridge! . . . At the time, after a feeling of panic when we heard the irregulars knocking at the door & had to go out to speak to them, one felt nothing but a curiosity to see how it was done & to try & save windows etc. But since then we have both felt rather ill & our hearts both hopping & stopping.

By the end of 1923, with the Civil War over, her husband having won the Nobel Prize and now a senator in the Irish Free State, with a house in Merrion Square (the equivalent of Berkeley Square in London, Yeats wrote to a friend), with the tower com- ing into shape, and two engaging children, and the Irish Sea between herself and her mother, who could irritate her, George Yeats had added to her happiness by having a number of Irish friends of her own. Like many women of her class, she was in need of a pair of homosexual men to confide in and gossip with, and these came in the guise of the playwright Lennox Robinson and the poet Thomas MacGreevy. Since most of Dublin suspected their homosexuality, "neither was a threat to the good name of Mrs. W. B. Yeats," Saddlemyer writes. She worked with both on the Dublin Drama League, which sought to produce more cosmopolitan work than was being put on at the Abbey. When MacGreevy moved to London in 1925, she wrote: "I wish you were back here. Willy said last night very solemnly: "Now MacGreevy's not here we have to do our own gossiping.'" In August of that year, the Yeatses spent time in Milan with Robinson and MacGreevy. Yeats, it seemed, did not enjoy the trip as much as George and her two new friends. He stayed in the hotel when the others went out sightseeing.

"Only six years older than she," Saddlemyer writes, "Lennox quickly became George's devoted pal. Together they gambled on the sweeps, went to the races (both horse and dog), the opera, the cinema and the theatre; they shared their experiences in gardening and breeding canaries." And they both drank a good deal, Robinson slowly becoming hopelessly alcoholic.

In London, MacGreevy, much to George's consternation, also befriended her mother, who immediately began to flirt with him. "You make me wish I were your own age," her mother wrote to him, "we could play a good game." By encouraging him to become an artist she seemed to feel that she had become one, too: "Love must be kept firmly in the present, it is a thing without past or future . . . The fact remains that, fundamentally and however painfully, we are artists and artists we shall remain, and we both know that art is the only thing that matters and the one thing that makes the world tolerable."

Soon George's mother and the young Irish poet were discussing George, much to George's annoyance:

Please please please, don't mention my name to my mother when you are writing to her more than is consistent with the usual necessities . . . My mother loves to make a whirlpool and especially if she can suck me in to it, and she has probably worked herself up into an annoyance with me in order to amuse herself over the Xmas holidays. That was why I said gaily to you in London: "you are not to discuss me with my mother."

Robinson and MacGreevy, in the early years of their acquaintance with George, thickened the plot by indulging in unrequited love. In 1919, Robinson, whose idol was Yeats, fell for Iseult Gonne, who rejected him despite Yeats's suggestion that they should marry. Yeats's sisters invited the unhappy couple to supper, but Lily remained doubtful that Iseult would change her mind. The following year Iseult married the eighteen-year-old Francis Stuart. George, Saddlemyer writes, sympathized with Robinson's "lingering affection for Iseult."

Both gentlemen then directed their attention towards the artist Dolly Travers Smith, with whose mother, Hester, a well-known medium, they were also friends, both having boarded with her at different times. (Hester's books included *Oscar Wilde from Purgatory: Psychic Messages*.) Hester and Dolly were to become the third mother and daughter in Yeats's circle who provoked interest in the same men. George thought Hester "the unbending hard essence of everything I loathe mentally, emotionally and temperamentally. She makes me think of lumpy beds, Russian fleas and ipecacuanha wine."

In the same years that she was getting to know Robinson and MacGreevy, George was also spending time at Thoor Ballylee. In March 1926, she wrote to MacGreevy: "I go to Ballylee Thursday morning for three glorious days of solitude & cabbage planting

& on my return will write you a sober & sane & reasonable letter." But there are also letters of complaint about conditions
there, and the amount of hard work required to keep the place
going. Yeats, in the meantime, was writing poems that used the
tower at Ballylee as symbol and icon. In February 1928 *The Tower*
was published. For the cover of the book Thomas Sturge Moore
had made an etching of Thoor Ballylee. "Now," Saddlemyer
writes,

with that magnificent volume and *A Vision* both published, from now
on, while still "this blessed place," the tower had become emblazoned
on his heraldic shield for all to recognize, assess and debate. Proud as
she might be of the poetry she had done so much to make possible, the
penalty was an inevitable dissipation of the original magic; by remaking
the imagery, Yeats had once again taken possession of the tower itself.

The tower had served its purpose; like the automatic writing,
Thoor Ballylee had delivered him metaphors for his poetry; it
had also allowed George to function in the domestic sphere while
at the same time empowering Yeats, offering him both comfort
and a charged environment. Once the book was published, neither she nor Yeats had any desire to go back there. Despite all the
specially commissioned furniture, the letters to the builder, the
planning and dreaming, after 1928 the tower remained closed, a
symbol of the way writers use houses for their magic properties
rather than their domestic space. Over the next few years, as
Lady Gregory's health was declining, Yeats spent a good deal of
time at Coole and "dutifully reported on regular inspections of
the rapidly deteriorating cottage and castle." When she grew
older his daughter, Anne, "tentatively asked whether she might
go there to paint, but George's monosyllabic refusal was so
abrupt that she gave up the idea of ever returning."

The abandonment of the tower may also be bound up with an
essential change in the relationship between George and Yeats.

Around 1928 and 1929 she ceased to have a close sexual relationship with him and became his nurse, the devoted mother of his
children and a great worrier on his behalf. Yeats and their children seemed to suffer from great numbers of illnesses. From the
time George and Yeats went on holiday to Spain in November
1927 until he died in January 1939, the state of his health and her
children's health became George's main preoccupation; her tone
in letters is often bitter and disappointed. In 1928 she wrote to
MacGreevy: "had I known that all this might happen I should
certainly never have had a family." She added "burn this when
read" at the top of the letter. When in Spain Yeats's lung began to
bleed, they made their way with difficulty to France and from
there to Rapallo. Yeats wrote to Olivia Shakespear that George
was "all goodness and kindness." George, as she tried to get the
children to Italy, wrote to Robinson: "I felt for years that life was
quite unnecessary & if only a landslide would remove me they
could have jointly a nurse a governess a secretary & a housekeeper & all get on so much better."

In March 1928, George signed a lease on a large flat close to
Ezra and Dorothy Pound overlooking the bay at Rapallo, where
they spent two winters. Anne and Michael were sent to school in
Switzerland. Yeats was released from being a "sixty-year-old smil-
ing public man" in Ireland. The company in Rapallo included the
German poet Gerhart Hauptmann and the American composer
George Antheil; others such as Max Beerbohm, Richard Aldington, Siegfried Sassoon and Basil Bunting passed through. In
Rapallo Yeats recovered and relapsed and needed constant care.
"Never was his dependence on George greater, or more pathetic,"
Maddox writes. "When told he needed a night nurse so that his
wife could get some relief, he wept." Mostly in these years she
was patient, but his helplessness sometimes exhausted her even
temper. When she sent him a lamp to Coole in 1931 and he wrote
to ask what oil to put into it, she replied: "The lamp of course

consumes lamp oil, paraffin. What in Heaven's name else could it consume?! Its very form shouts paraffin oil; you could surely not have imagined that it demanded Sanctuary oil, or olive oil."

In Ireland, the Yeatses gave up the house in Merrion Square for a flat in Fitzwilliam Square, and then in 1932 moved to a large house with a garden south of Dublin. When de Valera came to power Yeats flirted briefly with the Blueshirts, a semi-comic Irish Fascist group. George did not share his sympathies. She hated the Blueshirts. Unlike her husband, she was a de Valera supporter and voted Fianna Fáil.

After the Rapallo sojourn he bounced back, writing to Olivia Shakespear in 1933 that the writing of the Crazy Jane poems was "exciting and strange. Sexual abstinence fed their fire – I was ill yet full of desire. They sometimes came out of the greatest mental excitement I am capable of." Two years later he told Iseult Gonne, who told Richard Ellmann, that "everything was terrible. He and his wife had gradually been alienated – he said she was a mother rather than a wife – that she had humiliated him in public." By then he had had a vasectomy, and begun to receive injections that increased his sexual desire in the very years when he was mourning lost sexual opportunities in his youth. "Wonderful things have happened," he wrote to Olivia. "This is Baghdad. This is not London."

The old poet started then to make up for lost time. Just as in the 1890s he had moved between Dublin and London, reinventing himself at each crossing, now forty years later London was once more a place that offered freedoms not available in Dublin. In his seventies, with a few years left, he began to have love affairs. George nursed him when he returned exhausted, and seemed concerned that his friends should hear regular news about his condition before he set off again. In January 1935 she wrote to Gogarty: "I would rather he died in happiness than in invalidism. He may not have told you of all his past 18 months' activities.

One of them is that he has been very much in love with a woman in London." She told Richard Ellmann that she said to him: "After your death people will write of your love affairs, but I shall say nothing, because I will remember how proud you were." In June 1936, having left Yeats with Dorothy Wellesley, with whom he was having an affair, she returned to Dublin. Robinson wrote to Dolly: "W. B. is not coming back at the moment to G's relief, though Olive says she wants him back as soon as possible (she knows). I think I know that G at any rate wants to play roulette on Sat – and not have Willy." Earlier, however, when she went with him to Liverpool, but did not see him off on the boat for Spain, she wrote: "I felt too like the dog who sees his master going for a walk and leaving him at home."

In other words, her response to his affairs was ambivalent. She drank and was often ill; she was also lonely as Anne left home and Michael went to boarding-school. Nonetheless, she was practical and managerial and full of understanding, even writing to his new loves various accounts of his medical needs. She seems to have encouraged his regular decamping. When he read out loud to George a paragraph of one girlfriend's letter that suggested that he and the woman might not travel to France alone, "she laughed at the idea of our not going alone. That means her blessing . . . Other people's minds are always mysterious and I wanted that blessing."

Blessings might have come easy, but perhaps the most extraordinary aspect of her self-sacrifice was her willingness to cross the Irish Sea with him as far as Holyhead, accompany him through customs, get him on the train in the direction of one of his liaisons, and then return alone on the same day to Dublin. "It was," Saddlemyer writes, "a long day: an 8.25 train in order to catch the mail boat at Kingstown (now Dun Laoghaire), landing at Holyhead at 11.45, and departing again at 2.30 for arrival in Ireland at 5.25 p.m. This would become a regular routine." No wonder she was drinking.

By the beginning of 1939, Yeats was in the South of France with George; Dorothy Wellesley and her friend Hilda were close by; and Edith Shackleton, another of his lovers, soon arrived. On Friday 27 January, when he lapsed into a coma, Dorothy saw him for a few minutes, then Edith sat by his bedside; the following day, watched over by George, he died. All three women attended the poet's burial at Roquebrune near Menton on 30 January.

As George returned to Ireland, she must have known that she had deprived the nation of one of its greatest joys – a big funeral. There was always something wonderful about the way she kept apart from Irish patriotism and fanaticism and puritanism; her arrival home now without the body of the great poet was almost heroic. As she set about comforting her family, however, the country went into spasm. Maud Gonne wrote to de Valera, the President, and the Abbey Theatre, urging that Yeats be buried in Ireland. The poet F. R. Higgins, representing the board of the Abbey Theatre, replied: "We are making every endeavour to have the remains brought home to Ireland . . . I know personally he had a passionate desire to rest in Sligo." The theatre's message to George about the matter was, as Saddlemyer says, "aggressive in its urgency." The Dean of St. Patrick's in Dublin offered a grave in the cathedral. De Valera hoped "that his body will be laid to rest in his native soil." What was interesting about all this, besides the national ghoulishness in full flow, was that, since George Yeats had remained so private and reserved and in the background during her years in Ireland, no one felt a need to mention her in their statements. Clearly, the Englishwoman Yeats had married was not cut out to become the national widow.

Yeats did indeed wish to be buried in his native soil, but he had witnessed the funeral of George Russell, the poet Æ, in 1935, and been appalled by the level of pomp. Five months before he died he had written to Dorothy Wellesley: "I write my poems for the Irish people but I am damned if I will have them at my funeral. A

Dublin funeral is something between a public demonstration & a private picnic." In March 1939, George wrote to MacGreevy that Yeats had asked to be buried in Roquebrune "and then in a year's time when the newspapers have forgotten me, dig me up and plant me in Sligo." George waited until Richard Ellmann came to Dublin in 1946 to report that her husband had also said: "I must be buried in Italy, because in Dublin there would be a procession, with Lennox Robinson as chief mourner."

When the first biography appeared, she wrote to Frank O'Connor that she was "afraid now that it is on the market I will meet people in Dublin who will ask me what I think of the book, so I will slink as I did after Yeats's death round back streets to avoid the people who said: 'You will bring him back, won't you?'" His body was finally brought back in 1948, but, after much confusion in the graveyard in France and many versions of the story, it seems unlikely that the bones in the casket brought to Ireland did in fact belong to Yeats.

In 1965, the year of Yeats's centenary, three years before the death of George, Frank O'Connor made an oration over the grave in Sligo. He said: "Another thing he would have wished me to do – and which I must do since none of the eminent people who have written of him in his centenary year has done so – is to say how much he owed to the young Englishwoman he married, and who made possible the enormous development of his genius from 1916 onward."

In the same year, when Pound came to London for Eliot's memorial service, he announced that he wished to fly to Dublin on his way back to Italy. George, by then, only answered the phone at ten o'clock in the morning. On this day, by some miracle, she answered it when it rang at three o'clock in the afternoon, and took a taxi to the Royal Hibernian Hotel to meet Pound, who was travelling with Olga Rudge.

They had known one another for fifty-five years. During the

war, George had often listened to his broadcasts "in a humorous, half-conspiratorial sort of way." Now they sat in silence. When Anne Yeats arrived she could feel the affection between them, but neither said a word. There is a wonderful photograph of them in the hotel that day, Pound gazing at George fondly, almost adoringly, and she, an old lady wearing glasses and a battered hat, taking him in, her expression placid and candid and wise.

When she died in 1968, she was buried in the grave with her husband's bones, or others like them, under Ben Bulben in Sligo in the country she'd lived in for more than half a century. Her husband had been, as Frank O'Connor put it, "most fortunate in his marriage."

# New Ways to Kill Your Mother:
## Synge and His Family

In 1980, having been evicted from a flat in Hatch Street in the centre of Dublin, I was, by accident, offered temporary accommodation around the corner at No. 2 Harcourt Terrace. The house, three storeys over basement, was empty, having recently been vacated by its elderly inhabitant. It was early April when I moved in and the cherry tree in the long back garden was in full blossom. Looking at it from the tall back windows of the house, or going down to sit in the garden under its shade, was a great pleasure. The thought might have occurred to me that whoever had just sold this house could be missing it now, but I don't think I entertained the thought for very long.

The aura of the previous inhabitant of this house, in which I ended up living for almost eight years and where I wrote most of my first two books, appeared to me sharply only once. I was putting books in the old custom-made bookshelves in the house when I noticed a book hidden in a space at the end of a shelf where it could not be easily seen. It was a hardback, a first edition of Louis MacNeice's *Springboard: Poems 1941–1944*. I realized that these shelves must have, until recently, been filled with such volumes, and that the woman who had left this house and had gone, I discovered, to a nursing home, must have witnessed a lifetime's books being packed away, the books that she and her husband had collected and read and treasured. Books bought perhaps the week they came out. All lost to her now, including this one, which gave me a sense of her as nothing else did.

I asked about her. Her name was Lilo Stephens. She was the

widow of Edward Stephens, the nephew of J. M. Synge. In 1971 she had arranged and introduced Synge's *My Wallet of Photographs*. Edward Stephens, who died in 1955, was the son of Synge's sister, Annie. Born in 1888, when Synge was seventeen, he was aged twenty when his uncle died in 1909. Later, he became an important public servant and a distinguished lawyer. In 1921 he accompanied Michael Collins to London for the negotiations with the British that led to the Treaty which set up the Irish Free State. He was subsequently secretary to the committee that drew up the Irish constitution and thereafter became assistant registrar to the Supreme Court, and finally registrar to the Court of Criminal Appeal.

In 1939 on the death of his uncle Edward Synge, who had not allowed scholars access to Synge's private papers, Edward Stephens became custodian of all Synge's manuscripts. He began working on a biography of his uncle, which would partly be a biography of his family. "I see J. M. and his work as belonging much more to the family environment," he wrote, "than to the environment of the theatre." He had been close to his uncle, having been brought up in the house next door to him and spent long summer holidays in his company, and been taught the Bible by Synge's mother, as Synge had. But, in Synge's lifetime, not one member of his family had seen any of his work for the theatre. At his uncle's funeral, Edward Stephens would have had no reason to recognize any of the mourners who came from that side of his uncle's life. For his family, Synge belonged fundamentally to them; he was, first and foremost, a native of the Synge family.

"It was [Synge's] ambition," he wrote,

to use the whole of his personal life in his dramatic work. He ultimately achieved this . . . by dramatising himself, disguised as the central character or, in different capacities, as several of the leading characters, in some story from country lore or heroic tradition. It is in this sense that his dramatic work was autobiographical and that the outwardly dull story of his life became transmuted into the gold of literature.

In his work, Edward Stephens "transcribed in full," according to Andrew Carpenter in *My Uncle John*,

many family papers dating back to the eighteenth century; he copied any letters, notes, reviews, articles, fragments of plays, or other documentary evidence connected, even remotely, with Synge. He also recounted, with a precision which is truly astonishing, the events of Synge's life: the weather on particular days, the details of views Synge saw on his bicycle rides or walks and the history of the countryside through which he passed, the backgrounds of every person Synge met during family holidays, the food eaten, the decoration of the houses in which Synge lived, the books he read, his daily habits, his conversations, his coughs and colds – and those of other members of the family.

By 1950 the typescript was in fourteen volumes, containing a quarter of a million words. On Stephens's death in 1955, it had still not been edited for publication.

Lilo Stephens inherited the problem of the Synge estate. Out of her husband's work – "the hillside," as one reader put it, "from which must be quarried out the authoritative life of Synge" – two books came. Lilo Stephens made her husband's work available to David Greene, who published his biography in 1959, naming Edward Stephens as co-author. Later, in 1973, Andrew Carpenter would thank her "for her patience, enthusiasm and hospitality" when he edited her husband's work to a book of just over two hundred pages, *My Uncle John*. Lilo Stephens had also inherited Synge's papers, which had been kept for years in No. 2 Harcourt Terrace as her husband worked on them. In 1971 Ann Saddlemyer would thank her for first suggesting the volume *Letters to Molly* and providing "the bulk of the letters as well as much background material." Edward Stephens had purchased these letters from Molly Allgood so that they would be safe. Finally, Lilo Stephens ensured the safety of Synge's entire archive by moving it from Harcourt Terrace to Trinity College, Dublin, where it rests.

Synge's family remains of considerable interest, either because of the apparent lack of any influence on his work, or because they may or may not hold a key to his unyielding and mysterious genius. He seemed in his concerns and beliefs to have nothing in common with them – he stated that he never met a man or a woman who shared his opinions until he was twenty-three – and yet, for a great deal of his adult life, he lived with them and depended on them. Any version of his life and work has to take his family into account and understand the idea, in Edward Stephens's words, "that the context of his life . . . was quite different from any other writer of the literary movement. I tried to create a picture of a class or group in Irish society that has almost vanished."

If a writer were in the business of murdering his family, then the Synges, with their sense of an exalted and lost heritage and a strict adherence to religious doctrine added to dullness, would have been a godsend. Synge's great-grandfather, Nicholas Grene tells us in his essay on Synge and Wicklow in *Interpreting Synge: Essays from the Synge Summer School 1991–2000*, "owned not only Glanmore [in County Wicklow], with its fifteen hundred acres of demesne including the Devil's Glen, but Roundwood Park as well, an estate of over four thousand acres." His grandfather, however, managed to lose most of this property, a portion only of which was bought back by Synge's uncle. Synge's father, who became a barrister, died when Synge was one year old. He left a widow, four sons, a daughter and four hundred pounds a year. The first three sons were solid citizens, becoming a land agent, an engineer and a medical missionary to China respectively. The daughter married a solicitor. The youngest, it was presumed, despite his solitary nature and regular illnesses, would eventually find a profession to suit his family, if not his temperament.

In his book *Letters to my Daughter*, published in 1932, Synge's brother Samuel, the missionary, wrote:

There is little use in trying to say what if our father had lived might have happened different to what did happen. But I think two things are fairly clear. One is that as your Uncle John grew up and met questions that he did not know how to answer, a father's word of advice and instruction would have made a very great difference to him. The other thing is that probably our father would have arranged something for your Uncle John to do besides his favourite reading, something that would not have been too much for him but would have brought in some remuneration at an earlier date than his writings did.

This was to consign Synge's mother, Kathleen, to dust, to suggest a sort of powerlessness for her. She was, in fact, a very powerful person. Synge's mother was born Kathleen Traill in 1838. Her father was a clergyman of whom Edward Stephens wrote: "He spent his life, as he put it, waging war against popery in its thousand forms of wickedness, which did not always endear him to his ecclesiastical superiors." Finally he became rector of Schull in County Cork, where he died in 1847 from a fever caught from the people among whom he worked. His widow, who had been brought up in Drumboe Castle in County Donegal, moved to Orwell Park in the southern suburbs of Dublin. From here in 1856, her daughter married John Hatch Synge, the playwright's father. They lived in Hatch Street in the early years of their marriage, later moving to Rathfarnham, where John Millington Synge was born. Later, after her husband's death, Kathleen Synge moved her family to Orwell Park in Rathgar.

Synge's paternal grandfather and his uncle Francis, who had

bought back some of the family estates in County Wicklow, were members of the Plymouth Brethren. Mrs. Synge's father had held strong evangelical views, which his daughter also shared. She brought up her children according to strong religious principles, and her social life, such as it was, seemed to include only people who were of a like mind and background. Edward Stephens wrote:

Mrs. Synge conducted her household by a rule as strict as that of a religious order and supposed that her children would acquiesce without question. She was very well versed in the doctrine to which she adhered and she could support every tenet by citing scriptural authority. She believed the whole Bible to be inspired and its meaning to be clear to anyone who read with an open mind and faith in the Holy Ghost.

In an autobiographical essay composed in his mid-twenties, Synge wrote:

I was painfully timid, and while still young the idea of Hell took a fearful hold on me. One night I thought I was irretrievably damned and cried myself to sleep in vain yet terrified efforts to form a conception of eternal pain. In the morning I renewed my lamentations and my mother was sent for. She comforted me with the assurance that the Holy Ghost was convicting me of sin and thus preparing me for ultimate salvation. This was a new idea and I rather approved.

Between the ages of four and twenty-one Synge took part in his family's annual move to Greystones in County Wicklow, where his mother had friends and associates among the evangelical community. These "summer visits to the seaside," Synge remembered, "were delightful." His mother had the policy on holidays as well as during the rest of the year of gathering together as many members of her family as were available. When they were not available in large numbers, she invited friends, usually women of the missionary persuasion, to share the family sojourn in Wicklow, which often lasted for three months.

Nicholas Grene writes about Synge's relationship to his family: "There is nothing very unusual about a writer or artist from a conventional middle-class background diverging from his family's political, social and religious views. What is striking about Synge's case is that he maintained such close relations with the family in spite of his dissidence." However, while he spent most of his life in Ireland under his mother's roof, sharing even her holidays, he seems to have been seldom alone with her and this might have helped to maintain close relations. Mrs. Synge's house in Orwell Park had an entrance in the dividing wall to her mother's adjoining house, where her daughter, Annie, her husband and their children, including the young Edward Stephens, lived, as did Aunt Jane, Mr. Synge's sister. On 13 April 1890, after Mrs. Synge's mother's death, when the Stephens family decided to leave Rathgar, Mrs. Synge wrote to her son about her prayers to the Lord: "I am . . . asking Him to find us two houses together as we are here. He can do all things, so if he pleases to do that for me it is quite easy for Him."

The Lord came to her aid. He was assisted by Mr. Talbot Coall, the estate agent; they combined to find two adjoining houses at Crosthwaite Park in Kingstown, now Dun Laoghaire. Thus the extended family remained together and Mrs. Synge could continue to instruct her grandchildren in the ways of righteousness, as she had her children. While four of her five children carried her instruction faithfully into adulthood, it made her sad that John, the youngest, did not. In the letter quoted above, she also wrote: "Dear Sam is always a comfort when I see him. My poor Johnnie is not a comfort yet." Soon after the move she wrote: "John – poor boy. I am so sorry for him, he looks unhappy. He has not found the Saviour yet and until he does, how can he be happy?"

Her son, who had not found the Saviour, had found much comfort instead in the natural sciences and in his own imagination. In his autobiographical sketch, he wrote about an awakening that changed everything for him:

When I was about fourteen I obtained a book of Darwin's. It opened in my hands at a passage where he asks how can we explain the similarity between a man's hand and a bird's or a bat's wings except by evolution. I flung the book aside and rushed out into the open air – it was summer and we were in the country – the sky seemed to have lost its blue and the grass its green. I lay down and writhed in an agony of doubt . . . Incest and parricide were but a consequence of the idea that possessed me . . . Soon afterwards I turned my attention to works of Christian evidence, reading them at first with pleasure, soon with doubt, and at last in some cases with derision.

Synge was not naturally social. Because of ill health he had been educated at home for much of the time. Thus, when he went to Trinity College in Dublin, he took no great part in academic or student life. His reading had been intense and sporadic. His study of science and archaeology had been done for their own sake. His most notable attribute was his polite distance from those around him. By seventeen he did not seem to have shared his doubts and derisions with his mother, who wrote:

This is Johnnie's birthday. I can hardly fancy he is seventeen. I have been looking back to the time he was born. I was so dreadfully delicate and he, poor child[,] was the same . . . I see no spiritual life in my poor Johnnie; there may be some but it is not visible to my eyes. He is very reserved and shut up on the subject and if I say anything to him he never answers me, so I don't know in the least his state of mind – it is a trying state, *very* trying. I long so to be able to see behind that close reserve, but I can only wait and pray and hope . . .

But it was hopeless. He could not be spoken to about matters either spiritual or temporal. Within a year, she was writing again: "He does not know how to take care of his clothes and won't take advice; he has much to learn, poor boy; he is very headstrong." That summer she sent for a clergyman, who discussed religion with her son in private, leading her son to the view that he would have to come clean about his unbelief. The Sunday before Christmas, his mother wrote in her diary: "Fine, damp, mild day – church very hot – I felt overpowered. Johnnie would not come – very sad." And then on Christmas Day: "Very peaceful, happy day; went to church – my own sorrow Johnnie – he did not come."

Later, Synge wrote: "Soon after I relinquished the Kingdom of God I began to take a real interest in the Kingdom of Ireland. My patriotism went round from a vigorous and unreasoning loyalty to a temperate nationalism and everything Irish became sacred." This was a piece of easy subsequent self-positioning, however, and it is unlikely that a shift in faith as swift and facile as he suggests actually took place. It is much more likely that his religious faith, if replaced by anything, was replaced by an interest in music. As well as attending Trinity, he attended the Academy of Music in Westland Row where he studied the violin, becoming one of the many Irish playwrights whose first love was music. His mother was impressed by his musical ability. A month before his seventeenth birthday, she wrote: "Johnnie's ear is wonderfully good now, he hears if the piano is at all out of tune . . . [He] and I play together sometimes . . . He is greatly improved in time; at first he never kept with me and still runs *away* when he ought to rest, so I have to try and watch him as well as play my own part. We played some nice slow melodies last night, and it sounded wonderfully nice."

In these letters, written to her son Robert who was in Argentina, she compared her two youngest sons. "Johnnie certainly is the literary man of the family. I never saw such a love of reading as he has – he would spend any amount of money on books if he had it . . . I think Johnnie takes after my father." Sam, on the other hand, "can't help being slow. He is very like his dear father in that as well as other things." Sam followed his mother in religion "and his virtues make him a comfort to me." Yet John, who his mother believed had "a good opinion of himself," which she thought a pity, impressed her in ways that might have mattered to her more and that she could not take for granted. Mother and son did not fall out over his lack of religion and he was included in all family events and outings, the silent, stubborn dissenter at the table. Nonetheless, she lamented his state of ungrace year after year, in letter after letter; she was the only keener of the eastern seaboard. "Oh! My dear Johnnie is a great sorrow to my heart," she wrote in 1896 when he was twenty-five,

his belief or mis-belief has no joy in it and his residence abroad has been no help to him – he is wonderfully separate from us. I show him all the love I can. I pity him so much and love him so deeply – and I believe God is hearing my cry to Him, but the answer is delayed long. If we are all taken up to meet the Lord and he is left behind – how sad a thought but I won't think that – God can do all things – so I say to my doubts "be gone" . . .

Synge's aunt Jane, who lived in the extended household, had often dandled the young Parnell on her knee when they were neighbours in Wicklow; she now "piously wished she had choked him in infancy," as W. J. McCormack put it in his biography of Synge, *Fool of the Family*. The Synges were staunch defenders of the union and it is not hard to imagine their horror at the growing involvement of Synge in cultural nationalism. While his mother disapproved of his interest in archaeology, she did not object to his studying Irish at Trinity College. He took Irish with Hebrew, and these were seen as part of the

Divinity course, Irish being useful to those who wished to con-
vert the native speakers of the West of Ireland to the reformed
faith. His aunt Jane remembered how her brother Alexander,
who had ministered on the Aran Islands, had also learned Irish.
Like Lady Gregory, who began to study Irish in these years,
Synge and his fellow students used an Irish translation of the
Bible to help them. As for Lady Gregory too, some magic came
to Synge from the language he was learning, or some set of
emotions that were part of that decade. Both he and Lady Gregory,
in the same years and through the same influences, gradually
began to love Ireland, as though Ireland were a person. They
loved its landscape and its ancient culture; they loved the ordinary people they met in cabins or on the roads. It was as if their
own dying power in Ireland, the faded glory of their class, gave
their emotions about Ireland a strange glow of intensity. They
were both slow to turn this new emotion into politics. As Nicholas Grene has pointed out, "Synge canvassed for an Anti-Home
Rule Petition in 1893 and as late as 1895 was of the view that
Home Rule would provoke sectarian conflict." So too in 1893,
Lady Gregory published anonymously a pamphlet called *Home
Ruin*, essentially a piece of pro-unionist rhetoric. In time, however, they both realized that their project, if not political, was
bound up with politics. Synge would later write: "Patriotism
gratifies man's need for adoration and has, therefore, a peculiar
power upon the imaginative sceptic." And also: "The Irish
country rains, mists, pale insular skies, the old churches, manuscripts, jewels, everything in fact that was Irish had a charm
neither human nor divine, rather perhaps as if I had fallen in
love with a goddess."

The goddess came in many guises; flirting with her in these years
between the fall of Parnell and independence forced Lady Gregory
and Synge and others to deal in vast ambiguities, to turn a blind eye
to the irony of their own position. Lady Gregory collected her rents

at Coole from the same people from whom she collected folklore and with some of the same zeal. When they did not pay, she threatened them. W. J. McCormack writes in his biography:

As early as 1885, Synge's brother had been active as an agent, and in 1887 his services had been employed to dispossess tenants on the Glanmore estate in County Wicklow in an incident reported in the *Freeman's Journal*. According to the dramatist's nephew, "when Synge argued with his mother over the rights of tenants and the injustice of evicting them, her answer was 'What would become of us if our tenants in Galway stopped paying their rents?'"

When Synge was twenty-one his mother altered her summer routine, exchanging Delgany for the interior of County Wicklow. The fact that the house she rented was boycotted did not seem to bother her, nor did it prevent Synge from going with her. He read *Diarmuid and Gráinne* that summer and began to explore Wicklow with enormous enthusiasm. But, according to Edward Stephens, "they were not allowed to forget that they were staying in a boycotted house. In the evenings sometimes two constables came up the avenue and walked around the outbuildings to see that all was well." In 1895 when that house was not available, they rented Duff House on Lough Dan, but, as Stephens wrote, "it was with some misgivings ... for as the house was owned by Roman Catholics, she feared it would not be free from fleas."

Synge's writings about Wicklow, eight articles in all, represent in W. J. McCormack's phrase "a psychopathology of County Wicklow." He loved the idea of tramps and vagrants and saw his own class as doomed. "In this garden," he wrote,

one seemed to feel the tragedy of the landlord class ... and of the innumerable old families that are quickly dwindling away ... The broken green-houses and mouse-eaten libraries, that were designed and collected by men who voted with Grattan, are perhaps as mournful in the end as the four mud walls that are so often left in Wicklow as the only remnants of a farmhouse . . . Many of the descendants of these people have, of course, drifted into professional life in Dublin, or have gone abroad; yet, wherever they are, they do not equal their fore-fathers.

In one of the essays, as Nicholas Grene has discovered, he wrote and then omitted "his most telling condemnation of his own class": "Still, this class, with its many genuine qualities, had little patriotism, in the right sense, few ideas, and no seed for future life, so it has gone to the wall." Synge wondered what use such a decaying class could be to a playwright: "If a playwright chose to go through the Irish country houses he would find material, it is likely, for many gloomy plays that would turn on the dying away of the old families, and on the lives of the one or two delicate girls that are left so often to represent a dozen hearty men who were alive a generation or two ago."

His problem, as these ideas began to formulate in his mind, was his lack of worldly ambition. He wanted to be a musician. When his brother-in-law advised against it, his advice had not "the least effect." His brother Robert, returned from Argentina and now a land agent, offered to take Synge into his office and train him up to become a land agent too. This did not meet with any enthusiasm. His cousin Mary Synge, who was a professional musician, came to stay and advised him to go to Germany to study music. His mother agreed to pay. At the end of July 1893 he left for Koblenz, where he lodged with a family of four sisters whose company he loved, as he loved the company of most women. He stayed in Germany for almost a year, coming home in time to join his mother and the rest of the family for their annual holiday in County Wicklow.

That summer he renewed an acquaintance with Cherrie Matheson, a neighbour in Kingstown who came to stay with the Synges in Wicklow. His falling in love with her served to emphasize his own marginal position in his class. He had no prospects, just as he had no religion. Nonetheless, he wanted to marry her as he returned to Germany in October. From there, in January 1895, he went to live in Paris, where he remained until the end of June, teaching English, attending lectures in the Sorbonne and idling with others of his kind in the city. That summer and winter in Dublin were filled with his obsession with Cherrie, whom he saw a great deal. At the beginning of 1896 he returned to Paris. "He had left the woman he idealised," Edward Stephens wrote, "and had refused to engage in any money-making occupation which might have enabled him to offer her a home. He was going to Paris and to Rome with a general plan for studying languages and literature, inspired by the hope of developing his own productive powers in a way which, as yet, he could picture but dimly." After three months in Rome, he wrote to Cherrie proposing marriage. When she refused, he wrote to his mother. Her diary entry reads: "I got a sad *sad* letter from my poor Johnnie." He returned to Ireland, and soon began to see Cherrie once more. She remembered:

Sometimes we went to the National Gallery or some picture exhibition, sometimes to sit for an hour in St. Patrick's Cathedral and just drink in the beauty of the dear old place . . . He liked that part of Dublin more than the modern part and especially Patrick's Street, which runs between the two Cathedrals, and was then more like some queer continental street with little booths all down the centre of it.

Synge did not live long enough to reposition himself in a set of memoirs. It was clear, however, from his preface to *The Playboy of the Western World* that he would, had he lived, have easily joined Yeats, Lady Gregory, Sean O'Casey and many others in doing so.

He wrote: "When I was writing 'The Shadow of the Glen,' some years ago, I got more aid than any learning could have given me from a chink in the floor of the old Wicklow house where I was staying, that let me hear what was being said by the servant girls in the kitchen." This suggested that the girls were native Irish rural girls, proto-Pegeen Mikes. As Nicholas Grene has pointed out, they were "Ellen the cook and Florence Massey the maid, both of whom had been brought up in a Protestant orphanage and did not necessarily come from Wicklow at all."

Yeats outlived Synge by thirty years; Lady Gregory by twenty-three, and they both created versions of him that suited them. In the years when the three of them worked together, there was also a strange hostility lurking in the shadows while centre stage stood solidarity, mutual support and kindness. It was as though both Yeats and Lady Gregory harboured the view that Synge was on the verge of finding them out as they shifted ground and reinvented themselves in the early years of the twentieth century.

There was also the issue of class. In his essay "Good Behaviour: Yeats, Synge and Anglo-Irish Etiquette," Roy Foster pondered the relationship between Yeats and Synge when they first met in Paris in 1896, when Yeats was thirty-one and Synge twenty-five.

Yeats's background was an important notch or two down that carefully defined ladder. Synge's ancestors were bishops, while Yeats's were rectors; Synge's had established huge estates and mock castles, while Yeats's drew the rent from small farms and lived in the Dublin suburbs. Yeats had no money, while Synge had a small private income. Yeats had no university education, whereas Synge had been to Trinity . . . Another important difference between them, which reflects upon background and education, is that Synge, for all his unpretentiousness, was really cosmopolitan; whereas Yeats when they met was desperately trying to be.

Yeats had had bohemianism foisted upon him by his feckless father; Synge had done it all alone as a new way of killing his mother. Yeats later described their first meeting:

He told me that he had been living in France and Germany, reading French and German literature, and that he wished to become a writer. He had, however, nothing to show but one or two poems and impressionistic essays, full of that morbidity that has its root in too much brooding over methods of expression, and ways of looking at life, which come, not out of life, but out of literature, images reflected from mirror to mirror . . . life had cast no light upon his writings. He had learned Irish years ago, but had begun to forget it, for the only literature that interested him was that conventional language of modern poetry which had begun to make us all weary . . . I said "Give up Paris. You will never create anything by reading Racine, and Arthur Symons will always be a better critic of French literature. Go to the Aran Islands. Live there as if you were one of the people themselves; express a life that has never found expression."

Yeats wrote this account of their Paris conversations in 1905, claiming that they had taken place six years earlier, whereas they had taken place nine years before, shortly after Yeats's own first visit to the Aran Islands. Declan Kiberd in *Synge and the Irish Language* and Roy Foster, however, have pointed out more essential inaccuracies in what became, for many years, the standard account of Synge's impulse to go to the islands. Synge, through his study of the Breton language and his meeting with the Celtic scholar Richard Best, had been taking an intense interest in Celtic Studies in Paris in any case, as Declan Kiberd has emphasized. He knew about the islands because his uncle had been a minister there. "Doubtless," Kiberd has written,

the advice from Yeats was an important factor in Synge's decision; but the passionate studies in Breton culture must have awakened his enthusiasm for the Gaelic lore of his own country, to which he already held the key in his knowledge of the Irish language. It would be naïve to follow Greene and Stephens [David Greene and Edward Stephens, Synge's biographers] in asserting that he went to Aran at Yeats's suggestion. He was heading in that direction from the very beginning.

He wrote to his mother in Dublin about his new friends in Paris where he had returned, who included Yeats and Maud Gonne. (One of his friends later reported that "Synge gently hated Miss Gonne.") He explained that he had become interested in socialism, which his mother thought "utter folly." He became a member of the committee of Maud Gonne's Irish League, but politics did not interest him as much as culture, and he resigned after a few months. In the summer of 1897, despite his cosmopolitanism and his new friends, he came back to Ireland so he could go to Wicklow on holiday with his mother.

That summer, as he became ill, his hair falling out and a lump developing on his neck, some of his family put it down to unrequited love. But it was the beginning of the Hodgkin's disease that would kill him twelve years later. His mother wrote:

Johnnie is at home still. He has to get those large glands taken out of his neck, poor fellow. It is very unpleasant . . . Since his hair fell out he got cold in the glands, and they became so large they were, or rather are, quite disfiguring to him. He has been very anxious to go away to Paris. He has been advised by his friend Yeats, the Irish poet, to go in for reviewing French literature so John is working away with that end in view. His general health is very good and he is strong and able to walk, so I trust he may get over this time well, please God, and Oh I do ask Him to reveal Himself to my dear boy.

It is interesting that there is no mention here of the Aran Islands. The operation took place in December 1897. The doctors must have known that the symptoms could recur, but they told Synge and his mother, who both seemed to have believed them, that it was a success. His mother watched over him. On 3 January 1898 she noted in her diary: "John not well – made me anxious." Two days later she wrote to Robert: "Johnnie looks much better, but he is not strong, and I am anxious lest he should go to Paris too soon and be laid up again in some way, as the Hotel life is anything but comfortable or healthy. He is very silent, poor fellow, and spends all his time over his books except when he goes out for a walk." When he went back to Paris, writing fragmentary beginnings to a novel and attending lectures by a French professor on the connections between Irish and Greek literature, his mother wrote: "I heard from Johnnie; troubled by bugs."

On 23 April 1898 he came home. The difference between his life in Paris, where he spoke fluent French, lived alone and was deeply respected by his many associates, and his life in his mother's house, must have made him wonder. At least three times a day for meals in Ireland he had to listen to Mrs. Synge and her friends and other members of the family on the subject of religion and domestic life and their narrow political prejudices. She was teaching her grandchildren the Bible as she had taught her children, seeing it as part of her duty, according to Edward Stephens, to emphasize the horror of eternal damnation. "Sometimes," Stephens wrote,

our lessons were interrupted by his [Synge's] entering the room. I remember particularly his coming in once when we were having a Bible reading. He was twirling his pocket scissors on his finger chanting softly to himself, "Holy, Holy, Holy Moses." We greeted him and he sat in the window for a few minutes and then, feeling that he had caused an interruption, went quietly out again. Our grandmother said: "Don't put down your Bibles when Uncle John comes in," and resumed her reading.

In Paris, he was the earnest playboy of the western world; in Kingstown he was his mother's youngest son.

Just before Synge's first visit to the Aran Islands, he had a meeting with Cherrie Matheson, who told him that their differences were irreconcilable. Two days later, he called to her house and had what must have been a deeply dispiriting conversation with Cherrie and her mother. Mrs. Matheson, according to Edward Stephens, "with Cherrie's approval, rated him soundly for pressing a rejected proposal of marriage when he was not earning enough money to support himself. He left in despair . . . His mind was still distraught with anguish when, on the morning of Monday 9 May 1898, he left by the morning train for Galway."

He wrote of his visits to the islands over the next few years with beauty and reverence and restraint. It must have been a relief that first morning watching the sailors casting off in a fog from Galway pier and arriving in Aranmore after a three-hour journey, no one there knowing anything about Cherrie Matheson and her hectoring mother, or Mrs. Synge's worries about her poor Johnnie. He was now in the land of his dreams. Lady Gregory saw him on the island in 1898; she was in search, too, of nourishment from a primitive world that contained an astonishing life force and an ancient culture. She wrote:

I first saw him in the North Island of Aran. I was staying there, gathering folklore, talking to the people, and felt a real pang of indignation when I passed another outsider walking here and there, talking also to the people. I was jealous of not being alone on the island among the fishers and the seaweed gatherers. I did not speak to the stranger nor was he inclined to speak to me. He also looked on me as an intruder.

Later, she wrote about his work once he had arrived on the islands. He had, she wrote, "done no good work until he came back to his own country. It was there that he found all he wanted, fable, emotion, style . . . bringing a cultured mind to a mass of primitive material, putting clearer and lasting form to the clum-sily expressed emotion of a whole countryside."

Soon, he was invited to Coole and quickly joined the move-ment that resulted in the Abbey Theatre. He became, eventually, with Yeats and Lady Gregory, one of the three directors. He wrote five plays for them – *The Shadow of the Glen* (1903); *Riders to the Sea* (1904); *The Well of the Saints* (1905); *The Tinker's Wedding* (1907); *The Playboy of the Western World* (1907). He left one play unfinished, *Deirdre of the Sorrows*, which was first produced, in a completed version, in 1910. His imagination was powerfully autonomous; his plays combined the knowledge he had amassed through his study and his wanderings in Europe with a real open-ness and freedom and an immense natural talent. He delighted in language and character, in wild talk and massive abandon, as though he were concerned to dramatize and most portray what he himself in his own life kept in abeyance.

In these eleven years he took part in all the rows that ran at the theatre, seeming much of the time calmer, more focused, less vindictive and, on some matters, more determined than his col-leagues. He believed that Yeats was too impetuous to deal with the actors. In some of the correspondence, as Roy Foster has pointed out, "he sounds both older and wiser than Yeats; he appears more at ease in dealing with people." In 1908, when the Fays had left the theatre, Synge remarked: "Since then Yeats and I have been running the show, i.e. Yeats looks after the stars and I do the rest." The actors and workers in the theatre liked him. He appeared more natural, more in possession of himself than either of his colleagues. An Australian visitor in 1904 described him: "He was full of race and good breeding, courteous, sensitive, sincere . . . a simple man; but there was something strange and alluring about him, an indescribable charm expressed in his voice and manner and, above all, in his curious smile that was at the same time ironic and sympathetic." With the Abbey, as with his family, Synge was skilled at withdrawing. "I have often envied him his absorption," Yeats wrote, "as I have envied Verlaine his vice."

Lady Gregory disliked *The Playboy of the Western World*, although she defended it in public. She made sure that Yeats's play *The Pot of Broth* was not used as a curtain-raiser, which would be, she wrote to Yeats, foreseeing the riots, like "Synge setting fire to your house to roast his own pig." After Synge's death, she wrote a passage in her journal that she did not publish: "One doesn't want a series of panegyrics and we can't say, don't want to say what was true, he was ungracious to his fellow workers, authors and actors, ready in accepting praise, grudging in giving it . . . On tour he thought of his own play only, gave no help to ours and if he repeated compliments, they were to his own." Yeats in his journal wrote: "I never heard him praise any writer, living or dead, but some old French farce-writer."

The truth was that he understood the value of his own plays and did not rate very highly the work of Yeats or Lady Gregory for the theatre, although he admired other aspects of their work, such as Lady Gregory's translations. He made no secret of this, and of his profound irritation at Lady Gregory's tireless and fearless promotion of Yeats's work and her constant production of her own work. In December 1906 she told Synge that Yeats's dramatic work "was more important than any other (you must not be offended at this) as I think it our chief distinction." In March 1907, when *The Playboy of the Western World* had already been produced and Charles Frohman, an American producer, came to the Abbey looking for new work to tour in the U.S., Synge wrote to Molly Allgood:

I hear that they are showing Frohman *one* play of mine, "Riders," five or six of L.G.'s [Lady Gregory's] and several of Yeats. I am raging about it, though of course you must not breathe a word about it. I suppose after the P. B. [Playboy] fuss they are afraid of stirring up the Irish Americans if they take me. However I am going to find out what is at the bottom of it and if I am not getting fair play I'll withdraw my plays from both tours English and American altogether. It is getting past a joke the way they are treating me.

They, on the other hand, became increasingly sure that they had invented him. After his death Lady Gregory wrote to Yeats:

You did more than anyone for him, you gave him a means of expression. You have given me mine, but I should have found something else to do, though not anything coming near this, but I don't think Synge would have done anything but drift but for you and the theatre . . . I think you and I supplied him with vitality when he was with us as the wild people did in the Blaskets [which Synge also visited].

Synge's relationship to the islands of the west, however, came to him via his family as much as it did from Yeats's inspiration. As soon as he arrived on the Aran Islands in 1898, for example, he wrote to his mother, who wrote to his brother Sam:

I had a very interesting letter from Johnnie last week . . . The islanders of Aran found out that he was related to Uncle Aleck and came to see him and were quite pleased. He is now on Inishmaan island – went there in a *curragh* and is much pleased with his new abode, a room in a cottage inside the kitchen of a house . . . and he lives on mackerel and eggs and learns Irish; how wonderfully he accommodates himself to his various surroundings.

And parts of his vitality came to him from his mother as much as anyone else. When he returned to Dublin from the Aran Islands he accommodated himself to his mother's surroundings once more, joining her on holiday in County Wicklow. He would return to the family from his daily outings by foot or bicycle with stories of tramps he had met, including one who claimed to have known his grandmother and who had told him: "I never went there but Mrs. Synge offered me a glass of whisky." Later, when the young Edward Stephens mentioned the tramp to Synge's mother, she remarked: "I wish Uncle Johnnie would not encourage tramps; I don't know why he wants to talk to queer people. I'm sure that Mrs. Synge never offered a tramp whisky."

Once the summer was over, Synge followed his usual routine, returning to Paris for the winter. The following year, when he returned to Ireland for the annual long holiday with his mother in Wicklow, his mother had two young women, both interested in evangelical Protestantism, staying. Synge became close to them. His mother wrote: "Both girls are very lively and there is a great deal of joking and fun goes on between them and John. I have not seen him laugh so much for years." Edward Stephens remembered: "John had learned to enjoy their company so much that he never withdrew to read in his room when he had an opportunity of sitting with them on the steps looking at the view or, on wet days, on camp stools in the porch looking into the mist that hid everything but the tops of the trees below the house."

In September Synge returned to the islands and then in November to Paris, where he began to write his book about the Aran Islands. In May 1900 he returned once more not to miss his three months in Wicklow with his mother, who once more had invited young women, including one Rosie Calthrop, to stay and keep her son company, much to his delight. His mother, however, became jealous that summer of her son paying more attention to another woman than to her. She was not, it seems, content to play the Widow Quin to her guest's Pegeen Mike. She wrote to Sam:

She seemed to appreciate Johnnie's thoughtfulness and kindness very much! It is a pity he does not show it to me and not only to strangers. He was most attentive to both in little matters I could see, and he was always at their beck and call to walk or ride or escort them anywhere! So no wonder they like him, but it was rather aggravating to me; he wanted to put me aside entirely. But I told Rosie and then she did not fall in with his plans, though she loved to be out walking with him I know.

The idea of Mrs. Synge telling her guest that she was jealous of her son's attention to the guest is intriguing. It is hard to imagine what terms she used to make herself clear. It is also possible that the guest was forced to explain to Synge what the problem was, that the older woman was aggravated by his sudden success with strangers, his charm. Thus it is possible a central part of the action of *The Playboy of the Western World* was being played out in a rented house in Wicklow in the summer of 1900.

That September Synge set out again to charm strangers by returning to the Aran Islands. This was his third visit. He arrived in a particular state of gloom because Cherrie Matheson had been receiving a gentleman whom she would later marry. They had met on the street and Cherrie had introduced her new boyfriend to Synge. The following month when he returned, this visit having sown the seeds that would become *Riders to the Sea*, his mother wrote to Sam:

Johnnie came home last night from the Aran Islands. He has one very large gland on his neck just above his collar; he looks very well and the time on the islands agreed with him. I was glad to have him safe back. The sea has been very rough and great gales lately and it was hard for him to get away. He had a very rough passage to Galway and a miserable little steamer. The engines stopped several times and went on again.

That autumn Synge bought a portable typewriter, a Blickensderfer, which Richard Best chose for him. It came in a varnished wooden case. When he brought it home, he said that it spelt worse than he did. When he went back to Paris, his mother missed him. She wrote to Sam:

My poor Johnnie went off this morning; it is very calm, I am thankful to say, but raining and thick at sea . . . I miss Johnnie. As usual I have been very busy stitching and mending his clothes and getting him some new ones. The gland on his neck is very large, but back pretty far. He is getting rather anxious about it. I think he is improved; he has been more pleasant and chatty than usual of late, and I think his queer time in Paris always injures him, and he is so queer when he comes home and so out of all our ways, and then it wears off by degrees. I am trying to persuade him to give up his room in Paris and make a fresh start nearer home.

The gland in his neck was still swollen when he returned at the beginning of the summer; when he saw the doctor in Dublin he was given an ointment and a different medicine. His mother invited Rosie Calthrop to stay with them once more and wrote to Sam about the amount of money Synge and Rosie had spent on an outing. "John does not mind at all," she wrote, "of course it is my money and he has no scruples about that. However, I don't mind now and then, but I would not like it often." Synge had his typewriter with him and was working on the first draft of a play *When the Moon Has Set*, which dealt with his own class and was thinly disguised autobiography. He brought it with him when he went to stay at Coole but Lady Gregory told him that it was not good and of no literary interest. From Coole he went west to the islands and then back to Paris. That May of 1902 he was asked to review Lady Gregory's *Cuchulain of Muirthemne*, in which a version of the dialect spoken around Coole was used. Synge found this dialect close to the living speech he knew from rural Wicklow. In his review he described the language as "wonderfully simple and powerful . . . almost Elizabethan." The Elizabethan vocabulary, he wrote, has a force and colour that make it the only form of English that is quite suitable for incidents of the epic kind, and in her intercourse with the peasants of the west Lady Gregory has learned to use this vocabulary in a new way, while she carries with her plaintive Gaelic constructions that make her language, in a true sense, a language of Ireland.

He was working on the drafts of his early plays. In *The Shadow of the Glen* and *The Tinker's Wedding* he was, to some small extent, dramatizing the role of the artist, or the outsider, versus the role of the settled and respectable community; in other words, he made these plays as versions of his own plight at being turned down by Cherrie Matheson. Other aspects of these plays came from his own dreams and observations, especially in the summer months in Wicklow. Edward Stephens, who was fourteen at the time his uncle worked on these plays, wrote that the material

was derived from the lore of the country people, not from any direct association with the tinkers themselves. They were so dirty and in their mode of life so disreputable that it would have been impossible for John to mix with them at his ease. He warned me against dropping into conversation with them on the road.

By the beginning of October 1902 Synge had finished both *Riders to the Sea* and *In the Shadow of the Glen*. On his way to the Aran Islands for his final visit – his book on the islands still had not found a publisher – he stopped off at Coole to show the plays to Yeats and Lady Gregory, who described the plays as "both masterpieces, both perfect in their way." Later she wrote: "He had gathered emotion, the driving force he needed from his life among the people, and it was the working in dialect that set free his style." Yeats saw the language of the Bible as another influence.

Early the following year he decided to give up his room in

Paris. When he unpacked his French belongings in Dublin, Edward Stephens watched him taking out "the knife and fork and little frying pan that he had used in Paris, he showed them to me as if they were things he regarded with affection. I asked him whether they had ever been cleaned, he replied: 'A thing that is used by me only is never dirty.'" Because of attacks of asthma he spent that summer in Kerry rather than in Wicklow, returning to Dublin for the rehearsals of *The Shadow of the Glen*, which opened in October to considerable controversy. When Synge and his mother went down to breakfast the morning after the opening night, they read in *The Irish Times* that the play was "excessively distasteful" while the critic admitted "the cleverness of the dialect and the excellent acting of Nora and the tramp."

Edward Stephens wrote about his grandmother's response to the coverage of the play:

All she read in the Irish Times perplexed her. She had thought of John as being overpersuaded by his literary friends into praising everything Irish but, now that a play of his had been acted, the newspapers were censuring him for attacking Irish character. She disliked the kind of publicity his work was getting, she was sorry that he should have adopted a form of dramatic writing that was likely to prove no more remunerative than the Aran book, and she was sorry that any of his work should be connected with the stage.

Mrs. Synge also worried about her son, now aged thirty-two, being out late. She wrote in her diary: "After a dreadful storm last night, I had a headache from lying awake listening to the storm and watching for Johnnie who was not home until 3.30."

*The Irish Times* had nothing much good to say about *Riders to the Sea* either when the play opened in February 1904. The Synges disapproved of what they read about it. "The idea underlying the work is good enough," the critic said, but the treatment of it is to our mind repulsive. Indeed the play develops into something like a wake. The long exposure of the dead body before an audience may be realistic, but is certainly not artistic. There are some things which are lifelike, and yet are quite unfit for presentation on the stage, and we think that "Riders to the Sea" is one of them.

Edward Stephens remembered his father's response: "If they want an Irish play, why can't they act 'The Shaughraun'?"

The plays, however, were much praised by the London critics, but this made no difference to Synge's family, who were, Edward Stephens wrote, "serenely unaware of the importance of his work." After a time in the west, Synge decided in October 1904 to find his own lodgings in Rathmines and move out of the family home for the first time in Dublin. In January 1905 *The Well of the Saints* went into rehearsal with a walk-on part for a young actress, Molly Allgood, whose sister Sara was a well-known actress. She was nineteen. Soon she began to play important roles in the theatre's repertoire, including Synge's plays. Synge fell in love with her.

Both the Synge family and Lady Gregory disapproved of his relationship with Molly, the Synges for religious and social reasons, Lady Gregory because she did not want directors of the theatre consorting too freely with its employees. While he could not keep the relationship a secret from Lady Gregory, Synge could hide it from his family. On 5 November 1906, when he had moved back into his mother's house and given up his flat, he wrote to Molly: "My mother asked me again if I was alone, and I said I had 'a friend' with me. I must tell her soon." Seventeen days later, he wrote again: "I showed my mother your photo the other night and told her you were a great friend of mine. That is as far as I can go until I am stronger. I am thoroughly sick of this state of affairs, we must end it, and make ourselves public." That day, as he was suffering from influenza, Molly came to his mother's house. Later, Synge wrote to her: "My mother is too shy to say much about you, but I think she is pleased. She said you seemed very bright and she hoped I had asked you to come down on Sunday and cheer me up. I said I hadn't but I would write. Today she has reminded me several times not to forget my note to you."

The following month, when he told his mother he was engaged to Molly, he wrote:

I heard from my mother. She says she thought "the friend" I have been walking with was a man, but that my showing her the photo and the letters that came so often when I was ill made her think there was some thing. Then she says it would be a good thing if it would make me happier, and to wind up she points out how poor we shall be with only £100 a year. Quite a nice letter for the first go off. So that is satisfying.

While Synge sent Molly only the good news about his mother's response to his marrying a Catholic, it is easy to read between the lines of his letters. The following March, for example, he remarked that his mother "is much more rational about it than she was." This suggests that she had been, in the previous months, irrational in her response. Later that month, she began to ask in some detail about her future daughter-in-law: "My mother was enquiring about your temper today, she says my temper is so bad, it would be a terrible thing to marry a bad-tempered wife."

That January, as the rehearsals for *The Playboy of the Western World* started, Synge began to write to Molly about the possibility of finding a flat. Molly was playing Pegeen Mike. Willie Fay, who was producing, and his brother Frank realized how much indignation the play would provoke:

Frank and I begged him to make Pegeen a decent likeable country girl, which she might easily have been without injury to the play, and to take out the torture scenes in the last act, where the peasants burn Christy with lit turf ... Frank and I might as well have saved our breath. We might as well have tried to move the Hill of Howth as move Synge.

In her diary, once she had read the *Irish Times* account of the play and the opening night, Mrs. Synge recorded: "I was troubled about John's play – not nice." Synge himself was troubled by a cough that he could not shake off. In all these years he seemed to be suffering regularly from coughs and colds and other ailments. By April, he was making plans to get married. "I counted up my money last night and if all goes well I think we shall have £150 for our first year, if we get married soon, that is £3 a week." In January 1908 he found a flat in York Road in Rathmines for thirteen shillings and sixpence a week. His mother wrote:

Johnnie is on the move; he is at home today packing and sorting over books, clothes etc ... I feel his going *very* much: furnishing these rooms, trying to make a little home for himself on such a very small and uncertain income. I am giving him some old furniture etc, and he must buy some ... Johnnie says this move reminds him of his trips to Paris! Counting over his socks etc putting away things he does not want! However, he adds, it is not far.

Both Synge and his mother were ill that winter. Both had operations, and it must have been obvious to the doctors that both of them were doomed. In April, Mrs. Synge wrote to her son Robert about Synge's marriage, making clear that she must have been, up to recently, opposing it: "Johnnie came to see me on Friday last; he is seriously thinking of being soon married ... [and] as he is determined ... it is no use opposing him any more and we must only trust that he may get on." He was, however, too ill to remain in the flat he had dreamed of with Molly for so long. Once his operation was over, he came home to his mother once more: "We got [his] furniture all back from Rathmines yesterday," she wrote,

It was such a sad little flitting altogether. I remember now remarking how ill he looked when he was going away. He says those pains began in December! I think if he had been at home, I would certainly have thought there was something serious going on; but I saw him very seldom during the four months he was away, and I know he did not feed himself as he was accustomed and he used to be so very hungry for his dinners when he came. God has permitted it all to happen so I can say nothing.

In the time that remained to him, Synge travelled to London, returned to Koblenz to stay with the family who had hosted him years earlier, wrote tender letters almost daily to Molly Allgood and worked on his play *Deirdre*. Death was never far from his mind. On 2 November 1908 he sent Molly a draft of a new poem:

> I asked if I got sick and died, would you
> With my black funeral go walking too,
> If you'd stand close to hear them talk or pray
> While I'm let down in that steep bank of clay.
>
> And, No, you said, for if you saw a crew
> Of living idiots pressing round that new
> Oak coffin – they alive, I dead beneath
> That board – you'd rave and rend them with your teeth.

His mother died while he was in Germany. On 7 November, on his return to her house where he was to stay for the remaining months of his life, he wrote to Molly: "I am home at last. I am inexpressibly sad in this empty house." In February 1909 he went into hospital in the knowledge that he was dying. In his notebooks from his time on the Aran Islands, there is a passage that he did not transcribe fully when he came to write the book. He was in a curragh on a bad sea:

I thought almost enviously what fatiguing care I would escape if the canoe turned a few inches nearer to those waves and dropped me helpless into the blue bosom of the sea. No death were so delightful. What a difference to die here with the fresh sea saltness in my hair than to struggle in soiled sheets and thick stifling blankets with a smell of my own illness in my nostrils and a half paid death tender at my side.

During his long death battle, Molly came to see him every day until she went to play Pegeen Mike in Manchester where *The Playboy* was warmly received. On 23 March Yeats wrote to Lady Gregory:

I have just met M. [Molly] in the street and saw by her face that she had bad news. She told me that Synge is now so weak that he cannot raise himself on his arm in bed and at night he can only sleep with the help of drugs. For some days he has been too weak to read. He cannot read even his letters. They have moved him to another room that he may see the mountains from his bed.

The following day he died. He was buried in the family plot in Mount Jerome cemetery.

Before the funeral, Synge's brother Robert wrote in his diary: "Received a visit from Yeats and the Sec. of Abbey Theatre with a request which I refused as impossible." They wanted to have a death-mask made. Edward Stephens wrote: "Robert would have disliked it under any conditions but he . . . believed John's face to have changed so much during his last illness that no real likeness of him . . . could have been obtained." Stephens noticed that at the funeral the mourners were divided, "as they had always been in his lifetime," between family and the people among whom he had worked. Molly Allgood did not attend his funeral.

# Beckett Meets His Afflicted Mother

In his essay on the painter Jack Yeats, which he sent to Samuel Beckett in Paris in 1938, Thomas MacGreevy wrote: "During the 20-odd years preceding 1916, Jack Yeats filled a need that had become immediate in Ireland for the first time in 300 years, the need of the people to feel that their own life was being expressed in art." Beckett wrote to MacGreevy to say that he did "not think there is a syllable that needs touching" in the first eighteen pages, and that the rest, "though I do not find it quite as self-evident as the beginning, holds together perfectly." But then he said that "the political and social analyses are rather on the long side." He admitted his

own chronic inability to understand . . . a phrase like "the Irish people," or to imagine that it ever gave a fart in its corduroys for any form of art whatsoever, whether before the Union or after, or that it was ever capable of any thought or act other than the rudimentary thoughts and acts belted into it by the priests and by the demagogues in service of the priests, or that it will ever care, if it ever knows, any more than the Bog of Allen will ever care or know, that there was once a painter in Ireland called Jack Butler Yeats.

Like MacGreevy, Beckett was fascinated by Jack Yeats; in his letters Yeats the painter is almost alone among living Irish figures of the previous generation whom Beckett mentions with constant respect. In 1930 MacGreevy wrote of Beckett to Jack Yeats:

My last year's colleague . . . is still in Dublin for a little while. He's a nice fellow, the nephew of Cissie Sinclair [who had been a painter] . . .

It would be a charity to ask him round one afternoon and show him a few pictures and drop all the conversational bombs you have handy without pretending anything. But the luck will be all on his side, he says very little, especially at first, and you might find him not interesting, so don't do it unless you feel like doing nothing one day. Joyce does like him however, and I'm genuinely fond of him tho' he's maddeningly young.

After the visit, MacGreevy wrote to Yeats again: "Beckett wrote me about his visit to you. I'm glad you liked him. He was completely staggered by the pictures and though he has met many people through me he dismissed them all in his letter in the remark 'and to think I owe meeting Jack Yeats and Joyce to you!'" In February 1935 Yeats, alert to Beckett's solitary habits, wrote to MacGreevy: "I tried to get Beckett on the phone one day but he was away. I wanted to arrange a day for him to come here – when there wouldn't be other visitors as he doesn't so much like having them about."

Three months later, Beckett wrote to MacGreevy from Dublin:

Yesterday afternoon I had Jack Yeats all to myself . . . from 3 to past 6, and saw some quite new pictures. He seems to be having a freer period. The one in the Academy –"Low Tide" – bought by Meredith for the Municipal is overwhelming . . . In the end we went out, down to Charlemont House [the Municipal Gallery] to find out about Sunday opening, & then to Jury's for a drink. He parted as usual with an offer to buy me a Herald. I hope to see him again before I leave, but do not expect ever to have him like that again.

Early the following year Beckett saw the picture *Morning* in Yeats's studio; he wanted to buy it, despite his general lack of funds. "It's a long time since I saw a picture I wanted so much," he wrote to MacGreevy. In May 1936 he told MacGreevy that

Yeats had "brought up the subject of the picture . . . I since borrowed £10 which he accepted as a first instalment, the remaining £20 to follow God knows when, & have now got the picture. Mother & Frank [Beckett's brother] can't resist it much . . . It is nice to have Morning on one's wall that is always morning, and a setting out without the coming home." Later both men wrote separately to MacGreevy to say that they had bumped into one another at a donkey show in Dublin where Beckett had taken his mother, who was, Beckett reported, "the picture of misery." Yeats was making sketches for a painting.

In the early part of his essay on Yeats, which was finally published in 1945, MacGreevy touched on something that was crucial to Beckett in his twenties and thirties as he sought to get Ireland out of his system, or tried to find a way of including it in the work he would do without any reference to its mythology, its history, the amusing oddness of its people or the so-called lilt of its language. "Jack Yeats's people," MacGreevy wrote,

are frequently depicted in the pursuit of pleasure, at the circus or music-hall, at race meetings, or simply in conversation with each other. Yet often the expression on their faces suggests restraint, thoughtfulness, an inner discipline. Outwardly they so obviously belong to a more primitive state of society than has ever been depicted without condescension in Western European painting that their attitude to existence, their human significance, may easily be overlooked . . . the figures in his pictures are not elegant – their clothes bag about their lean bodies; they are not sensual – their faces are ascetic, thin and careworn; and their expression is thoughtful – they are bemused as much as amused.

In other words, Yeats was attempting to move beyond what MacGreevy called "mere stereotyped inventions." There was a melancholy and a mystery at the heart of all the movement and gaiety he depicted. He painted Irish light using colours and textures that belonged to his dreams as much as to the actual landscape or to the palette or systems of previous painters. Nothing in his paintings was idealized simply because it was Irish. He could easily, especially in the years when Beckett knew him, have been a German painter. There was a mixture in him of someone rigorous, watchful and solitary and someone fascinated by swirl, swift movement and pure excitement; his canvases were filled with theatricality and crowds, and also with reverie, solitary figures lost in bare, windswept places, tramps and loafers beneath the high, haunted, visionary sky. Yeats personally was elusive and reticent, despite his sociability; it was said that he seldom discussed with anyone, or even generally mentioned, anything of emotional importance to him. He had other things to talk about. And this might have been useful to Beckett. Yeats also wrote experimental plays and novels, and it was he who found Beckett a publisher in London for his first novel, *Murphy*, after it had been rejected by several firms.

Like Yeats and his brother the poet, and the playwrights Shaw, Synge and O'Casey, Beckett was a Dublin Protestant. The fact that he played no part in the development of the Abbey Theatre, and did not write about Ireland directly or suffer from patriotism or indulge in nationalism, and seemed in ways deracinated, a citizen of nowhere, does not mean that Ireland, its light and its landscape, and to some extent its so-called heritage, did not form him, or have a deep effect on him. His Protestantism shows up in some lovely moments, however, such as when he bathes at the Forty Foot in Dublin in 1936 and sees a Father McGrath, "red all over with ingrowning semen & exposure." The footnote offered by the editors in Volume I of his *Collected Letters* remarks drily: "It is not known to which Father McGrath SB refers." Beckett's South Dublin Unionist background emerges also in some wonderful comments, such as an attack on the police force of the Free

State: "There is no animal I loathe more profoundly than a Civic Guard, a symbol of Ireland with his official Gaelic loutish complacency."

Beckett's problem was that, as a literary artist, he knew that what his predecessors in Ireland had done with the island's hidden or invented personality would be of no use to him. What Jack Yeats had done had a greater influence on him than the work of any Irish writer. In 1937, he wrote to his aunt Cissie Sinclair, a kindred spirit, about Yeats's work as though he were writing about the work he himself would begin creating a decade later:

Watteau put in busts and urns, I suppose to suggest the inorganism of the organic – all his people are mineral in the end, without possibility of being added to or taken from, pure inorganic juxtapositions – but Jack Yeats does not even need to do that. The way he puts down a man's head & a woman's head side by side, or face to face, is terrifying, two irreducible singlenesses & the impassable immensity between. I suppose that is what gives the stillness to his pictures, as though the convention were suddenly suspended, the convention & performance of love & hate, joy & pain, giving & being given, taking & being taken. A kind of petrified insight into one's ultimate hard irreducible inorganic singleness. All handled with the dispassionate acceptance that is beyond tragedy.

In the years after Beckett met Yeats he set about finding further sources of inspiration not in literary texts or traditions but in the study of European paintings. In the 1930s he was looking at paintings and writing about them with an intensity and sense of discovery. In his interest in art, and his efforts to write a poetry filled with radiant or fragmented statement, the language unadorned, personal, sometimes obscure and strangely beautiful, he came across a soul mate in Thomas MacGreevy. MacGreevy, born in Tarbert, County Kerry, in 1893 and so thirteen years older than Beckett, was an art critic and a poet. His poem "Exile" began:

> *I knew if you had died that I should grieve*
> *Yet I found my heart wishing you were dead.*

This found echoes in an untitled poem by Beckett, written first in French:

> *I would like my love to die*
> *And the rain to be falling on the graveyard*
> *And on me walking the streets*
> *Mourning the first and last to love me.*

MacGreevy had fought in the First World War, seeing active service at Ypres and the Somme, where he was wounded twice. By the time he met Beckett, he already knew Joyce and his circle in Paris and had met Eliot in London. Besides his short book on Jack Yeats and some poems, a few of them masterpieces of their kind, he wrote books on Eliot and Richard Aldington for the same series as Beckett's book on Proust, the publication of which he arranged. He later wrote a monograph on Poussin and was director of the National Gallery of Ireland from 1950 to 1963. MacGreevy flits in and out of the lives of various figures in these years. He was a friend of W. B. Yeats's wife, George, and of Joyce's wife, Nora; he corresponded with Wallace Stevens, who dedicated a poem to him. Richard Aldington called him "a paradox of a man if ever there was one. He looked like a priest in civvies." MacGreevy chatted and gossiped a lot, knew a great deal about art and music and literature and was charming and cheerful. He disliked England, even though he retained a British passport and had no objection to actual English people. Like many before and after him, he was homosexual abroad but celibate in Ireland. (When he mentioned his sexual inclinations to a priest, he was told to kick himself every time he had such thoughts.) He was a dapper little fellow who wore a bow-tie; he managed to be Catholic and queer, patriotic and cosmopolitan all at the same time. When he lived in Paris, he often went for a walk during the day to "make sure the world was where [he] had left it the evening before." In the years between Beckett's arrival in Paris in 1928, where he and MacGreevy taught at the École Normale Supérieure, and the outbreak of the Second World War, MacGreevy was Beckett's confidant and his closest friend.

Although Beckett was brought up in what was effectively suburban Dublin, the house was close enough to the mountains south of the city, and to the sea and the bare Wicklow Mountains even further south, to make this landscape one of abiding importance to Beckett, who, like his father, was a great walker. The letters in the first volume of his correspondence make clear that, despite his lack of interest in Ireland or Irishness, he loved the Irish landscape. In 1932 he wrote to MacGreevy about a trip to the west of Ireland with his brother Frank, describing Galway as:

a grand little magic grey town full of sensitive stone and bridges and water. We . . . spent a day walking on Achill right out over the Atlantic . . . Altogether it was an unforgettable trip and much too short, through bog and mountain scenery that was somehow far more innocent and easy and obvious than the stealthy secret variety we have here. I would like to go back to Galway and spend a little time there.

Ten days later, he described the Wicklow Mountains:

I walk immeasurably & unrestrainedly, hills and dales, all day, and back with a couple of pints from the Powerscourt Arms under my

Montparnasse belt through the Homer dusk. Often very moving and it helps to swamp the usual palpitations. But I disagree with you about the gardenish landscape. The lowest mountains here terrify me far more than anything I saw in Connemara or Achill.

This habit of walking would fill one of Beckett's miraculous late pieces, *Company*, in which he described his narrator walking ("Sole sound in the silence your footfalls") but also his own father's setting out on a long day's walk as his mother was giving birth:

It being a public holiday your father left the house soon after his breakfast with a flask and a package of his favourite egg sandwiches for a tramp in the mountains. There was nothing unusual in this. But on that particular morning his love of walking and wild scenery was not the only mover. But he was moved also to take himself off and out of the way by his aversion to the pains and general unpleasantness of labour and delivery. Hence the sandwiches which he relished at noon looking out to sea from the lee of a great rock on the first summit scaled. You may imagine his thoughts before and after as he strode through the gorse and heather.

Beckett seems to have had an uncomplicated relationship with his father. In April 1933 he wrote to MacGreevy:

Lovely walk this morning with Father, who grows old with a very graceful philosophy. Comparing bees & butterflies to elephants & parrots & speaking of indentures with the leveller. Barging through hedges and over the walls with the help of my shoulder, blaspheming and stopping to rest under colour of admiring the view. I'll never have any one like him.

Two months later, when his father died, Beckett wrote to MacGreevy:

He was in his sixty first year, but how much younger he seemed and was. Joking and swearing at the doctors as long as he had breath. He lay in the bed with sweet pea all over his face, making great oaths that when he got better he would never do a stroke of work. He would drive to the top of Howth and lie in the bracken and fart . . . I can't write about him, I can only walk the fields and climb the ditches after him.

Beckett's father's late interest in not doing a stroke of work made its way with many complications and much guilt to his son. Lassitude is one of Beckett's great subjects. In August 1930, as he worked on his book on Proust, he wrote: "I can't do the fucking thing. I don't know whether to start at the end or the beginning." In December, the book finished, he wrote to the editor in London to say that he had added nothing. "I can't do anything here – neither read nor think nor write. So I am posting it back to you within the next day or two with practically no changes made. I must apologise for the absurdity of the entire proceeding. I expected more generous rifts in the paralysis." The following month he wrote to MacGreevy: "You know I can't write at all. The simplest sentence is a torture." Soon, he wrote to MacGreevy again from London: "If I could work up some pretext for writing a poem, short-story, or anything at all, I would be all right. I suppose I am all right. But I get frightened sometimes at the idea that the itch to write is cured. I suppose it's the fornicating place & its fornicating weather." Two weeks later, nothing had changed: "I don't believe I could put a dozen words together on any subject whatsoever." A year afterwards, back in Ireland, there was still no advance. "I find it more and more difficult to write and I think I write worse and worse in consequence." In 1934 he wrote to his cousin: "I can't do any work, no more than a man can pick his snout and thread a needle at the same time. So I've nearly given up trying." In 1936 he wrote from Hamburg to the writer Mary Manning in further despair:

My next work shall be on rice paper wound about a spool, with a perforated line every six inches and on sale in Boots. The length of each chapter will be carefully calculated to suit with the average free motion. And with every copy a free sample of some laxative to promote sales. The Beckett Bowel Books, Jesus in farto.

(He referred to his Proust book as "my Proust turd.") His interest in the toilet might have been awakened by what he described to Arland Ussher early in 1936 as "a sebaceous cyst in my anus which happily a fart swept away before it became operable." As late as 1939 he was writing to MacGreevy: "I drowse through the days & do nothing. I try now & then to get started, but it comes to nothing. If it is to be like that, let it be like that."

His problem in these years was very simple and not easy to solve: it was how to live, what to do, and who to be. He was clever, well educated, he spoke French and Italian fluently; his German was very good. But his first book of stories had not sold and he could not find a publisher for his novel. He had no idea how he would earn a living, and he was also deeply unhappy. He was not always the saintly figure, full of shy politeness and withdrawn courtesy, that he subsequently became. His loathing for the poet Austin Clarke emerges freely in his letters. He openly satirized him in *Murphy* as Austin Ticklepenny and attacked his work in an essay for the *Bookman* in 1934. Nor was he known for his personal courtesy in the years before he left Dublin. When one night the playwright Denis Johnston asked him for a lift to Foxrock, where they both lived, Beckett replied rudely: "No."

His famous despair is not always on display here, though there are hints of it. In a letter to his cousin in 1934, he wrote about the coming of spring:

The strange, gentle pleasures I feel at the approach of spring are impossible of expression, and if that is a sentence inviting ridicule, so much the worse for me. I have positively never watched it coming with so much impatience and so much relief. And I think of it as a victory over darkness, nightmares, sweats, panic and madness, and of the crocuses and daffodils as the promise of a life at least bearable, once enjoyed but in a past so remote that all trace, even remembrance of it, had been almost lost.

At times in his letters, it is easy to see him slowly and laboriously becoming the writer and the man he later was; at other times, it is clear that he could have become someone else. In 1933 he wrote to MacGreevy about the possibility of a career in advertising ("It has been in my mind for a long time"). In 1936, when he was thirty, he thought of training to be a commercial pilot ("I hope I am not too old to take it up seriously"). He also considered training to be a film-maker and sent a letter to Eisenstein that same year asking to be admitted to the Moscow State School of Cinematography. As well, he applied to be a lecturer in Italian at the University of Capetown. In the end, in a splendid ruse, he decided to be an art critic and convinced his mother that she should pay for a lengthy stay in Germany so that he could look at pictures.

His letters to MacGreevy about paintings are serious and well informed. He writes about paintings in his early letters better than he writes about anything else, including his own life. There is a sense of his complex personality – on the one hand, his stern-ness of judgement, on the other, his ability to take pleasure in what he saw – in the way he goes into exacting detail about the paintings he was looking at, including work in the National Gallery of Ireland, which was around the corner from the office in Clare Street where the family quantity surveying business was run. In December 1931, he took in Perugino's *Pietà*, newly acquired by the gallery.

It's buried behind a formidable barrage of shining glass, so that one is obliged to take cognisance of it progressively, square inch by square inch. It's all messed up by restorers, but the Xist and the women are lovely. A clean-shaven, potent Xist, and a passion of tears for the waste ... Rottenly hung in rotten light behind this thick shop window ... a lovely cheery Xist full of sperm, & the woman touching his thighs and mourning his jewels.

In his story "Love and Lethe" in *More Pricks than Kicks*, Ruby Tough from Irishtown is likened to the Mary Magdalene in this picture: "Those who are in the least curious to know what she looked like at the time in which we have chosen to cull her we venture to refer to the Magdalene in the Perugino Pietà in the National Gallery of Dublin, always bearing in mind that the hair of our heroine is black and not ginger." The following year he wrote: "I seem to spend a lot of time in the National Gallery, looking at the Poussin Entombment and coming stealthily down the stairs into the charming toy brightness of the German room to the Brueghels and the Masters of Tired Eyes and Silver Windows. The young woman of Rembrandt is splendid." In his story "Ding-Dong," he described the face of the pedlar woman: "Yet like tormented faces that he had seen, like the face in the National Gallery in Merrion Square by the Master of Tired Eyes, it seemed to have come a long way and subtend an infinitely narrow angle of affliction, as eyes focus on a star. The features were null, only luminous, impassive and secure, petrified in radiance."

His letters from Germany, too, are filled with the names of paintings and a sense of his fierce concentration on the task in hand. Sometimes, the descriptions and lists go on for pages. Although he wrote mainly from Germany about paintings he saw and his own melancholy, he didn't ignore what was happening around him. From Hamburg he wrote to Mary Manning in 1936: "All the lavatory men say Heil Hitler. The best pictures are in the cellar." Soon afterwards, he wrote to MacGreevy: "I have met a lot of friendly people here, mostly painters . . . They are all more or less suppressed, i.e. cannot exhibit publicly and dare sell only with precaution. The group was broken up in 1933, their library confiscated." In January 1937 he noted that Thomas Mann's citizenship had been rescinded. The following month he wrote about an art historian he had met: "He was removed from his post in the Real Gymnasium here at the Gallery in 1933, like all the others of his kidney."

While this might seem like nonchalance, it should be placed beside Beckett's general refusal to write letters filled with news of the day and his subsequent determination to stay in France once war broke out and become involved in the Resistance. It is hard not to underline the passages where Beckett took pleasure in the image of the *Pietà*, in pictures of the tearful mother and her headstrong son who was lying finally in her lap, hers at last. Beckett was the sort of young man who was made to break his poor mother's heart. Home from Paris and then London and then Germany and feeling very sorry for himself, he must have been an awful nuisance lounging around the house, or in bed with hangovers – he was drinking a lot – or other unnamable complaints. His mother was neurotic enough in any case, and sad, often depressed, after the death of her husband. Beckett's brother, Frank, who was as solid as his father, took over the family business, and he was now on the point of getting married. For Beckett's mother, her wayward son became the focus of her worry.

There is an interesting letter written from London in 1935 to MacGreevy that deals with Beckett's reason for undergoing psychoanalysis there. He went three times a week. "For years," he wrote,

I was unhappy, consciously & deliberately ever since I left school & went into TCD, so that I isolated myself more & more, undertook less & less & lent myself to a crescendo of disparagement of others & myself . . . It was not until that way of living, or rather negation of living, developed such terrifying physical symptoms that it could no longer be pursued, that I became aware of anything morbid in myself . . . It was with a specific fear & a specific complaint that I went to Geoffrey [Thompson, a shrink], then to Bion [Wilfred, also a shrink] to learn that the "specific fear & complaint" was the least important symptom of a diseased condition that began in a time which I could not remember, in my "pre-history."

In other words, it was all about his mother.

In October 1937, when his mother had left him alone (with a cook, of course) in the family house, he wrote a letter marvelling at the pleasantness of Cooldrinagh without her.

And I could not wish her anything better than to feel the same when I am away. But I don't wish her anything at all, neither good nor ill. I am what her savage loving has made me, and it is good that one of us should accept that finally . . . I simply don't want to see her or write to her or hear from her . . . Which I suppose all boils down to saying what a bad son I am. Then Amen. It is a title for me of as little honour as infamy. Like describing a tree as a bad shadow.

In Paris in January the following year, when he was recovering from being stabbed in a serious assault, he wrote to MacGreevy about a visit by his mother and brother: "Hope you met Mother & Frank in London. He was relieved to be getting back, and she sorry. I felt great gusts of affection & esteem & compassion for her when she was over. What a relationship!" In May, when he heard that she had burned her hands badly, he wrote: "Of course she kept it from me. I feel sorry for her often to the point of tears. That is the part that was not analysed away, I suppose." The following month he wrote: "As you can imagine I am not anxious to go to Ireland, but as long as mother lives I shall go every year."

Beckett's mother disapproved of her in-laws, the Sinclairs, as much as she would have disapproved of the Joyces, had she heard much about them. Beckett, however, was closely involved with both families: they offered him a way out of his own family; they opened paths for him towards certain freedoms that he sought, though they created problems for him along the way. The Becketts had a lovely habit, over the generations, of producing one or two really sensible members of the family, such as Beckett's father and his brother, who never put a foot astray, and then various complex figures, such as Beckett's aunt Cissie and Beckett himself and indeed his first cousin John Beckett, whose serious, intelligent and eccentrically minimalist style of conducting Bach cantatas in Dublin, and wonderfully laconic and informative introductions, were, for me, one of the very great pleasures of the city in the 1970s. Cissie Sinclair was Beckett's father's only sister. She had studied art in Paris with Estella Solomons and Beatrice Elvery, later Lady Glenavy, both artists who regularly showed in the Dublin galleries. Cissie married Boss Sinclair, a Dublin antiques dealer and friend of the painter William Orpen; in the early 1920s the Sinclairs moved to Germany, where they dealt in contemporary German art, as well as antiques. Beckett often visited them there and became emotionally involved with their daughter, his first cousin Peggy, who died of tuberculosis in 1933 aged twenty-two. Her ghost is all over his collection of stories *More Pricks than Kicks*, and there are stray references to her throughout his work. (And there are elements of Cissie's last years, when she was confined to a wheelchair and watched the world through a telescope, in Beckett's play *Endgame*.) When Hitler rose to power, making life for Jewish art dealers impossible, the Sinclairs returned to Dublin.

They were serious art collectors and interested in music and literature. Both Boss and his son Morris played the violin. Their priorities were rather different from the stolid, dull ones that dominated Beckett's own household. They were bohemians. They gave parties at which, as Anthony Cronin noted in his biography of Beckett, "people sat on the floor and afterwards quite possibly slept on it." No one among the Sinclairs minded Beckett staying in bed all morning and having no worldly ambitions and many vague and high-toned dreams. Beckett could write to them easily about art and music. There is a marvellous letter to Morris from London in 1934, written in French, in which Beckett describes a concert he went to:

I have had to put up with a huge composition by [Bach], humorously entitled: Suite for Orchestra, conducted by the ignoble Furtwängler, who, it appears, has had the better part of his nudity covered with interwoven swastikas. He has the charming modesty of letting himself be led by his brass-players, who blow as only beer-drinkers can, while making with his left hand very daring gestures towards his first violins, who fortunately paid not the least attention to them, and swinging the soft fleshiness of his posterior as if he longed to go to the lavatory. Hardly had I recovered from this assault when he had the impertinence to launch into Schumann's Fourth Symphony, which is less like a symphony than like an overture begun by Lehár, completed by Goering, and revised by Johnny Doyle (if not his dog).

A small rift with the family arose after Beckett published the story "The Smeraldina's Billet Doux," in which he used a letter from Peggy Sinclair just a year after her death. In a letter to Morris, Beckett wrote: "Glad to hear that Boss bears me no ill-will. But that I knew beforehand." James Knowlson writes in his biography:

His uncle seems to have understood better than his aunt the needs of fiction and not been too cross. As for Cissie, she was very upset at first. But she quickly forgave him, after he wrote a letter pleading with her to see him during his summer trip home. The reconciliation was so successful that, after meeting her during the summer, he could write to MacGreevy that all was well "with only a minimum of constraint with Smeraldina's Ma."

In her biography, Deirdre Bair wrote: "Yet he seems to have had little remorse for deeds such as this, complaining only of the loss of visiting privileges, as if someone else, a complete stranger, had committed the transgression."

A problem arises in the edition of his letters with the sources for this information. Beckett insisted that only letters "having bearing on my work" needed to be published after his death. Edward Beckett, Beckett's nephew, who represents the estate, is cited in the introduction to Volume I of his letters as "a working partner in the preparation of this edition." The editors acknowledge that "he has responded generously where there was disagreement over what counts as 'having bearing on the work.'" But they also make clear that while they followed a policy of including as much as possible, there were disagreements between them and the estate. "To take one example," they write, "it is the editors" view that Beckett's frequent, at times almost obsessive, discussion of his health problems – his feet, his heart palpitations, his boils and cysts – is of direct relevance to the work; with this the Estate of Samuel Beckett has disagreed." The editors point out that while there are "some ellipses" in the letters as published, they have "tried to limit these." Calling Cissie Sinclair, whom Beckett dearly loved, "Smeraldina's Ma," just a year after the death of her daughter Peggy, the model for Smeraldina, in a letter to MacGreevy may not improve Beckett's status among right-thinking people. But for the rest of us, who are interested in his work, it is not merely of prurient interest, though it is that as well. It is of importance how Beckett dealt with people in his family who objected to real people being used as models for characters. In the case of Beckett, whose relationship with the world of "real people" would become increasingly strained as he produced his masterpieces after the war, this early use of his dead cousin, and his own response when problems arose, has "bearing on the work," whether his estate likes it or not.

Bair, in her footnotes, cites "the papers of Thomas Mac-Greevy" for her information on the strain between Beckett and the Sinclairs over the use of Peggy's letter. Knowlson cites two different letters to MacGreevy written in August 1934, only one of which is included in the edition of his letters. The one here is printed with three ellipses, and there is no use of the term "Smeraldina's Ma" to describe Cissie Sinclair. The first paragraph reads:

My dear Tom, Your letter this morning. Somehow things at home seem to be simpler, I seem to have grown indifferent to the atmosphere of coffee-stall emotions [ . . . ] But people's feelings don't seem to matter, one is nice ad lib. to all & sundry, offender & offended, with a basso profundo of privacy that never deserts one. It is only now I begin to realise what the analysis has done for me.

The next paragraph also begins with " . . . ," and another " . . . " appears at its end.

The problem for the reader, in a book so filled with detailed and informative footnotes, is that in this case there is no footnote, no clue given as to who might be offender or the offended here. In May 1937, after the death of Boss Sinclair, Beckett wrote to MacGreevy: "I suppose you have read about the action for libel that Harry [Boss Sinclair's twin brother] is taking against [Oliver St. John] Gogarty. I am in it up to the neck. And gladly in so far as Boss wanted it done, having seen the offending passage some weeks before his death." Gogarty had written an autobiography, *As I Was Going Down Sackville Street*, and included a passage about

an old usurer who had eyes like a pair of periwinkles on which somebody had been experimenting with a pin, and a nose like a shrunken tomato, one side of which swung independently of the other. The older he grew the more he pursued the immature, and enticed little girls into his office. This was bad enough, but he had grandsons, and these directed the steps of their youth to follow in grandfather's footsteps, with more zeal than discrimination.

There were also references to "the twin grandchildren of the ancient Chicken Butcher" and to an antique dealer called Willie (William was Boss's original name).

In his statement of claim, Harry Sinclair accepted that his grandfather had in fact enticed little girls into the back room of his premises and interfered with them sexually, but denied that he and his brother had followed in their grandfather's footsteps, as it were, in this matter. He insisted that he and his brother were easily identifiable and were clearly libelled.

Beckett came back from Paris to give evidence that he recognized the Sinclairs as the subject of Gogarty's libel. Earlier he had written to MacGreevy: "All kinds of dirt will be raked up & I suppose they will try & discredit me as author of the Pricks." He was right. The barrister for the defence read out a passage from *More Pricks than Kicks*, which had been banned in Ireland, that referred to Jesus's "interference in the affairs of his boyfriend Lazarus." He also made mention of *Whoroscope*, a book of poems, and forced Beckett to correct his deliberate mispronunciation of the name Proust and admit that he wasn't a Christian, a Jew or an atheist, alienating the jury as much by his French accent as by his lack of religion or his non-religion. In the summing-up, the barrister referred to Beckett as "a bawd and a blasphemer" and this was used the next day as a column subheading in *The Irish Times*. In his summing-up the judge said that he himself would not put much faith in the evidence of "the witness Beckett."

In his biography Knowlson writes: "Although he rarely discussed the case in his correspondence with friends, his remarks about Ireland became more and more vituperative after his return to Paris." It is easy to imagine his mother's view on the matter as she read about the trial daily in *The Irish Times*. Beckett did not stay with her when he returned to give evidence. When the trial was over, he went to see his brother, who advised him to go back to Paris without seeing her. Beckett did so. His mother, in retaliation, never spoke to the Sinclairs again.

Although Beckett wrote many letters – 15,000 have been found and transcribed by the editors, and there may be more – he was not, on the evidence of the first volume, a great letter-writer. We are lucky that he put his real energies into his work. And yet there are passages and entire letters in this volume that throw significant light on the development of his thinking about language and prose, as much as about art and music. The most interesting is his letter from Dublin to the writer and translator Axel Kaun, written in 1937 in German:

It is indeed getting more and more difficult, even pointless, for me to write informal English. And more and more my language appears to me like a veil which one has to tear apart in order to get to those things (or the nothingness) lying behind it. Grammar and style! To me they seem to have become as irrelevant as a Biedermeier bathing suit or the imperturbability of a gentleman. A mask . . . Of course, for the time being, one makes do with little. At first, it can only be a matter of somehow inventing a method of verbally demonstrating this scornful attitude vis-à-vis the word. In this dissonance of instrument and usage perhaps one will already be able to sense a whispering of the end-music or of the silence underlying all.

He went on to say: "In my opinion, the most recent work of Joyce had nothing at all to do with such a programme."

In these years, however, what Joyce was doing continued to fascinate him; he was nourished by his association and friendship with Joyce and his reading of Joyce's work. Despite his admiration for Shem, as he often calls him in his letters, and indeed his affection for him, the relationship was not simple, not least perhaps because of the class difference between them as Irishmen. Just before Christmas 1937 he wrote to MacGreevy about working on the proofs of *Finnegans Wake*: "Joyce paid me 250 fr. for about 15 hrs work on his proofs. That is needless to say only for your ear. He then supplemented it with an old overcoat and 5 ties! I did not refuse. It is so much simpler to be hurt than to hurt." It is hard to know what Joyce was thinking of. And the idea that a notorious scrounger of Irish Catholic origin, great writer or not, was offering acts of charity to Beckett in Paris would not have brought cheer to May Beckett in her large, posh house in Foxrock.

Beckett was invited to dine with the Joyces on Christmas night 1937. Joyce wanted a collection of critical essays on his work in progress to appear in the *Nouvelle Revue Française* and asked Beckett to do one of them. Beckett wrote to MacGreevy:

I have done nothing more with the NRF article and feel like dropping it. Certainly there will be no question of prolegomena or epilegomena when the work [*Finnegans Wake*] comes out in book form. And if that means a break, then let there be a break. At least this time it won't be about their daughter, who by the way as far as I can learn gets deeper & deeper into the misery & less & less likely ever to emerge.

Soon, however, he was writing in a different mood about Joyce. On 5 January 1938: "He was sublime last night, deprecating with the utmost conviction his lack of talent. I don't feel the danger of the association any more. He is just a very lovable human being." After the stabbing, he wrote to MacGreevy from hospital: "The Joyces have been extraordinarily kind, bringing me round everything from a heating lamp to a custard pudding." When he arrived home, he found "an immense bunch of Parma violets from Joyces."

There is very little about Beckett's relationship with Lucia Joyce, James Joyce's daughter, in his letters, although the short biography of Lucia at the back of the book is helpful. ("Lucia Joyce, who is widely considered to be the model for the Syra-Cusa in SB's *Dream of Fair to Middling Women*, became increasingly infatuated with SB, but in May 1930 SB made it clear that he did not reciprocate her interest. This caused a temporary falling-out with the Joyces.") When Beckett and Lucia met in London in 1935, Beckett wrote to MacGreevy: "The Lucia ember flared up & fizzled out. But more of that viva voce."

In early 1938 Beckett reported that Joyce was very worried about Lucia; the footnote informs us that she was "in treatment for mental illness." In April 1939 he wrote: "I see the Joyces now & then. I go every week to Ivry to visit Lucia, who I think gets slowly worse. She sees nobody but her father & myself."

The edition of the first volume of Beckett's letters has been annotated with knowledge and care, using vast research. It will, for the most part, please admirers of Beckett's art and satisfy those who respect his wishes that only letters that have bearing on his work should appear. There is no spilling the beans, or mad gossip; it was not his style. There is no detailed account of what it was like to be a witness in the Gogarty libel action. Nor is there much fanfare when Beckett meets Suzanne Deschevaux-Dumesnil, with whom he was to live for almost half a century and with whom he would spend the war years in France, the years immediately after this first volume of letters. In April 1939 Beckett wrote to MacGreevy with his typical dry, stoical wisdom: "There is a French girl also whom I am fond of, dispassionately, and who is very good to me. The hand will not be overbid. As we both know that it will come to an end there is no knowing how long it may last."

# Brian Moore: Out of Ireland Have I Come, Great Hatred, Little Room

In the second chapter of Brian Moore's early novel *The Lonely Passion of Judith Hearne*, Miss Hearne gets to know her fellow boarders, especially the landlady's brother, the returned Yank, Mr. Madden. They discuss the difference between men and women in Ireland and America. "Guys beating their brains out to keep their wives in mink," Mr. Madden complains. "It's the women's fault. No good . . . Me, I wouldn't have nothing to do with them." Miss Hearne, deeply alert to nuances of education and class, thinks to herself that he can't be very well educated if he can speak like that. And then she replies: "Oh, that's not like Ireland, Mr. Madden. Why, the men are gods here, I honestly do believe." As Mr. Madden continues, Miss Hearne becomes aware of his maleness: "He was so big, so male as he said it that she felt the blushes start up again. His big hand thumped the table."

Brian Moore began to think about Judith Hearne when he was twenty-seven, in exile from Belfast, and trying to write short stories in a remote part of Ontario: "I thought of this old lady who used to come to our house. She was a spinster who had some Civil Service job to do with sanitation and she lived most of her life with her 'dear aunt.' They'd not been 'grand' but they had pretensions, and she had very genteel manners." The novel is full of Joycean moments. It is set in a Catholic Ireland that is half-genteel and oddly insecure; it allows Judith Hearne's vulnerable consciousness great dramatic power; it uses different tones and cadences and voices; and it takes from "Clay," the most mysterious story in *Dubliners*, the idea of a single, middle-aged woman visiting a family and finding both comfort and humiliation there. As Moore moved from a short story to a novel he wrote to his sister in Belfast (as Joyce wrote to his sister in Dublin looking for details of the city) asking for her memories of Miss Keogh, the visitor on whom Judith Hearne was based. However, he disregarded most of what he was told. (The original Miss Keogh had a job, for example.) He used merely the "speech and mannerisms" of the original and he surrounded them with something else, elements of his own isolation as a non-achiever in a family obsessed with achievement, and as an emigrant in Canada. His own loss of faith becomes hers, and his memory that his original had "a little weakness for the bottle" becomes her alcoholism.

Yet none of this explains the intensity of the novel, the versions of spiritual suffering and abject despair set beside tiny instants of pure social embarrassment and nuanced social observation. The novel manages to make the large moments in the book – Judith running at the tabernacle in a Catholic church in a fit of drunken despair, for example – as credible and powerful as the smaller pieces of self-delusion and social comedy. "It is also a book about a woman," Moore wrote to his publisher, "presenting certain problems of living peculiar to women. I wrote it with all the sympathy and understanding that I am capable of."

Moore knew that you could achieve certain effects by writing about a woman in the Ireland of his time that you could not achieve in writing about a man. A man can swagger with drink, his drunkenness, even in a genteel context, will not bring disgrace, but pity maybe, or tolerance, or a sort of liberation. A middle-aged woman, however, who gets drunk alone in her room in a genteel boarding house and does not remember that she sang all night and has to face her landlady and her fellow boarders the next day is a piece of dynamite. In a society where, as Miss Hearne says, men are gods, how do you go about dramatizing them? In a society where female vulnerability is open and public, where women are alert to their shifting position, watchful, under the bony thumb of the Church, in charge of intimate domestic details but nothing else, women are a godsend to a novelist, living, as Moore told an interviewer:

in a personal world, a very, very personal world. Men, I find, are always, as they say in America, "rolling their credits" at each other. They come on telling you what they've done, and who they are, and all the rest of it. Quite often, women don't do that, because life hasn't worked out that way for some of them. But when a woman tells me a story about something that happens to her, [I] often get a sudden flash of frankness which is really novelistic. It is as if a woman knows when she tells a story that it must be personal, that it must be interesting.

It is no coincidence, then, that the three finest novels to appear in Ireland between the mid-1950s and mid-1960s were about middle-aged women suffering. They were Moore's *The Lonely Passion of Judith Hearne* (1955), John McGahern's *The Barracks* (1963) and Aidan Higgins's *Langrishe, Go Down* (1966). It is no coincidence, either, that the best novels about men in the period after independence dealt with figures in extreme and exquisite isolation, as in the novels of Beckett and Francis Stuart, or offered elaborate comedy, as in Flann O'Brien. In Irish fiction after Joyce, the women suffered and the men were antisocial, and the tone is one of unnerving bleakness.

The problem for Moore, McGahern, Higgins and many others was how to create a male character who was neither comic nor lying on his back in the dark. In a society that was merely half-formed and had no sense of itself, a society in which the only real choice was to leave or live in a cowed internal exile, the failure to create a fully formed male character in fiction was emblematic of a more general failure.

The four novels that Brian Moore wrote after *Judith Hearne* struggle with this, and all of them bear the mark of the problem more clearly than any sign of its resolution. These novels are *The Feast of Lupercal* (1957), *The Luck of Ginger Coffey* (1960), *An Answer from Limbo* (1962) and *The Emperor of Ice-Cream* (1965). The last of these is a coming-of-age novel set in wartime Belfast; the second and third have as protagonists Irishmen in exile in North America; and the first tells the story of Diarmuid Devine, a teacher, who stayed behind in Belfast.

"The climate of Northern Ireland . . . is such as to encourage weakness of character," Moore wrote.

The interesting thing about Devine was, compared to Judith, who had all the bases loaded against her, he has some choice and therefore is a less admirable character, because you feel he is in some way master of his fate, which she really wasn't . . . I wanted Devine to be a character who had choice, and who had failed in the choice.

Devine has something in common with Mr. Madden and Bernard Rice, the landlady's son, the two male figures in *The Lonely Passion of Judith Hearne*. He is underimagined; there is a crudity and lack of subtlety in his creation. When he overhears two colleagues undermining his masculinity, we are told that "he had never been so mortified in his life" and, a few sentences later, "He was very upset." Devine's response to every single moment is predetermined by the author's vision of him: thus his response is always dull and afraid; his consciousness, through which we see the world, is limited in a way that Judith Hearne's is open-ended. Like Judith and Mr. Madden, he, too, has views on the man/ woman question: "Character assassins, every blessed one of them," his mind tells us. "That was a thing he couldn't help noticing about women, they always had a bad word for one another. Men had far more sense, at least they shut up when they didn't like a person."

This last passage seems to offer us a key to the problem with these four novels. The men's attitudes are not only stereotyped and tiresome but dated in a way that Leopold Bloom's responses to women, or Stephen Dedalus's, don't seem dated. There is no element of richness or surprise, and there is a terrible ironic distance and jauntiness (more noticeable in *The Luck of Ginger Coffey* and *The Emperor of Ice-Cream*). Clearly, the passage quoted above could not be easily written now, but Devine would be a more interesting figure had these words not been put into his consciousness in the first place.

Is it a golden rule of fiction that an author cannot create a character whose way of noticing is significantly and emphatically less rich than the author's own? The problem always is: what colours and nuances to leave out, what tricks and twists of voice or consciousness to throw aside? This question arises when reading the four novels Moore published between 1957 and 1965 and reading Denis Sampson's biography. Moore became increasingly fascinated by failure, by the idea of the painful case, the more successful he became. All four of these novels deal in failure, and he himself, from early on, was alert to what dull failure in a novel looked like compared to melodrama, say, or, in the case of Judith Hearne, a sort of tragedy. In 1957 in a letter to Diana Athill, his editor at André Deutsch, he wrote:

I always want to give my character more diversity, more intellectual strength – something of that wonderful Dostoevskian quality of the unexpected, which, on examination, turns out to be the logical, the underlying truth in their behaviour. But, so far, each time I simply lack the ability to bring this off and, lacking it, settle for what my pessimism and my experience tell me is possible. So the characters become smaller, duller in a way and without the stature of tragedy.

Brian Moore was born in Belfast in 1921 into what can almost be described as a ruling-class Catholic family. His father was a surgeon, the first Catholic to be nominated to the Senate of Queen's

University Belfast and a pillar of society. His father's sister Agnes was married to Eoin MacNeill, who became leader of the Irish Volunteers on their foundation in 1913, countermanded the order for the 1916 Rising and later became Professor of Early Irish History at University College Dublin. Moore's mother, twenty years younger than his father, had been a nurse at the hospital where his father worked. She came from an Irish-speaking background in Donegal, from a family of nineteen children. "My mother seemed to be more in sync with me," Moore later said. "I was very fond of my mother. I think the fact that I had six sisters and that I was one of my mother's favourite sons, if not her favourite son, had an effect on me."

All his life Brian Moore loathed his old school, St. Malachy's in Belfast, and he attempted revenge on it in several of his novels. The tone and quality of this loathing must have been enriched by the fact that his father was founder and president of the past pupils' union. His father was also, Sampson writes, "custodian of the prestige and tradition of the school, and so his expectations of his sons' behaviour and academic achievement carried this burden in addition to the common expectations of an academically successful parent." Moore took his own academic failure and his loss of faith in Catholicism immensely seriously. He became a socialist in a deeply conservative household, in a city where more than sixty years later mild socialism is still a sour dream. "I began to think of myself as a failure at an early age," he said, "and I began to think of myself as someone who was concealing something."

Moore shared the dream of many adolescents worldwide: he wanted to blow his homeplace sky-high. The difference was that his homeplace already had its explosive elements. Moore said that he "reacted against all that nationalistic fervour," because he saw that his father's and uncle's "dislike of Britain extended to approval of Britain's enemies." In *The Emperor of Ice-Cream*, which

he described as his most autobiographical novel, Moore dramatized the gap between Gavin's idealism (and failure to study for
exams) in the early years of the war and his family's conserva-
tism. Gavin's mother thinks that General Franco is a saint and
Gavin's father is jubilant about Hitler's prospects, just as our
young hero, a member of the ARP, a local defence unit, comes
more and more to understand what is happening in Europe.
Moore offers perfect set pieces between father and son. ("I won't
go into the fact that you're the first member of this family to fail
any examination, I won't mention that when I was your age anything but honours marks would have been inconceivable to me."
And then: "Wipe that grin off your face. After your performance
today, I see nothing to smile about, do you?") A Christmas Day
scene between father and son during the early years of the war
must have been impossible to resist, and as he smokes cigars after
his Christmas dinner, Gavin's father tells him that the war will
soon be over: "Oh, the English are going to find out that their
troubles are only beginning. Mark my words, Hitler won't be an
easy master. He won't spare them, not after the way they turned
down that perfectly reasonable offer he made last summer."

The last fifty pages of the novel deal with the German air-raids
on Belfast in 1941. Brian Moore, like Gavin, worked in the morgue.
"I found myself being punched from adolescence into a volunteer job coffining dead bodies for weeks. And that experience
naturally had a strong effect on me." The father in the novel flees
Belfast for the safety of Dublin with all the family except Gavin,
but not before he has a sudden, crude and unconvincing change
of heart: "I've said it before and I'll say it again. The German
jackboot is a far crueller burden than the heel of old John Bull."

In reality, Moore's father, aged seventy-four, worked day and
night during the air-raids and frequently slept in the hospital,
worried that he would not be able to get there if there were further attacks on the city. "My father," Moore said, "who was

pro-German, when he saw what the Germans were able to do, when he saw what modern warfare was really like, when they blew up your home, that was all, things were over." In the novel, the father's change of heart is rendered as another, almost comic aspect of his pomposity; in the real world, Dr. Moore's change of heart is more likely to have occurred slowly and silently. In the novel, the cowardly and hypocritical father returns to hear news of his heroic son, who has braved the bombs to bury the bodies. The book ends: "His father seemed aware of this change. He leaned his untidy, grey head on Gavin's shoulder, nodding, weeping, confirming. 'Oh Gavin,' his father said. 'I've been such a fool. Such a fool.' The new voice counselled silence. He took his father's hand." In the novel, the playboy of the Antrim Road got to kill his father. In the real world, Moore's father died in 1942 "thinking I was a wimp, that I was a person who wasn't going to achieve anything in life and that was very sad. I've had to live with my father's disappointment."

Brian Moore had an interesting war. In 1942 he left the ARP and joined the National Fire Service in Belfast and from there he got a job with the Ministry of War Transport in Algiers. After Algiers, he became assistant port officer for Naples, following the Allied taking of the city. Later, he was posted to Marseilles and Sète near the Spanish border. From January 1946 to November 1947 he worked in Warsaw with the United Nations Relief and Rehabilitation Administration. He saw the camp at Auschwitz and then witnessed the Communist takeover of Poland. He did not write immediately about these events: "In Europe," he said, "I had been a spectator at events that were not my events." More than forty years would pass before he wrote his terse dramas about belief and power and treachery in Poland and France in *The Colour of Blood* and *The Statement*. Nonetheless, these experiences affected him, made him sceptical and wary, a hardened observer. "Working with Polish government officials I discovered that Polish Communists were almost always as anti-semitic in their views as the rest of their countrymen." He began to develop an eye for detail, for the exotic:

Above all, Warsaw was for me . . . an exciting visual confirmation of my readings of Tolstoy, Gogol and Dostoevsky. Here were *drozhki*, the horse-drawn street cabs we had read about in Russian novels. Here were filthy peasants in fur-trimmed coats, driving long carts through the muddy streets; here were Russian soldiers singing gypsy chants, bearded beggars (or were they priests?) begging alms outside ruined churches. Here was the heart-stopping sound of a piano playing Chopin on a quiet Sunday morning in a deserted square.

Moore spent five years in Europe. It is not hard to imagine his plight when, at the end of 1947, he was forced to return to Belfast and to his family, once more with no job, no prospects, no qualifications. In the 1930s, as Moore later recalled, Sean O'Faolain argued that the only possible dénouement of an Irish novel was that "the hero gets on the boat and goes to England." Moore, who from an early age had wanted to be a writer, had two reasons for going to Canada. One, he had fallen in love with a Canadian woman; two, in his interview for a visa, he was told that he could become a journalist. In 1948 he started his long North American exile.

He began in Toronto, trying to find newspaper work, his love affair falling apart, but moved soon to Montreal, where he was hired, like Ginger Coffey in his novel, as a proofreader. He liked the city; its provincial energy and divided culture reminded him of home. Slowly, he found better newspaper work and a group of friends. In 1951 he married a fellow journalist, Jacqueline Sirois; their son was born in 1953. That year, too, he became a Canadian citizen. He began to write thrillers for money. Published under pseudonyms, they were immensely successful. They financed the writing of *The Lonely Passion of Judith Hearne* and subsequent literary novels, and together with his work as a journalist and his personality, which was modest, hard-headed and non-flashy, they helped establish his prose style, which increasingly favoured the non-poetic and pacy, the clear and terse, the brisk and sharp.

*The Lonely Passion of Judith Hearne* won instant critical success in England, Canada and the United States. It was banned in the Republic of Ireland, and this, at the time, was also a kind of critical success. The letter Moore received from his mother in Belfast concentrated on the more sexually explicit parts of the novel: "You certainly left nothing to the imagination, and my advice to you in your next book is leave out parts like this." That, too, was part of the rite of passage for an Irish novelist of that time. In her recent memoir, *Stet*, Diana Athill describes Moore in London in 1955:

He was fat because he had an ulcer and the recommended treatment in those days was large quantities of milk; and also because Jackie was a wonderful cook . . . They were both great gossips – and when I say great I mean great, because I am talking about gossip in its highest and purest form: a passionate interest, lit by humour but above malice, in human behaviour.

In 1959 the Moores moved to New York. In Canada, Brian had become friends with many writers, especially Mordecai Richler; now he became friends with Philip Roth and Neil Simon. He and his wife divided their time between Manhattan and Long Island. Moore won prizes, sold movie rights and began to achieve a sort of fame, but he lived in those years in a world he grew to distrust: "I lived in Greenwich Village . . . and I noticed that the serious writers there were quite interested in bestsellerdom, publicity, immediate personal fame, that they were . . . shameless little puffers-up of their talents and muggers-in-public for anyone who would write them up." This world gave him the background for his protagonist Brendan Tierney in *An Answer from Limbo*, but the novel is damaged by Moore's raw disapproval, and is wooden and not quite credible.

Brian and Jacqueline Moore met Frank and Jean Russell in New York in 1963, and the two couples, all of them interested in journalism and writing, began to hang out together. In the summer of 1964, Jacqueline and their son Michael went to Long Island while Brian stayed in New York working on *The Emperor of Ice-Cream*. Frank Russell, who had won a Guggenheim for his nature writing, also left New York. Brian and Jean became lovers that summer, and not long afterwards Jacqueline and Frank also became lovers. Brian dedicated *The Emperor of Ice-Cream* to Jean (as he would all his subsequent books) as Frank Russell dedicated his next book to Jacqueline and Michael. It all seemed neat and amicable, but slowly, in fact, became bitter and difficult. Moore broke with friends who supported Jacqueline, including Diana Athill and André Deutsch, to whom he wrote a letter announcing that he was going to find a new publisher.

But the letter did not end there. It went on for another page and a half, and what it said, in what appeared to be a fever of self-righteous spite against the woman he had dumped, was that I had sided with Jackie, and no one who had done that could remain his friend . . . Mordecai [Richler] told me at the time that other friends of the Moores had been taken aback by this "He who is not with me is against me" attitude.

Within a year Brian and Jean had begun their long sojourn in California, having been enticed there by Alfred Hitchcock, for whom Moore wrote the screenplay of *Torn Curtain*. (Moore, after all, knew much more about corpses than Hitchcock.)

The California the Moores inhabited was an isolated stretch of coast at Malibu. Moore worked hard on his novels. He had written five, all of which dealt in various ways with his own background. Now he needed new styles, new subjects and no interruptions. The Moores travelled a bit each summer, going to the West of Ireland, the South of France and Nova Scotia, but mainly they lived in solitude and isolation. Consciously and with deliberation, they both withdrew from the world. Denis Sampson writes superbly about some of the strange elements of Moore's transformation:

As I examined the notes Moore wrote in 1965–66, during the first year of their life together in California, I was struck by a sudden change in his handwriting. For more than fifteen years, the journalist-turned-novelist recorded his thoughts in a quick scrawl written with a fine-nibbed fountain pen or typed headlong, the text replete with misspellings and crossings out. Suddenly, notes for the novel he is working on take on the character of a monk's script. The novelist becomes a calligrapher, practising his self-conscious and stylised lettering on the back of plot outlines. By summer 1966, the transformation is complete: he now writes personal letters in a carefully crafted hand and signs with a new signature.

It is unclear whether Moore ever believed that he had lost anything by his long exile. He certainly believed that he had gained a great deal. In the 1970s, in a review of John McGahern's collection of stories *Getting Through*, he wrote:

For those writers born and brought up within its shores, Ireland is a harsh literary jailer. It is a terrain whose power to capture and dominate the imagination makes its writers for ever prisoner – forcing them, no matter how far they wander in search of escape, to return again and again in their work to the small island which remains their true world.

Brian Moore did not witness things changing in Ireland, except as a tourist, and he also missed the slow changes in the way men were treated in Irish writing. In the 1960s playwrights such as Eugene McCabe in *King of the Castle*, Tom Murphy in *A Whistle in the Dark* and John B. Keane in *The Field* began to work on the mixture of violence and impotence in the Irish male psyche. And in the 1970s John McGahern published two novels, *The Leave-taking* and *The Pornographer*, that opened new ground. *The Leavetaking* tells almost exactly the same story as *The Feast of Lupercal*: the protagonist is a teacher and the background is a fearful, authoritarian and Catholic Ireland. In *The Leavetaking* McGahern found a tone that was poetic, melancholy, slow-moving and serious to describe an adult male protagonist living in an Irish city. More and more, McGahern focused on a tiny territory, using the same motifs, the same landscape down to the same trees and the same shadows, the same set of emotional circumstances. If Ireland was a harsh literary jailer, then McGahern had become its model prisoner.

In the solitary confinement of his own choosing, Moore worked hard during his years in Malibu. Between 1968 and his death in 1999, he wrote fifteen novels. He had clearly discovered certain things about his own talent. The last fifty pages of *The Emperor of Ice-Cream* showed that he had extraordinary skills at pacing, handling time and action, creating credible excitement. *The Lonely Passion of Judith Hearne* showed how good he was at dealing with failure, isolation and loneliness.

The first novel he wrote in his new guise as recluse and cosmopolitan was *I Am Mary Dunne*, and it was his first since *The Lonely Passion of Judith Hearne* to deal with a woman's drama, his first story with North American characters, and of all his books the most fraught and intense. The scene between Mary and her friend Janice in a Manhattan restaurant is a display of pure skill: full of careful revelation, memory and reflection, placed beside the comedy of being in the wrong restaurant at the worst table. The two women are bright and upmarket; Mary is perhaps too obviously on the verge of a nervous break-down. Yet her own account of her adultery and sexual treachery is breathtaking in its detail. This story would be enough for any novel; beside it, the story of Mary's paranoia and breakdown and loss of identity is not as convincing. In other words, her North American fate of ruthlessly seeking happiness is more dramatic and interesting than her fate as victim, as imagined by an Irish novelist – what Brian Friel, in a letter to Moore, called "Gaelic gloom."

From the beginning of Moore's career a problem existed that came increasingly to damage his novels – a willingness to work in broad strokes. Some of Mary Dunne's perceptions as she moves around New York are crude and hackneyed. So, too, in his later novels about women, *The Doctor's Wife* (1976) and *The Temptation of Eileen Hughes* (1981), the social detail, the dialogue and even the characters are brisk, with a strange lack of nuance and shadow. Sheila, the doctor's wife, has various conversations with her husband that read like early, hastily written drafts. Her American lover has no presence in the book, and the two observers of the scene in the South of France are pure fictional contrivances. Similarly, the rich Northern Irish Catholics in *The Temptation of Eileen Hughes* are created in very broad strokes indeed, and Eileen's first sexual experience is a jaded Irish cliché.

Yet there is something fascinating in all three novels. Moore is able to render consciousness itself, the mind's free flow, as a sort of innocence. Nothing his women do in these books seems worthy of judgement or blame. They appear to the reader as they do to themselves; we experience them at first hand (even though *The Doctor's Wife* and *The Temptation of Eileen Hughes* are written in the third person). All three are books about quest, about intense yearning, and there is a core of deep and sharp feeling in them that survives, after a long struggle, the quickly fixed fictional world around them.

Moore did not lack confidence. He said of *The Doctor's Wife* that the character of Sheila, who abandons her husband, had to be Irish and not Californian because there is really no past to escape in California; it wouldn't have had that ring I wanted in the book. I wanted, as I've done before, to contrast the American and the Northern Irish character and the crucial thing is that you have to be very strong in your feelings for both these lifestyles. For example, I couldn't do a middle-class English woman, because I don't have her speech rhythms, I couldn't hear her voice; but I know that I can still create Irish characters because it's in my bones and I know that my ear won't mishear them.

In a 1967 interview there is a chilling sentence about the mother in *An Answer from Limbo*, who comes from Ireland to New York to look after her grandchildren and save her son and his wife some money: "I could do the mother with my eyes closed." The mother is, in fact, a collection of stereotypes out of central Irish casting. Moore may very well have had his eyes closed when he imagined her. His sense of Irish character and Irish speech becomes weaker and weaker, culminating in *Lies of Silence* (1990), a novel set in a contemporary Belfast that has as much truth and local flavour as a CNN news report. Also, many of Moore's North American characters have a strange hollowness and lack of urgency.

He had left the Irish prison and sat alone in his cell in an odd imaginative nowhere. The house in Malibu became even more isolated when the State of California decided to clear that stretch of coast of its inhabitants. The Moores refused to leave, but by 1976 all their neighbours had gone and they were alone. Their nearest friends were Joan Didion and John Gregory Dunne. In her essay "Quiet Days in Malibu," Didion described "the most idiosyncratic of beach communities, 27 miles of coastline with no hotel, no passable restaurant, nothing to attract the traveller's dollar."

Moore's two best novels since *The Lonely Passion of Judith*

*Hearne* are set in wildernesses, where no knowledge of a society, its mores or manners or peculiar speech rhythms is required. The first of these is a very short novel, *Catholics*, published in 1972. It deals, in oblique ways, with the concerns of Moore's earlier novels, especially the relationship between the Catholic mother and the agnostic son in *An Answer from Limbo* and Judith Hearne's loss of faith. The novel is set in the future, there has been a fourth Vatican Council, but a small band of monks on a remote Irish island are adhering to the old traditions. A man is sent from Rome to deal with them, and the novel tells the story of his confrontation with the Abbot, who is created with the same complexity and richness as Judith Hearne and a subtlety absent from many of Moore's other novels.

As he worked on the novel Moore wrote to the Irish Jesuit Michael Paul Gallagher: "I find myself sympathetic to both sides of this argument (the Ecumenical and the Traditional) and so perhaps the story will work out." The drama is between the Abbot's own worldly authority and the monks' aggressive faith, between his wavering conscience and his wavering leadership. The tone is dark, the conclusion is poetic rather than forced, and the general atmosphere in its intensity and its interest in poetic moments is very far indeed from most of Moore's work, and closer to the work of other Irish writers such as John McGahern and John Banville.

In an interview about *Catholics* quoted by Sampson, Moore is almost prepared to solve the riddle of why this book and the later *Black Robe* work in ways his other fictions do not:

I've felt as a writer that man's search for a faith . . . is a major theme. For one kind of novelist it's the big and ultimate theme. If you're an English novelist you write novels of manners, novels of society, novels of class. If you look at Ireland and Irish literature, there are very few Irish novels [of this sort] because society and class don't operate the same way in Ireland. And so I think that this Irish tendency is to pick on the meaning of life. The Gael is interested in the meaning of life and he's usually pessimistic about it.

In the 1970s Moore made contact with other Gaels interested in the meaning of life, among them the poets Seamus Heaney and Derek Mahon and the playwright Brian Friel. He had met Friel for the first time in Ireland in 1969 and the two began to correspond. They had much in common. Both had attempted works in which young men deal with their fathers. Both were interested in faith and exile; both were also interested in the creation of women characters. Both had reinvented themselves as distant and reclusive figures. Friel admired Moore's courage in writing *I Am Mary Dunne* and wrote a screenplay for *The Lonely Passion of Judith Hearne*, in which Katharine Hepburn was to play the lead. (It was never used; many years later the role was played by Maggie Smith.) Moore wrote to Friel: "I know this sounds un-Ulster and extreme, but as it is much easier for me to say it in print than to your face, I am first among your many admirers." The correspondence contains a great deal of the banter that passes for communication between men in Ireland and elsewhere. When Moore took a job one day a week at UCLA, Friel wrote: "We'll overlook the shabby detail that you've gone over to Them. As long as you are handsomely paid and the pool is convenient." When Moore bought a fancy car, Friel wrote: "I can't see you in that Mercedes Sports (you're a Raleigh and trousers-and-socks man at heart) but Jean is born for it." Sometimes Friel was more serious and supportive: "I am genuinely concerned about your reaction to other people's reaction" to *The Great Victorian Collection*, the novel Moore published in 1975. ("I have had this experience so often. One fluctuates between despair and arrogance.") When Moore wrote to Friel about his play *Faith Healer*, Friel replied:

I was delighted with your response ... Because, as you know, one finally holds the press/reviewers/critics in disdain; and the reaction of one's fellow artists is the important response. And it occurred to me that there are many similarities – in attitude, in objectivity and by God in overall gloom – between *F. H.* and *The Great Victorian Collection*.

When the film of *Judith Hearne* was postponed, Friel wrote:

You know, of course, that what has screwed up the whole thing ever since John Huston was a nipper is *your* lousy ending to the book. What is needed is a Beautiful Upsurge – Judith as international president of AA, or plunging back into the arms of mother church and becoming a stigmatist, or eloping with the Professor's wife ... I'm sick of them all [film producers]. They don't believe in anything. They know the value of nothing. They are all sustained by the energies of their own pretences.

The late 1970s was a period of astonishing creativity for Friel. Although *Faith Healer* did not win critical acclaim when it was first performed in New York with James Mason as Frank Hardy, a later production in Dublin with Donal McCann in the part made clear that Friel had created one of the most subtle and memorable male characters in Irish writing. But it was his play *Translations*, first performed in 1980, that seems to have made the greater impact on Moore as he began to work on what is probably his own best novel, *Black Robe* (1985). Both works deal with a central moment in the colonial drama, Friel with the changing of place names in nineteenth-century Ireland, Moore with the arrival of the Jesuits in seventeenth-century Canada. Both deal with the idea of an intact native culture colliding with a more technologically advanced colonial dream. Both bring the colonist and the native face to face; there is a powerful sense of the two watching each other, with violent and tragic results. Both works represent a great stylistic departure for the two writers.

"I've discovered that the narrative forms – the thriller and the journey form – are tremendously powerful," Moore said. "They're the gut of fiction, but they're being left to second-rate writers because first-rate writers are bringing the author into the novel and all those nouveau-roman things." And also:

I went into the wilderness of this book I suppose, compared to my other books, because I'd never written a book like this before. I didn't want to write a historical novel because I don't particularly like historical novels ... I wanted to write this as a tale. I thought of it in terms of authors I admire, like Conrad. I thought of *Heart of Darkness*, a tale, a journey into an unknown destination, to an unknown ending.

He also said in an interview that "the whole thing could be a paradigm for what is happening" in Northern Ireland.

Originally, I'd have said that wasn't true, but maybe subconsciously I was thinking of it. The only conscious thing I had in mind when writing it was the belief of one religion that the other religion was totally wrong. The only thing they have in common is the view that the other side must be the Devil. If you don't believe in the Devil, you can't hate your enemy and that may be one of the most sinister things about Belfast today.

Moore's view of the art of fiction and those "nouveau-roman things" takes him close to the man on the golf course in E. M. Forster's *Aspects of the Novel*: "You can take your art, you can take your literature, you can take your music, but give me a good story." Although this view was to be the making of *Black Robe*, it was to ruin his subsequent work. The landscape of *Black Robe* was very close to him: "I would go into my room and my mind would go back to the Montreal winter I remember and the cold and the St. Lawrence River. When I thought of the river I could see it, because I had gone up and down it so many times." As he was writing the novel, Moore also visited, according to Sampson, "various sites and museums of Iroquois, Algonquin and Huron cultures, in particular Midland, Ontario, where the original Jesuit mission of Sainte Marie among the Hurons has been reconstructed, complete with Huron longhouses and villages."

Moore managed in *Black Robe*, in a way that Conrad did not in *Heart of Darkness*, to make the natives, as he says, "among the strongest characters in the book." But the figure of the Jesuit Father Laforgue remains a towering and haunting presence. Moore allows him to be the central consciousness of the book. He gives him faith, but more importantly, he gives him fear. Moore was interested in clashing systems of belief, but it is the sense of the physical in the book – the river, the forest, the cold – and the sense of threat and violence that gives *Black Robe* its power. The violence is terrifying, almost unbearable. Against a background of implacable nature and inevitable disaster and with the immediacy of Moore's tone, Laforgue's faith and the reader's knowledge of who will finally prevail seem very small things indeed.

Moore was in his mid-sixties when he published *Black Robe*. "I'm entirely conscious that most novelists don't do their best work past sixty and often seem to run out of material. What keeps me going as a writer is the belief that I can write new kinds of books," Moore said in 1995, four years before his death. After *Black Robe*, he produced five more novels, set in Poland, Ireland, Haiti, France and Algeria. He adapted the style of the thriller and the tale, using clipped sentences, briskly set scenes, dramatizing crises of conscience for individuals and societies. Economy was all. He did not revisit Poland to write *The Colour of Blood*, but used scenes from Graham Greene's account of his visit in the 1950s. (A review by Greene gave him the original idea for *Black Robe*. He and Greene admired each other greatly.) He did not visit Haiti to write *No Other Life*. "There's too much information in most novels," he said. "Novelists showing off."

Brian Moore was not, by any stretch of the imagination, a novelist showing off. In the sentences he wrote and the life he lived, he almost made a display of avoiding show. He remains a fascinating case because he had nothing to go on when he began, no tradition to call on, no example except that of Joyce, who was not much use to him save as an example of sheer dedication. Moore was clearly damaged by exile because the sort of novel he wanted to write required a detailed knowledge of manners and morals; imaginatively, he lost touch with Ireland and never fully grasped North America. Yet he could not have stayed in Ireland: his independent spirit and questing conscience had no place on either side of the Irish border. Out of this sense of loss and exile and displacement, he produced three masterpieces and an emotional territory filled with loners and failures, faith and unbelief, cruelty and loss of identity and a clear-eyed vision of man's fate.

In the early 1990s Moore and his second wife began to build a house on the coast of Nova Scotia where Jean had been brought up. The house was finished in 1995. Thus Moore spent his last summers in sight of the Atlantic Ocean: "It's beautiful. It looks out on a bay that looks just like Donegal. It's very wild there and empty. I love it for its emptiness. It's like Ireland probably once was. Now that I'm old it seems so crazy to build another house, I know. Especially there. But I'm very happy I did all the same." That October, he revisited Belfast, walked through his old school for the first time in sixty years and saw the site of the family house on Clifton Street, which he had first described as the professor's house visited by Judith Hearne forty years earlier. The house had been demolished a month before his visit:

I think as a writer it is very symbolic. Your past is erased. Now it's as if it's completely died. I was here a few years ago to film a documentary and I stood in front of the shell and I could remember my father's brass plate at the door, the patients to-ing and fro-ing. Now what is it? It's a paradigm of man's existence on earth. The earth remains and man does not.

# Sebastian Barry's Fatherland

In the first years of the new century the young Irish playwrights wrote about bad fathers. In May 2000, for example, Marina Carr's play *On Raftery's Hill*, in a joint production by Druid in Galway and the Royal Court in London, was performed at the Kennedy Center in Washington, D.C., as part of a festival of Irish culture. Some in the audience at the opening night were old Kennedy stalwarts; others were loyal devotees of Irish culture. It was clear from the silences and the gasps and the shocked comments at the interval that this Irish father on the stage was not familiar to them. "The kitchen of the Raftery household," where the play was enacted, lacked charm, to say the least. There was no dancing at Lughnasa; there were no wild or comic Irish characters; there was even no bitter melancholy; the language was colourful in ways that did not seem to appeal to the audience. The dark cruelty of the father was relentless. Incest, rape, violence, vicious attacks on animals were all central to the drama and its impact. It was an Ireland recognizable to anyone who attended to page four of *The Irish Times*, which by the mid-1990s was daily covering cases of family horror. But for those whose image of Ireland came from their memory or from the glories of *The Quiet Man* or *Riverdance*, this dark Ireland was new and strange.

In 2004 three first plays by Irish writers dramatized a world dominated by bad or mad fathers. In these plays, fatherhood was to be mocked, subverted, shown in all its madness and perversion. Stuart Carolan's *Defender of the Faith*, for example, was, once again, set in a rural kitchen. The setting was South Armagh in 1986. As in Marina Carr's play, Foucault rather than Freud was the dominant spirit, where power over others was the goal, where mindless control and cruelty lay in a fierce embrace on the hearth-rug. Foul statement made a constant raid on the inarticulate.

In Mark Doherty's *Trad*, first performed at the Galway Arts Festival in 2004, the word "Da" became almost a chant in the play, as a mad father, well past his sell-by date, led his dim-witted son into the temptation offered by hideous prejudices, many non-sequiturs, hilarious wild goose chases and bizarre urges and desires. In *Take Me Away* by Gerald Murphy, produced by Rough Magic, the father was a manic figure, unprotected, asking absurd questions, lacking all forms of authority, a joke on the stage. As in *On Raftery's Hill*, *Defender of the Faith* and *Trad*, the mother in *Take Me Away* was entirely absent. Thus the father was left exposed in his foolishness, his exaggerated needs, his mad requests, his ultimate humiliation.

In his play *Hinterland* Sebastian Barry sought to move the drama about fathers and their failures from a purely domestic space into the public realm, or into what seemed at first like the public realm. For an Irish audience the character of Johnny Silvester was clearly, and also deceptively, a closely researched version of Charles J. Haughey, who became Taoiseach in 1979 and held that position through some of the 1980s until he was ousted in 1992. Later, in his retirement, Haughey was plagued by allegations, which he himself subsequently confirmed under oath, that he had taken large sums of money from prominent businessmen for his own private use, and had held an enormous overdraft at Allied Irish Banks. If Ireland needed a public figure to become its disgraced father, then Charles Haughey auditioned perfectly for the role and played it with tragic dignity in a lonely exile in his Georgian mansion in North County Dublin.

This was the house of *Hinterland*. The stage directions set the play in "the private study of a Georgian mansion, outside Dublin. All the paraphernalia of a successful political life – citations, presentations, election posters framed." The opening speech, however, offered a clue to the great ambiguity that would surround the text and its dramatic intentions. In what was, ostensibly, a stilted letter to his aunts in Derry – Haughey also had family in Derry – about the effects of partition, Silvester mentioned his father, who was "hardly the same man after partition, and his physical breakdown may well have been hastened by the same imposition." Partition, he wrote, separated "father from fatherland"; the play dealt over and over with the matter of fathers – Silvester was haunted by his own father's failure, his wife by her own father's reputation, and their son by Silvester's own disastrous fathering.

What distinguished these fathers in Irish plays of the first years of the twenty-first century was that none of them was a tragic hero; they were not caught between two worlds as one collapsed and the other took its place. In these plays, there was only one world, the one that had collapsed and had brought down a reign of terror, or a reign of madness, with no other world come to replace it. These men were static villains, caught in dramatic headlights, willing to destroy, living in a dream of the past. They would always do their worst, and there would be no moments of redemption or recognition or reconciliation. These fathers did not change; they acted and they remembered and they justified their actions. They and those around them were frozen in a ritual in which there was no exit. They were like figures in a Trojan horse, which does not move, which has no Troy in sight.

The act of not killing the father became the core of both *On Raftery's Hill* and *Hinterland*. Letting the father live, against all dramatic expectation, became a powerful and intriguing way of offering no resolution, no easy hope, and an increased tension. It is important to note that both of these plays were written in a time of great and obvious social change in Ireland, a time of new money, new social and sexual freedom and many bright expectations. These plays became a message from the strange, dark, hidden soul of the society. But they were also plays which dealt with both the private and the public. The unrepentant exile of Charles Haughey was a godsend to a playwright concerned with the dramatic possibilities of intractability; he is a hero who is unready for change, on whom everything is lost. Johnny Silvester's kingdom in *Hinterland* has already been taken from him; his house, where his wife weeps, is his prison. As his servant leaves him for the night, Silvester uses precisely the same phrase from *Othello* as Charles Haughey used in the Dáil on the day of his resignation. "I have done the state some service." Just as he begins then to quote Yeats's lines about "an aged man" he is visited by Cornelius, a dead colleague, instantly recognizable to an Irish audience as Brian Lenihan, who held many ministerial portfolios in Fianna Fáil governments, and was defeated for the Presidency by Mary Robinson in 1990. One of Silvester's earliest comments to his old friend mentions his heart transplant; Brian Lenihan, as an Irish audience would know, had a liver transplant.

*Hinterland* thus contains large numbers of references to details from the career of Charles Haughey that are given to Johnny Silvester as part of his past. Both Silvester and Haughey, for example, were praised by pensioners for giving them free travel. Both men gave a silver teapot to a female British Prime Minister. As Silvester had betrayed Cornelius during his bid for the presidency, so too Haughey betrayed Brian Lenihan in the 1990 presidential campaign. Both Haughey and Silvester have to face tribunals to investigate their financial affairs.

These clues to the emotional or political core of the play are, however, deeply misleading; they represent a sort of decoy to distract the audience from what is really happening. Almost any imaginative writer who creates a set of motives and signature tones for a character from history ends by writing a sort of auto-biography. Sometimes this can happen unconsciously; the character begins as a set of facts, and slowly melts into a set of fictions. The process is gradual and tentative; it may have its origins in speculative drafting, seeing how some new ingredient might work, realizing that, while the main character need not be changed, some of the surrounding circumstances will not fit the drama. Gradually, the play, or the novel or the story, becomes a dramatization of an aspect of the secret self.

In considering the relationship between *Hinterland* and Sebastian Barry's secret self, it might be useful to quote in full the second stanza from a poem from his collection *The Pinkening Boy*, which was published in 2004, and written in the same few years as the play. The poem is called "The Trousers." The first stanza deals with the poet's interest in joining the Royal Marine Yacht Club, his inability to join because his father was not a member, his plans with his father to buy

> *a yacht*
> *and sail*
> *wherever the spirit took us, to Dalkey island,*
> *to the inland mysteries of the French canals*
> *though neither of us knew a sail from a bedspread,*
> *and still don't.*

The second stanza reads:

> *So what a surprise to meet him in Dawson Street*
> *last Friday, after years of separation,*
> *family troubles keeping us apart. He passed*
> *like a retired sea-captain with a long white beard,*
> *the trim of his coat quite sailorlike,*
> *the hint of the South Seas in the sun creases*
> *about his eyes, his tentative and nautical hello –*

*not sure of his ground, the tilt of the hard earth.*
*As if in the intervening years he had indeed*
*gone off to the Caribbean or rounded the Horn*
*nonchalantly enough, and the Royal Marine Yacht-club*
*owed me an apology. And as he hurried on,*
*quite shipshape at sixty-seven,*
*his sea-legs not yet attuned to land,*
*it was his neat trousers particularly I noticed –*
*the cut of his jib, the breeze athwart the main.*

*Hinterland* is as concerned with the failures of fatherhood and the surrounding grief and estrangement as the poem "The Trousers." Just as Johnny Silvester summons up his father in his opening speech, so his wife, Daisy, does hers almost as soon as she arrives on stage. Daisy's father, like Charles Haughey's actual father-in-law, was a politician, "the soul of probity." Both Johnny and Daisy will continue throughout the play to make reference to their respective fathers, as though they are desperately trying to eke out an identity for themselves, even one that depends on myths and shadows. So too Aisling, who comes to interview Johnny, refers over and over to her own father. ("My father is a good decent person, I have to say. As fathers go.") As Daisy bemoans her husband's infidelities, she mentions the needs of their son Jack:

A little boy waiting for his father to come home. Do you know what a little boy is, Johnny? I'll tell you. He's a tiny contraption of bones and skin, tuned like a radio to give out and receive certain signals. When a little boy is sick, his whole body strains to broadcast a special signal, he wants a very simple thing, to be cuddled in the arms of his father.

Daisy carries on discussing the power of the absent father to do damage in a set of speeches that are the most emotionally forceful in the play:

I pity all the little boys of this world. Because, when the signal is not answered, the pain is so great, so oddly great . . . A true father would feel that call from three thousand miles and travel all day and night to reach his child. Nothing can put that little scenario back together again and time goes on swiftly and then there is nothing but a tangle of broken wires, good for nothing because it can finally neither receive nor send a signal.

When Jack arrives on stage, it is clear that he is a tangle of broken wires, still half a child demanding and offering love. Daisy, by this time, has mentioned a particular mistress of her husband's who had written a book. For an Irish audience, this would have been seen as a reference to the journalist Terry Keane, who published a series of articles in the *Sunday Times* about her long affair with Charles Haughey and who made no secret of the affair in her column in the *Sunday Independent*. Once more, a precise reference to an actual event in the life of Charles Haughey had been inserted into the play.

The problem, however, was not this reference to Haughey's personal life, but the presence of Silvester's son Jack on the stage. Charles and Maureen Haughey, as is well known, have three sons, all of whom benefit from exceptionally strong mental health; there has not been a sign of a breakdown or a hint of a twitch among them. But healthy children, in general, are no use to a playwright. Suddenly, with the son Jack, the play had moved into areas dictated by its own necessities, the proper realm of fiction. In one sense, the play had always been there, since its emotional life arose not from a set of public events but from a series of meditations about fathers and fatherhood. But in scene after scene, the connections between the Silvesters and the Haugheys had been made abundantly clear. Now the script had departed from the story of the Haugheys to tell another story, one of grief and estrangement and the damage fathers cause to their sons, which belonged more to the emotional life of the poem "The Trousers," in which a son inspects his father as he passes him silently on the street, than to the many volumes by journalists that told the story of Haughey's reign and his downfall.

The controversy surrounding the play thus centred on the use of Haughey as a central character and the distortion of the facts for dramatic purposes. It simmered in the newspapers and on radio and came to a head at a post-show discussion in the Abbey Theatre on 20 February 2002. The actors, the director and the theatre's literary manager took part, the author watching from the wings.

Jocelyn Clarke, the literary manager, remembers "an unusually full post show discussion house" in which the first speaker from the audience disagreed with the director's statement that the play had "grace." "The characters," she said, according to Clarke, "were small-minded and petty, especially the politician, and his relationship with his wife and son was not credible." Clarke remembers that a young man then stood up "and wondered how Barry could use the life and figure of a still living politician for his play – what right had he to do that to Charles Haughey's family, and to a lesser extent Brian Lenihan's family." Clarke set about defending the play:

I replied that *Hinterland* was not a biographical drama about Charles Haughey's life and times but about an imaginary politician whose life and times were based on figures and events in Ireland's recent political history, which were very much in the public domain. That a playwright chooses to write a play about a political figure whose life story has similarities to the story of a living or dead politician does not make it a play about that politician's life or career.

"The audience," Clarke remembers, "grew more restive."

"That's not true," cried somebody. "It's about Charles Haughey," shouted somebody else. "It's all been in the newspapers." I replied . . . that it had not been Barry's intention to write a play about Charles Haughey. Indeed, *Hinterland* should be seen in the broader context of his work, and his ongoing theatre project to explore a nation's history through the prism of Barry's own family and its history. It could be argued that *Hinterland* is a biographical play in the sense that Barry primarily uses elements from his own biography rather than Haughey's or any other politician's and that as far as I was aware Haughey was still happily married, and he has several sons, none of whom suffer from a mental illness.

Thus the ambiguities surrounding the play and its intentions were spelt out. Its emotional shape came from the author's private life and that of his family; some of its detail came from the public domain, from aspects of the life of the former Taoiseach. Some of the audience believed that the author had no right to confuse the two, and the play had been damaged by the confusion. The theatre's literary manager suggested that to see *Hinterland* as solely about Haughey or as a distortion was a fundamental misreading of the play.

Act 2 of *Hinterland* centres on Jack's father-fed neurosis and Johnny's affair with Connie, the woman whom the audience recognized as Terry Keane. The act opens with Jack trying to hang himself. When Daisy comes in on this scene, she says to her husband: "Listen, you can be the king that ruined his country but I won't let you be the father that ruined his son." And it is this sense that the personal is all that matters that impels *Hinterland*, with Daisy as a sort of chorus, musing always on the career of her husband as a father rather than as a party leader. His neglect of his son is offered as an event that supersedes politics, but stands for the rot at the heart of the public realm as well:

You were running for office, or running the country. Ah, yes. But it denies something at the heart of life. At the heart of families, of countries, of political parties even. If that slight signal [that the child in need gives out] is not attended to, there is really no family, party or country. Because the oldest law on earth has been violated.

Thus Barry subtly works the connection between a man who calls himself "the father of the nation" and the domestic father, insisting on the failure of the latter as a poison that infects the nation. But he is also using elements in the career and personality of Charles Haughey as a metaphor for what is essentially a private ache. This might seem, as it did to some of the Abbey audience at the discussion, a sort of confusing battle between private and public, an invasion of Haughey's privacy and the privacy of his wife and children, a distortion of the facts for mere artistic purposes, a dishonest and misleading play on public affairs while all the time masking a personal, private pain. Many of these accusations that were made about the play missed the point, which is that all fiction comes from a direct source and makes its way indirectly to the page or the stage. It does so by finding metaphors, by building screens, by working on half truths, moulding them towards a form that is both pure and impure fabrication. There is simply no other way of doing it. Most plays, novels and stories use the same stealthy process. Barry, by stealing Haughey, simply exposed an age-old system. Fiction, by its very nature, is a form of deceit. *Hinterland* inhabits beautifully and controversially the interstices between the world as we know it, raw and shapeless, and the world as imagined, tested richly and suggestively by private and hidden experience.

# Roddy Doyle and Hugo Hamilton:
# The Dialect of the Tribe

1

It seemed beyond belief that our neighbour Seamus Doyle, who tended roses, and his wife, Gretta, who went to Mass every day, had once led a revolution, that he had been sentenced to death by the British, and that she had, with two other women, raised the Tricolour, the Irish flag, over one of the main buildings of the southern town of Enniscorthy in the 1916 Rising. It seemed even more astonishing that Marion Stokes had been one of the other flag-raisers; she came to our house every evening during Easter Week 1966 to watch a drama on television about the events of fifty years earlier.

She was the least likely ex-terrorist you could imagine, polite and sedate and distantly smiling. My uncle, who fought in the subsequent War of Independence and went on a hunger strike in prison during the Irish Civil War, also gave not a hint in his manners and his attitudes that he had, when he was young, taken on the might of the British Empire in pursuit of a dream that those around him viewed as foolish and fanatical.

The third woman who put up the flag in the town in 1916, Una Bolger, was married to Robert Brennan, one of the leaders of the Rising; he later became Irish ambassador to Washington and a close associate of Eamon de Valera. (Their daughter was the novelist and short-story writer Maeve Brennan, who wrote for the *New Yorker* for many years.) Una's brother Jim Bolger, also involved in the struggle against the British, was Roddy Doyle's grandfather, the father of Ita, who tells her story and that of her family in *Rory & Ita*, which Doyle edited for his parents' fiftieth wedding anniversary.

The story of the revolutionary generation in Ireland remains complex and powerful and difficult to tell. My uncle, who died in 1995, confined himself to chance remarks and jokes on these matters; I have no memory of our neighbours, who took part in the Rising, discussing their years as revolutionaries in private conversations. They were quiet and conservative people; their years of living dangerously made them grumpy, it seemed to me, rather than garrulous. But since the IRA ceasefires of the late 1990s, the commemoration of what happened has become easier now that the events are not re-enacted in Northern Ireland on a daily basis. When the *Enniscorthy Echo*, the local newspaper, celebrated its centenary, it produced a supplement with articles proudly stating that it was "once a hive of nationalists," printing a photograph of Robert Brennan in paramilitary uniform, his wife standing behind him, and articles about Jim Bolger's arrest for sedition in 1915 and my uncle's hunger strike. All three worked for the newspaper, which, its centenary edition stated proudly, "assumed a notorious reputation with the authorities" in the decade before the creation of the Irish Free State.

In the 1940s, the Irish government asked those involved in the Rising and the War of Independence to write down their memories, which would be locked away until an indeterminate time in the future. More than seventeen hundred obliged, including Seamus Doyle and Robert Brennan. In March of this year, the archive was opened for the first time to scholars and researchers. Having read a sample of the accounts from Enniscorthy, including the memoirs of Doyle and Brennan, full of flat statement and unadorned prose, I found it fascinating to imagine the conditions under which the statements were written. These men sat down to record their memories in the relative comfort of neutral Ireland, in domestic harmony, in a world about which no one will ever, it seems, need to take further statements to lock away. Seamus Doyle must have walked in from his rose garden and sat quietly at a table in the front room of his semi-detached house to describe a meeting in prison with Patrick Pearse, who had led the 1916 Rising, shortly before Pearse's execution. "He rose quickly when the door was opened and came forward to meet us and shook hands with us. He appeared to be physically exhausted but spiritually exultant . . . When the soldier was out of the cell Pearse whispered to us, 'Hide the arms, they will be wanted later.' We then bid him goodbye."

"On the inception of the new state," Roddy Doyle writes in *Rory & Ita*, "Jim Bolger became a civil servant, at the Department of External Affairs . . . His first task was to sit outside a room with a gun while the new Minister, Gavan Duffy, was inside the room." Ita, Roddy's mother, remembers that her father "never lost the idea of what he had fought for, but he wasn't a diehard." By the time she was born in 1925, three years after the foundation of the state, her father was working by day and studying accountancy at night. Roddy Doyle's father was born in 1923 and was called Rory, the Irish for Roderick, after the patriot Rory O'Connor. O'Connor was one of four leaders, one from each province, taken out and shot a year earlier by the Irish Free State forces in the beginning of a series of reprisals in the Civil War. These executions caused immense bitterness among the opponents, led by Eamon de Valera, of the 1921 treaty with the British, which left the North behind under British control. In 1936 the poet Austin Clarke wrote:

> *They are the spit of virtue now,*
> *Prating of law and honour*
> *But we remember how they shot*
> *Rory O'Connor.*

Rory Doyle's own father, as a member of the IRA, was involved in burning down the Custom House in Dublin in 1921, but did not take part in the Civil War, although two of his brothers fought on opposite sides, one being killed in the war. "He couldn't face up to fighting the men he'd been with; he just couldn't do it," Rory remembers, "but he was still close to the Republican fellows who were causing the trouble." In 1926 his father joined Fianna Fáil, the party founded by de Valera, which held power in Ireland for much of the time between 1932 and recently.

Roddy Doyle's parents, then, being born in the short time after the struggle for independence ended and before the revolutionaries began to grow roses, are Irish versions of midnight's children. Doyle has attempted to write a book about a most elusive subject, using their two voices; he has attempted to evoke ordinary life in peacetime amounting in its modest way to happiness. He has kept the revolution and its spirit in the background, placing instead his parents' courtship, marriage, the raising of their children, their domestic life in the foreground. He has also attempted to capture their particular tone, interrupting merely to explain a small matter or move the story on, but never to argue with them. He is interested in the detail of things; the book is full of proper names, brand names, precise memories, simple anecdotes.

He is concerned to dramatize a number of subjects uncommon in Irish writing, including his own previous work – niceness, decency, love, harmony, gentleness, kindness, prosperity, gentility. Thus cooking and going to work in the morning, acquiring a first refrigerator or a first washing machine, the buying of a dress or a suit, the going to a dance or visiting friends, in all their mundane detail, are central events in the book, are allowed the space normally reserved for bitterness and violence in Irish books. This move into sweetness may arise partly from the genuine affection that Doyle feels for his parents, but it also comes from the sort of politics that has been central to his work from the beginning.


2


In November 1979, two months after the Pope's visit to Ireland, Roddy Doyle, aged twenty, first came to public attention. He wrote an article for the magazine *In Dublin* stating that the Virgin Mary, who had appeared at Knock in the west of Ireland one hundred years earlier, had thereafter travelled to Dublin where she had, he was sure, given birth to Patrick Pearse, whose centenary we were also celebrating. The delay of two months between the two events, Doyle explained, was due only to the bad state of the roads at the time. Doyle's remarks, funny and bitterly irreverent in a time of great piety, made him something of a hero for those of us who worked for the magazine. His status was much enhanced when he was denounced soon afterwards by the Irish-language magazine *Inniu*, which pointed out that there were countries in the world who knew how to deal with such blasphemies. Clearly they meant Iran, since the Ayatollah and his punishments were in the news every day. Doyle had taken a cheeky swipe at Knock, the very shrine the Pope had visited, and at one of the martyred icons of Irish nationalism at the same time.

A year or two later, when the IRA hunger strikes were causing an upsurge of sympathy for the movement and its martyrs, someone told me that Roddy Doyle was writing a comic novel called *Your Granny's a Hunger Striker*. Although brought up in the bosom of the Fianna Fáil party and the Catholic Church, I looked forward to the novel. Like many of our generation, I had had my fill of Irish piety and wished only for jokes on these matters. This was, perhaps, one of the rights for which the earlier generation had fought, and one of the inevitable consequences of their struggle, even if it did not seem like that at the time.

*Your Granny's a Hunger Striker* was never published, but in 1987 Doyle's novel *The Commitments* appeared, followed by *The Snapper* (1990), *The Van* (1991), *Paddy Clarke Ha Ha Ha* (1993) and *The Woman Who Walked into Doors* (1996). The novels, and the movies that were made from some of them, were original in their tone, fast-moving, sharp, irreverent. They also became, in the images they created of Dublin, immensely influential.

The city of Dublin has always stood apart from the Irish nation. When Roddy Doyle's great-uncle, Robert Brennan, heard in prison about the extent of the 1916 Rising in Dublin, his informant told him: "Dublin was grand. No longer shall we hear [the] jibe about the city of 'bellowing slaves and genteel dastards.'" By the time Rory, Roddy Doyle's father, began his apprenticeship as a printer twenty-five years later, working with men from Dublin city, however, the city seemed to have returned to its old self. "It was an eye-opener for me, like being in a different country. The philosophy was profoundly anti-Republican, anti-Gaelic, almost anti-Irish. As far as they were concerned, they were Dublin men, not Irish. They bought and read English newspapers . . . They spoke of nothing but soccer, all the Dublin and English teams."

This, then, was the world in which Rory's son set his novels, a world in which there was no mention of the struggle for independence or its legacy, and no mention of the conflict in Northern Ireland, at its most intense in the years the novels were published, and no mention of the Catholic Church. It was a world stripped of the props that readers most associated with Ireland, and filled instead with rock 'n' roll, much wit and shouting, and sex and swearing and soccer. It could have been Liverpool or Birmingham or Manchester, except for something absolutely central to it, which was the spirit of the city, which everyone who knew Dublin recognized. Making this image of the city popular, almost official, as Doyle did in these years, was a seriously political project in a country whose self-image was rural and Catholic and conservative and nationalist. In doing this, Doyle came in a distinguished line of Irish novelists who sought to reinvent Ireland, from Joyce, who placed a Jewish hero in his irreverent capital city in *Ulysses* in 1922, to John Banville, who made Irish history into a great burlesque and a set of comic sequences in *Birchwood* fifty years later. The novelists sought to reassemble the nation.

In 1999, in his novel *A Star Called Henry*, Roddy Doyle came to deal for the first time with the nationalism of his grandparents and the heritage and history that provide the background to *Rory & Ita*; he made an effort to apply his comic skills to the lives of his grandparents. Henry, his hero, who plays a crucial part in most events in Irish history, is also a Dubliner who comes in contact with the members of the nationalist movement:

They hated anyone or anything from Dublin. Dublin was too close to England; it was where the orders and cruelty came from . . . Ireland was everywhere west of Dublin, the real people were west, west, west, as far west as possible, on the islands, the rocks off the islands, speaking Irish and eating wool . . . they were more Irish than I was; they were nearer to being the pure thing.

*Rory & Ita* quietly and subtly dramatizes the lure of this Dublin life and its softening effect on the nationalists who settled in the city after independence. Rory did not join the Fianna Fáil party because of his nationalist sympathies; he said he

became involved in Fianna Fáil because I was born into Fianna Fáil. I never joined; I was born into it. I never joined and I never left. My father was one of the Republicans who followed de Valera when he founded the party in 1926 . . . Anyone who belongs to Fianna Fáil, just look at them; they don't need a card – they are who they are.

Fianna Fáil has managed since 1926 to be many things to many people. It soaked up nationalist energies, diverted the old brigade from fighting wars into fighting elections. In theory, it sought to restore Gaelic as the national language, to reunify Ireland, and to represent the lower middle class and the small farmers, but slowly it put most of its energy into staying in power. It began to represent big business and corruption. It managed to offer allegiance to both Brussels and Boston. My father, who was a staunch member, having also been "born into it," always said that if you voted for the opposition, your right hand would wither away. He too believed that you could tell a Fianna Fáil person by looking at them. He, like Rory, put enormous energy into election campaigns and derived great pleasure from winning them. "Election campaigns are highly emotional – soaring adrenaline and non-stop hard work," Rory says. In 1977 Rory set about organizing the campaign to replace Conor Cruise O'Brien, who was a Labour member of the Irish parliament, with a Fianna Fáil candidate. "I'm sure he was a charming man to meet, but I never did meet him, and we took his seat," he says.

Rory manages to be charming also, and mild-mannered and funny. Like many other ordinary members of Fianna Fáil, he embodies a certain low-key decency, excited by local rivalry as much as large ideologies, lacking zealotry. These are the very qualities that made the party very difficult to unseat. Even those of us who, despite being "born into the party," loathe its politics, find it hard to dislike its actual members. This makes killing your Fianna Fáil father a rather onerous task; Roddy Doyle has been wise, perhaps, to try to do it to his with kindness.

Despite Fianna Fáil's interest in restoring Gaelic as the national language, neither Rory nor Ita took the matter too seriously. When Rory bought a new suit of Donegal tweed he wondered if he might be mistaken "for one of those Gaelic League people who went around talking Irish out loud. I wasn't talking Irish out loud but I was going around in this lovely suit, and enjoying myself." So too Ita and her friends, when they were ignored at an Irish traditional dance, "ended up dancing with each other and more or less jeering and sneering at the Irish zealots around us."

3

The father of the writer Hugo Hamilton also went around in the same streets and attended the same dances during the same years as Rory and Ita. But he did so, his son tells us in *The Speckled People*, "talking Irish out loud" and becoming one of the "Irish zealots" sneered at by Ita. Unlike the Doyles, who brought merely their deep affections and modest ambitions into the domestic sphere, Hamilton's father in *The Speckled People* carried his politics into the house, burdened his family with his fierce views on Ireland, and made the home into a state under siege.

Hugo Hamilton, who was born in 1953, published his first three novels in the early 1990s. They were set in Germany, where his mother came from, and dealt with the large subjects of history and treachery and memory. The tone was stylish and restrained and ironic, the drama subtle. It was as though his own upbringing in the Dublin middle-class suburbs in the years when nothing happened did not seem in itself worthy of his attention, being too quiet and settled, too contented perhaps to be useful to a novelist interested in large historical and political subjects. His two subsequent novels, set in the Dublin underworld, served to confirm that his own comfortable background did not offer him material for fiction.

A happy childhood may make good citizens, but it is not a help for those of us facing a blank page. In 1996 Hamilton published a story, seven pages long, called "Nazi Christmas" in a collection called *Dublin Where the Palm Trees Grow*. It told a story that was so unbelievable that it could not have been made up. The three Dublin children in the story with a German mother are harassed by their neighbours. "It began with the man in the fish shop saying 'Achtung!' and all the customers turning around to look at us." As the family in the story appear in public: "There was something about us that made people laugh, or whisper, or stop along the street quite openly to ask the most bizarre questions; something that stuck to us like an electronic tag." Soon the children are attacked and beaten up.

The story was written in that distant style that Hamilton used in his first three novels, where all judgement is withheld and the emotion, coiled and ready to spring, is buried in the coolness of the tone. His memoir *The Speckled People*, a bestseller in Ireland, has that same masterfully suppressed rage. It is as artful and deliberate in its textured use of voice as Roddy Doyle's book is intentionally artless. The world here is viewed through the eyes of a child who does not judge, merely details and describes. But each detail and each description convey enormous and carefully measured levels of concealed emotion and blocked-out pain.

Language itself has been the ground of the child's suffering, not only the language of his mother, which causes the events of "Nazi Christmas" to be retold here as memoir, but the English language itself, which the father has decided his children should not speak or listen to, even though it is the only language spoken in their Dublin suburb. The father wishes his children to speak and hear Irish, and in order to fulfil these wishes he will need to keep them away from the outside world, from radio and television and popular music and playmates. He will also need to mould them according to the ideology that he has decided to bring home, unsoftened by the atmosphere all around him, by the city of Dublin in all its diversity, but also by the spirit of compromise that took over from the revolutionary spirit in Ireland as soon as the British departed.

The debate between Hamilton and his father is the same

debate as occurs between Gabriel Conroy and Miss Ivors in James Joyce's story "The Dead." When Miss Ivors encourages Gabriel to go to the west of Ireland on his holidays, Gabriel tells her that he wishes to go to the European continent instead, "partly to keep in touch with the languages and partly for a change." When she challenges him with "And haven't you your own language to keep in touch with – Irish?" he replies, "Well, if it comes to that, you know, Irish is not my language." Finally, she accuses him of being a "West Briton."

In his memoir, Hamilton adopts the style of Stephen Dedalus in the early pages of *A Portrait of the Artist as a Young Man*, in which the world is described through the eyes of a child: "When you're small you're like a piece of white paper with nothing written on it," he writes. "My father writes down his name in Irish and my mother writes down her name in German and there's a blank space left over for all the people outside who speak English . . . My father says your language is your home and your country is your language and your language is your flag."

The Hamiltons, an island of non-English speakers in a West British city, imported Aine, a servant from the west of Ireland, whose tasks included the speaking of Irish, which is her first language, to the children. "What good is that to them?" Aine asked when Hamilton's mother insisted that she speak only Irish to them. That is the question that haunts any account of the slow decline in the use of the Irish language over the past two centuries. "Irish doesn't sell the cow," is the reason advanced why the language was abandoned in favour of English by family after family until it was spoken as a first language only by a small number of people along the west coast of Ireland.

"By the late 1970s," the historian J. J. Lee writes in *Ireland, 1912–1985: Politics and Society*, "the population of the real Gaeltacht . . . was calculated to be only 32,000, compared with more than ten times that number at the foundation of the state." The official Gaeltacht was, during all these years, much larger than the real one. In the late 1980s, when a friend of mine made a journey through the parts of Ireland officially designated Irish-speaking, he found that the most mountainous regions of County Kerry, completely uninhabited, were marked as Irish-speaking by the government. He supposed that the rain came down in Irish and the wind blew in that language, and when snow began to descend it changed its name to *sneachta* as it hit the ground. But there was no one listening.

No historian of the language's decline has managed to explain why those who wished to sell cows did not become bilingual, why so many abandoned the language completely. The economic argument, Joe Lee has written, would

strictly speaking . . . explain the acquisition of English, but not the loss of Irish, unless it be assumed that Irish brains were too small to accommodate two languages, or that the Irish were simply too lazy, or too utilitarian, to be bothered with the less materially useful one . . . The burden of the small language did not suffice to prevent Sweden, or Norway, or the Netherlands, or Flanders, from exporting successfully to Britain, from growing more rapidly than Britain since the late nineteenth century, and from overtaking British living standards in the course of the twentieth century.

Lee suggests that one reason why Ireland adopted English with such zeal had to do with the sheer intensity of emigration to both Britain and the United States from the time of the Great Famine. Parents needed to do something radical to prepare their children for separation. It is also possible that the levels and grades of poverty were so enormously varied and so minutely structured – and knowledge of Irish was associated with poverty – that abandoning the language was a way of moving upwards, however strangely and imperceptibly.

In the years after independence, while Irish remained associated with poverty in the west, in the rest of the country it became associated with school, with long hours of a grammar badly taught and only half-understood by some of the teachers, with politicians beginning and ending their dull speeches with a few words of the language. "The children," Joe Lee writes, "were given no incentive to master Irish as a living language, only as a dead one. The charade of Irish language tests for public employment, when everyone knew the language would hardly ever be used again . . . inevitably left its mark." Irish, for those who knew it and loved it, was, in the words of Arland Ussher, "the great language of conversation, of quips, hyperboles, cajoleries, lamentations, blessings, cursings, endearments, tirades. Its unsuspected rhythm had even given an intimate and personal quality to the great Irish writers of English. It was the winged word in its flight that was beautiful. Stuffed and mounted on the page of a school book, it stank."

Thus when Roddy Doyle's father wanted to be made permanent in his state job as a teacher, finding himself "the only man in Ireland qualified" for a vacancy to teach printing, having both the experience as a printer and the technical knowledge, he had to do an Irish test, although all his teaching would be done in English. When it came to the oral part and he was not doing too well, the examiner said to him, "'What is this at all? Sure, any of the labouring men down in Connemara can speak Irish.' So I said, 'Why don't you get them to teach printing?' At that, he hit the table a belt of his fist, nearly broke it, and I was thrown out." Rory got the job only on the insistence of a trade unionist who said: "'The apprentices are sent to the school by their employers to learn printing, not fuckin' Irish. My man is fully qualified to teach printing, and if that man isn't reinstated, you won't have any apprentices next Monday.'" Such were the battles fought for strange freedoms by the first generation to be born in the Irish Free State.

At more or less the same time in another part of the city, Hugo Hamilton's brother Franz had learned some words of English and was innocently singing them to himself as their father was digging in the garden. The father "hit him on the back of the head so that Franz fell off the wall and his face went down on the bricks. When he got up, there was blood all around on his nose and mouth." His nose was broken.

My father said he was very sorry, but the rules had to be obeyed. He said that Franz was speaking English again and that had to stop. Then my mother and father had no language at all. My father went outside again and my mother brought Franz upstairs. Even when the blood stopped, he was still crying for a long time and my mother was afraid that he would never start talking again.

Hugo, too, brought English words into the house. When he repeated a line from a popular advertisement, his father picked out a stick from the greenhouse and prayed "that he was doing the right thing for Ireland. We kneeled down and asked God how many lashes he thought was fair and my father said fifteen." Since the children could be punished for listening to English, even if spoken by neighbouring children, their playmates had to be imported from the few like-minded families in the city:

Even they thought it was stupid to play in Irish and didn't want to come back again, even for the biscuits. You couldn't be cowboys in Irish. You couldn't sneak up behind somebody or tie somebody to a chair in Irish. It was no fun dying in Irish. And it was just too stupid altogether to hide behind something and say "Uuuggh" or "hands up" in Irish, because there were some things you could only do in English, like fighting and killing Indians.

Thus Stephen Dedalus's famous musings on the relationship between Ireland and the English language are subverted and played with. When Stephen encounters the English dean of studies in Dublin, he notes: "His language, so familiar and so foreign, will always be for me an acquired speech. I have not made or accepted its words. My voice holds them at bay. My soul frets in the shadow of his language." By the end of the book, however, Stephen discovers that the disputed word "tundish," which the Englishman had never heard in his life and knows only as "funnel," is not an Irish word at all: "I looked it up and find it English and good old blunt English too. Damn the dean of studies and his funnel! What did he come here for, to teach us his own language or to learn it from us? Damn him one way or the other." And in Samuel Beckett's play *All That Fall*, the questions surrounding Irish and English are offered further mocking glosses. When Mr. Rooney says to his wife, "Sometimes one would think that you were struggling with a dead language," Mrs. Rooney replies, "Well, you know, it will be dead in time, just like our own poor dear Gaelic, there is that to be said."

"The relationship between language and national identity is notoriously complex," Joe Lee writes:

Without language, only the most unusual historical circumstances suffice to develop a sense of identity. Those unusual circumstances existed in Ireland for perhaps two centuries. As that phase broadly characterized by the reality, or the memory, of an obtrusive imperial presence, of a national revival, of a struggle for independence, draws to a close, the importance of the lost language as a distinguishing mark becomes more rather than less evident. As circumstances normalize, only the husk of identity is left without the language.

Perhaps the importance of Roddy Doyle's *Rory & Ita*, besides the efforts to revive domestic bliss as a subject for Irish writers, is to suggest that Irish identity in a time of normality is almost miraculously and unselfconsciously intact, so much so indeed that neither Rory nor Ita has occasion to mention it, nor the reader to notice either its significant absence or its obvious presence. It is simply there in how they think and speak, how they remember, how they live. It is part of Doyle's tact that he does not draw any attention to this, but he is too political a writer not to have deliberately left it like that.

"It is," Joe Lee continues, "unusual for descendants of a destroyed culture to join in the disparagement of a lost language. It smacks of a parricidal impulse." It does indeed. It offers Hugo Hamilton a whole new way to kill his father, not only by telling the story of his own persecution in the name of the destroyed culture, and by telling of his discovery of anti-Semitic articles, written by his father in 1946, in the bottom of a wardrobe, but by doing so in an English sonorous and refined, perfectly modulated and moulded. And in a final chapter he can struggle with language until he has it by the throat, and offer one more blow for Irish freedom: he can describe his father's death with some of the same conjuror's relish with which the young Alexander pictures his stepfather's death in Ingmar Bergman's film *Fanny and Alexander*. Hamilton's father was stung by bees, who re-enact rather more violently what he has been doing subtly in his book:

Maybe my father was not meant to be a beekeeper. Maybe he wasn't calm enough to be a father. Maybe the bees knew he was still fighting and thinking about the time when he was a boy and nobody liked him except for his mother. Maybe they could feel anger in the air from the time when Ireland was still under the British, or when Ireland was free but could remember nothing but being under the British. Maybe they could smell things like helpless anger, because they kept trying to kill him.

When the father ran out into the street, screaming in Irish, the "neighbours ran back into their houses because they were scared of bees and scared of the Irish language." Soon afterwards, he died of a heart attack. "People said there was nobody like my father left in Ireland now," Hamilton comments. His tone is held so carefully in check that the reader is not sure whether to laugh or to cry. But, either way, it is clear that on his father's death, one of the last and strangest vestiges of the Irish revolutionary spirit was laid to rest.

PART TWO

*Elsewhere*

# Thomas Mann: New Ways to Spoil Your Children

Thomas and Katia Mann had six children. It was obvious from early on that Katia most loved the second child, Klaus, who was born in 1906, and that Thomas loved Erika, the eldest, born in 1905, and also Elisabeth, born in 1918. The other three – the barely tolerated ones – were Golo, born in 1909, Monika, born in 1910, and Michael, born in 1919. Erika remembered a time during the shortages of the First World War when food had to be divided but there was one fig left over. "What did my father do? He gave this fig just to me alone . . . the other three children stared in horror, and my father said sententiously with emphasis: 'One should get the children used to injustice early.'"

Some things ran in the family. Homosexuality, for instance. Thomas himself was gay most of the time, as his diaries make clear. So were three of his children: Erika (also just most of the time; she made an exception for Bruno Walter, among others), Klaus and Golo. Suicide was a family theme too. Both of Thomas Mann's sisters committed suicide, as did his sons Klaus and Michael, as did the second wife of his brother Heinrich. Also, gerontophilia. Bruno Walter was almost as old as Erika's father when she had an affair with him; and in 1939 Elisabeth married the literary critic Giuseppe Antonio Borgese, who was thirty-six years her senior.

And then there is the small matter of incest. Much interest in this was fuelled by incidents in Thomas Mann's own work. In her useful and sympathetic book about the Mann family, *In the Shadow of the Magic Mountain*, Andrea Weiss writes: "Just how much Katia and Klaus Pringsheim loved each other was the subject of public gossip and private distress, especially when Thomas Mann, married to Katia for only a few months, used his wife's relationship with her brother as the basis for one of his novellas." The novella, *The Blood of the Walsungs*, dealt with the incestuous relationship between a twin brother and sister; Katia's father attempted to have the story suppressed.

Such rumours also existed about Erika and Klaus, much encouraged by Klaus's play on the subject, *The Siblings*, and made their way into Gestapo reports when the siblings went into exile and FBI reports about them once they arrived in America. (In the mid-1920s Klaus helped to keep things in the family by having an affair with Erika's first husband, Gustaf Gründgens.) In his novel *The Volcano*, Klaus allowed the character based on his sister to marry the character based on his father. In Thomas Mann's *The Holy Sinner*, the hero, Pope Gregorius, marries his mother – who is also his father's sister.

In his diaries Thomas Mann explored his own sexual interest in Klaus: "Am enraptured with Eissi," he wrote in 1920, when Klaus was fourteen (Eissi was his nickname), "terribly handsome in his swimming trunks. Find it quite natural that I should fall in love with my son . . . It seems I am once and for all done with women? . . . Eissi was lying tanned and shirtless on his bed, reading; I was disconcerted." Later that year he "came upon Eissi totally nude and up to some nonsense by Golo's bed" and was "deeply struck by his radiant adolescent body; overwhelming." He used some of this same language to describe Jacob's interest in the young Joseph in *Joseph and His Brothers*, and in the novella *Disorder and Early Sorrow*, written when Elisabeth was seven, the relationship between the bookish father and his young daughter, clearly based on Mann's relationship with Elisabeth, is heated and fervid enough to make any reader marvel at what a wonderfully daring imagination the old magician was in possession of.

By the time Hitler came to power in 1933 Thomas Mann, at

fifty-eight, was in possession not only of this daring imagination but of the Nobel Prize, which he had received in 1929. He lived in a large and beautiful house in Munich and owned an idyllic summer house on the Baltic that he had built three years earlier – a house subsequently requisitioned by Goering. Mann had a reputation as the most serious-minded and respectable German alive. He enjoyed his fame and his family, his bourgeois comforts and his mornings alone in his study writing essays and fiction. The Manns lived well, their son Golo later wrote, thanks to the Nobel Prize and the tremendous earnings of *The Magic Mountain*. They took trips, they ate and drank well, and two large cars stood in the garage: an open American car and a German limousine. When they went to the theatre, the chauffeur waited in the lobby with their fur coats at the end of the performance. This style of life, which they went to no trouble to conceal, made their growing number of political enemies hate them all the more.

Thomas Mann was unprepared for exile. In a letter, he wrote: "I am too good a German, too closely involved with the cultural traditions and language of my country for the prospect of a year-long or perhaps life-long exile not to have a hard, ominous meaning for me." He was so unprepared that, on leaving the country less than a month after Hitler became chancellor, he failed to take his diaries and the pages of the novel he was working on. Publication of the diaries would have considerably dampened the warm welcome he was to receive in America.

By 1933 Erika and Klaus Mann were famous too. Thomas Mann had not encouraged Klaus to become a writer, noting in his diary that his fourteen-year-old son's intention to send stories to magazines was "a folly from which he must be dissuaded." As adolescents, Erika and Klaus wrote plays and stories. While still teenagers, they made their way to Berlin, where Erika was determined to become a famous actress and Klaus a famous writer. As soon as he began to publish essays and stories, Klaus traded on his father's fame with a mixture of brazenness and unease. A car-toon appeared in a satirical magazine showing him in short pants next to his father. The caption read: "I am told, Papa, that the son of a genius is never a genius himself. Therefore, you can't be a genius!" Bertolt Brecht wrote: "The whole world knows Klaus Mann, the son of Thomas Mann. By the way, who is Thomas Mann?" When *The Magic Mountain* appeared in 1924, Thomas Mann wrote in his son's copy: "To my respected colleague – his promising father." Klaus was foolish enough to show it to a friend and it was quoted regularly in the press. Klaus, as he entered his twenties, was both a wunderkind and a joke.

Thomas Mann, unlike his son, was an immensely complex fig-ure, conservative in his manners and ambiguous in his politics and, for many years, in his German nationalism. He could have been a senator and businessman like his father had it not been for something rich and almost hidden in his nature that set him apart. It was not merely a hidden sexuality, or something inher-ited from his slightly daft mother, but an imaginative energy and dark daring that, combined with an astonishing steely ambition and solidity, enabled him to produce *Buddenbrooks* when he was twenty-five.

Klaus was always simpler to read. He was fluid and generous and flighty. He kept nothing in reserve, and this, despite his obvi-ous literary talent, made him melancholy. His father's deep, almost obsessive interest in death was entertained and kept at bay because Thomas Mann placed it at the service of his work; a sense of doom and disease filled the pages and the spirit of the characters in *Buddenbrooks*, *The Magic Mountain*, *Doctor Faustus* and many of Mann's best stories. Mann comes to us a writer of many layers and guises. Much can be read into his work, and it is easy to understand the interest of scholars in finding a key to his peculiar artistic systems and to hidden aspects of his life. He had to be careful, once he arrived in the United States, about his sexuality and his shifting relationship with aspects of Germany that, after 1933, had become deeply unsavoury and shameful. In *Bluebeard's Chamber: Guilt and Confession in Thomas Mann* (2003), Michael Maar argued, however, that Mann was, for much of his life, especially with his family, his friends, and in his work, unusually open about his sexuality.

Instead, searching for secret elements in his fiction, Maar insisted that one theme impelled and nourished Mann's imagination more than any other. He found image after image from the beginning to the end of his work of murder, blood, knives and sexual pleasure. He suggested that this was the key to Mann's work and perhaps to his life. "We can venture," he wrote, "the thought experiment that if Thomas Mann had committed an actual crime and sought to give an account of it in his fiction, the work would not have taken a different form than it actually has." He suggests – almost convincingly – that in Naples, in the mid-1890s, when he was a very young man, Thomas Mann did something, or witnessed something, or was closely implicated in something that involved sex and murder. And that what he did, or what he witnessed, both maimed and energized him and made its way into what he wrote over sixty years. It hardly matters whether Maar's hypotheses are true or not. What is more interesting is the way Mann's work continues to be examined and reread, as though the key to it remains in some furtive, cloaked part of his dark and exotic psychosexual being. "It is as well," Mann wrote in *Death in Venice*, "that the world knows only a fine piece of work and not its origins."

Klaus, on the other hand, had no secret crimes, real or imaginary, on his conscience; instead of writing about death as his father did, he allowed the aura of death to enter his own spirit. As early as 1932 he wrote in his diary that he had thought about suicide. In February 1933 he wrote: "In the mornings, nothing but the wish to die. When I calculate what I have to lose, it seems negligible. No chance of a really happy relationship. Probably no chance of literary fame in the near future . . . Death can only be regarded as deliverance." What makes Klaus a subject of great fascination in Germany now, however, is not his dance with death but rather that he saw the rise of Fascism more clearly and presciently than his father did and bravely set about opposing it in every way he could while also managing to take drugs and have lots of sex. As the prevaricating father struggled with ambiguities, both political and sexual, he made masterpieces from the fight. The son was a simpler soul, more open about his sexuality, more certain of his beliefs. Out of that he made a few almost interesting books.

At the end of 1924 Klaus Mann wrote *Anja and Esther*, a play about a neurotic quartet of four boys and girls who were in love with each other. The following year he was approached by the actor Gustaf Gründgens, who wanted to direct the play with himself in one of the male roles, Klaus in the other; Erika Mann and Pamela Wedekind, the daughter of the playwright Frank Wedekind, would be the two young women. The ambitious Gründgens had a reputation in Hamburg but not in Berlin. At one point, as they worked on the play, Klaus planned to marry Pamela, with whom Erika fell in love, while Erika arranged to marry Gustaf, with whom Klaus began an affair. At Erika and Gustaf's wedding reception, Erika noted that her mother's brother was, as she wrote to Pamela, "flirting with Gustaf." The honeymoon was spent in a hotel where Erika and Pamela had stayed not long before as man and wife (Pamela had checked in dressed as a man).

*Anja and Esther*, which opened in Hamburg in October 1925, attracted vast amounts of publicity, partly because of its scandalous content and partly because it starred three children of two famous writers. One magazine put them on the cover, cropping out Gründgens's face, emphasizing his status as outsider amid all this fame. His marriage to Erika ended soon after it began. "A cynical explanation," Weiss writes, "would point out that Erika's theatrical career had flourished to the point where she no longer needed Gustaf as stepping-stone; that Gustaf had finally realized his marriage to Erika would not bestow on him her father's impeccable social credentials."

Pamela Wedekind married a man old enough to be her father, and the foursome returned to being the twosome of Erika and Klaus Mann. Although Erika played the part of Queen Elisabeth in Schiller's *Don Carlos* at the State Theatre in Munich, she longed for greater excitement. And since Klaus was bored and his next play a flop, they decided to go to America, where they were ready to have their genius fully recognized. To amuse themselves, they told the U.S. press that they were twins and thus began the American myth of "The Literary Mann Twins." They went on a tour of the country. "Whenever they were stuck for funds," Weiss writes, "Klaus would write articles and Erika would write letters to organizations, seeking lecture engagements. They often arrived in town with no change in their pockets." Soon, they decided to tour the world. They stayed at the Imperial Hotel in Tokyo for more than six weeks – "kept in that luxurious prison by the evil spell of our unpaid bill" – and, on being rescued by their father's publisher, agreed to write a book about their travels as a way of paying him back.

They returned to Germany in 1928 and over the next five years wrote articles and books and made outrageous statements; they travelled, they had many lovers. Erika worked in the theatre and appeared in films, Klaus wrote more plays. In other words, they took full advantage of the freedoms offered by the Weimar Republic. For many in the Nazi Party, they were the epitome of all that was wrong with Germany. And their mother's Jewish background didn't endear them to the National Socialists either. Despite the fact that they often seemed in these years to be the silliest pair of people alive, they came nonchalantly and almost naturally to believe that their right to freedom and fun and half-baked opinions was something worth preserving. It was their silliness that made them serious. Once the right to go on being silly was threatened, they would respond with considerable urgency and earnestness.

Erika took almost no direct interest in politics until, in January 1932, she was asked to read a poem by Victor Hugo to a women's pacifist group. As she stood on the stage she was shouted down, one young Brownshirt screaming: "You are a criminal . . . Jewish traitress! International agitator!" She later wrote: "In the hall, everything became a mad scramble. The Stormtroopers attacked the audience with their chairs, shouting themselves into paroxysms of anger and fury." The Nazi newspaper later called her "a flat-footed peace hyena" with "no human physiognomy"; she didn't increase her popularity with the party by suing for damages and winning. "I realised," she later wrote, "that my experience had nothing to do with politics – it was more than politics. It touched at the very foundation of my – of our – of the existence of all."

That winter, Erika, now out of work and living in her parents' house, conceived the idea of starting a cabaret in Munich. Her father came up with the title. *The Peppermill* opened on New Year's Day 1933. It ran for two months next door to the local Nazi headquarters, and, since it was so successful, was preparing to move to a larger theatre when the Reichstag went up in flames. Erika and Klaus were on a skiing holiday while the new theatre was being decorated and arrived back in Munich to be warned by the family chauffeur, himself a party member, that they were in danger. Later, Klaus wrote that the chauffeur "had been a Nazi spy throughout the four or five years he lived with us . . . But this time he had failed in his duty, out of sympathy, I suppose. For he knew what would happen to us if he informed his Nazi employers of our arrival in town."

Erika and Klaus made contact with their parents, who were in Switzerland, and warned them not to return to Munich. As soon as she could, Erika drove over the border to Switzerland, where she began to prepare her parents for the idea that they were going to lose everything that they owned in Germany, including not only their houses and cars, but the manuscripts of Thomas Mann's books and such invaluable sources as Katia's letters to her husband from the sanatorium in Davos.

Klaus didn't travel with his sister. Instead, he took the night train to Paris. The day he arrived, he wrote in his diary: "Feeling of loneliness always, whenever SHE isn't there." The "she" was Erika. And Erika, it seemed, was now ready to transfer her loyalty from her brother to her father. She began by returning to Munich, putting herself in some danger, once she discovered that a section of Mann's novel-in-progress, *Joseph and His Brothers*, had been left behind. She sneaked back into the family home and, without turning on the lights, found the handwritten manuscript on her father's desk. Hiding it among the tools under the seat of her car, she made her way once more across the border. (It isn't clear why Mann didn't ask his daughter to take his diaries too. Eventually, he sent Golo a key to the safe where they were, imploring him not to read them. "My fears," he wrote in his diary when their arrival was delayed, "revolve first and foremost almost exclusively around this threat to my life's secrets. They are deeply serious. The consequences could be terrible, even fatal.")

Erika had a strength of will that Klaus lacked, an urge to look after others, a need, which was often irritating, to put her considerable physical and emotional energies to use. Until this point, the siblings had been inseparable, Klaus constantly falling in love with Erika's friends. With the shock of exile, Erika for much of the time left Klaus unprotected. Her attention was now directed at political action, at her own survival and at ensuring the happiness and comfort of her father. Her bossiness and her ability to organize things meant that she thrived in exile. Klaus, on the other hand, drifted. In July 1933 he wrote in his diary: "Thought about how sad I am to be alone . . . Erika has Therese [the actress Therese Giehse, who worked with Erika on *The Peppermill*] . . . By the rules of our bond, I too should be permitted to seek relationships elsewhere. I reflect on all the failed or half-failed attempts." He was living on money sent to him by his mother. In October he wrote: "Hope to receive November money – I am not, like my sister, able to manage without it, on the contrary – alas."

It was clear that Klaus couldn't go back to Germany. He thus had nothing to lose by denouncing the Nazi regime and saw it as the duty of all writers to do what they could to undermine Hitler. "Neither pleasure nor pain," he wrote, "ever makes me forget the inexorable gravity of the situation and the weight of my responsibility. Every anti-Fascist German writer must exert his whole strength today to the very utmost, and I know that, for particular reasons, I am under an especially great obligation." He decided to publish, from Amsterdam, a monthly literary journal, *Die Sammlung*, and began to ask the main German writers for contributions. He knew what he wanted to achieve. The problem was that his father, now in the South of France, was considerably more ambivalent about his duties.

Some of this arose from Mann's fears of losing his readers in Germany and having his assets confiscated. But it also had to do with an old argument about Germany that Mann had had with his brother Heinrich. In August 1914 Mann was enthusiastic about the war. He wrote to a friend: "One feels that everything will have to be new after this profound, violent anguish and that the German soul will emerge stronger, prouder, freer, happier from it. So be it." Heinrich believed from the beginning that Germany would lose. In an essay written in 1915, ostensibly about Zola, he launched an attack on his brother:

The whole nationalistic catechism, filled with madness and crime – and those who preach it, is it out of eagerness or, even worse, vanity . . . Because you're eager to please you become poet laureate for half a lifetime, if you don't run out of breath beforehand, desperate to run with the crowd, always cheering it on, high on emotion, with no sense of responsibility for – and no awareness of – the impending catastrophe like a loser! . . . It does not matter now that you take an elegant stance against truth and justice; you oppose it and belong to the base and fleeting. You've chosen between the moment and history and concede that in spite of all your talents you are just an amusing parasite.

By that time Mann had ceased work on *The Magic Mountain* and begun writing a reply to his brother, called *Reflections of a Nonpolitical Man*. It was six hundred pages long. Golo remembered him writing it:

We had once loved our father almost as tenderly as our mother, but that changed during the war. He could still project an aura of kindness, but for the most part we experienced only silence, sternness, nervousness or anger. I can remember all too well certain scenes at mealtimes, outbreaks of rage and brutality that were directed at my brother Klaus but brought tears to my own eyes. If a person cannot always be very nice to those around him when he is devoting himself exclusively to his creative work, must it not be much more difficult when he is struggling day after day with *Reflections of a Nonpolitical Man* in which the sinking of the British ship *Lusitania* with twelve hundred civilian passengers on board is actually hailed, to name just one of the book's grimmest features . . . This work, coming into being only for itself, or for its author, was a castle laid out like a labyrinth, meant to be torn down no sooner than it was built.

Even as late as March 1920 Mann was unrepentant. "Heinrich's position," he wrote, "no matter how splendid it appears at the moment, is basically already undermined by events and experiences. His orientation towards the West, his worship of the French, his Wilsonism etc are antiquated and withered."

In his biography of Mann, published in 1999, Hermann Kurzke traces the ironies, the contradictions and the changes of opinion in Mann's politics between 1918 and 1922, when, in a speech called "The German Republic," he seemed to recant. Kurzke writes that Mann, in these years, developed friendships, some of them close, with figures such as Ernst Bertram, Elisabeth Mann's godfather, who later became supporters of the Nazis or fellow-travellers with the regime. Kurzke is cautious, however, about making too much of this:

Does that make Thomas Mann a precursor of Fascism? He certainly made an effort to stay out of the way of the resurgent right-wing movement of the time. Very early on in the summer of 1921, he took note of the rising Nazi movement and dismissed it as "swastika nonsense." As early as 1925 when Hitler was still imprisoned in Landsberg, he rejected the cultural barbarity of German Fascism with an extensive, decisive and clearly visible gesture.

In May 1933, when "un-German" books were being burned, Heinrich Mann's were on the bonfire. Thomas Mann's were not. He was still being protected by Bertram, among others. But his main protection was his own silence. When the first issue of *Die Sammlung* appeared, it had a provocative essay by Heinrich Mann and an editorial by Klaus: "The true, valid German literature . . . cannot remain silent before the degradation of its people and the outrage it perpetrates on itself . . . A literary periodical is not a political periodical . . . Nevertheless, today it will have a political mission. Its position must be unequivocal."

Goebbels, in retaliation, stripped Heinrich of his citizenship, and the following year Klaus, too, was declared stateless. In 1935, five days after her marriage to W. H. Auden, her second husband, Erika was also stripped of her citizenship. (Auden seemed to get infinite amusement from his relationship with the Manns. "What else are buggers for?" he replied when asked why he had married the soon-to-be-stateless Erika. "I didn't see her till the ceremony and perhaps I shall never see her again," he wrote to Stephen Spender. "Who's the most boring German writer? My father-in-law." He said about Klaus: "For an author, sons are an embarrassment, as if characters in his novel had come to life.")

Thomas Mann confined his views on what was happening in Germany to his diary. On 10 April 1933 he wrote:

But for all that, might not something deeply significant and revolutionary be taking place in Germany? The Jews: it is no calamity after all . . . that the domination of the legal system by the Jews has been ended. Secret, disquieting, persistent musings . . . I am beginning to suspect that in spite of everything this process is one of those that has two sides to them.

On 20 April he wrote:

I could have a certain understanding for the rebellion against the Jewish element were it not that the Jewish spirit exercises a necessary control over the German element, the withdrawal of which is dangerous; left to themselves the Germans are so stupid as to lump people of my type in the same category and drive me out with the rest.

While it is important to read these musings as musings, they were of a type that Heinrich Mann never went in for, nor did Erika and nor did Klaus; they were certainly not shared with Thomas Mann's wife and were never aired in public; they were countered by such remarks as: "Anti-Semitism is the disgrace of any educated and culturally engaged person."

When Mann found that his name was first on the list of future contributors to *Die Sammlung*, he wrote in his diary that "Klaus has played a trick on us by including Heinrich's article in the first issue." When a German trade magazine reprinted an official warning to booksellers not to stock books by anyone associated with *Die Sammlung*, Mann sent them a telegram that was widely reproduced in Germany: "Can only confirm that the character of the first issue of *Die Sammlung* does not correspond to its original programme." He had openly repudiated his son's magazine. The following month Mann moved to a large three-storey villa in Switzerland and Erika opened *The Peppermill* in Zurich. Klaus was on his own in Amsterdam. "Long letter from the Magician" – his father – "the most humiliating sensation . . . Sorrow and confusion," he wrote in his diary. He was taking heroin and morphine, and wrote in his diary about longing for death.

Thomas Mann continued to be published in Germany until 1936. When Bermann Fischer, his German publisher, was denounced by exiles as a Jewish protégé of Goebbels, Mann's fervent public defence of him was too much for Erika. She wrote to her father:

You are stabbing in the back the entire émigré movement – I can put it no other way. Probably you will be very angry at me because of this letter. I am prepared for that, and I know what I'm doing. This friendly time is predestined to separate people – in how many cases has it happened already. Your relation to Dr. Bermann and his publishing house is indestructible – you seem to be ready to sacrifice everything for it. In that case it is a sacrifice for you that I, slowly but surely, will be lost for you – then just never mind. For me it is sad, and terrible. I am your child, E.

More than sixty years later Elisabeth remembered the confrontation. Erika, she said,

threatened never to want to see him again, I mean she went as far as that in her letter. She was full of real and deep political passion, Erika was. And quite, quite uncompromising. Klaus didn't ever have the same kind of intellectual violence. He also had strong convictions, he also felt betrayed when he did not get the support for his journal that he hoped he would get. That was a bitter disappointment for him, but he never had the aggressiveness that Erika had, never.

Klaus sent his father a telegram beseeching him to make a statement in solidarity with the émigré writers. Katia, in the meantime, tried to dissuade Erika from breaking with her father, telling her that, aside from Elisabeth and Katia herself, she was "the only person on whom Z.'s heart really hangs, and your letter hurt deeply and made him ill." Z. is *der Zauberer*, "the magician."

Thomas Mann replied to Erika asking for time to consider what she had said. This caused Erika to become even angrier. She blamed her father for doing more harm to Klaus in the row over *Die Sammlung* than the Nazis had ever done. Her mother had had enough and began a draft of an open letter under the name of Thomas Mann. While mild in its tone, it was his first public statement from exile against the Nazis. Once he had released it, he wrote to a friend: "I am finally saving my soul." He was immediately notified that his honorary doctorate from Bonn University had been rescinded. He, his wife and their four younger children lost their German citizenship.

While all this was going on, Klaus was working on the novel for which he is best known, *Mephisto*, which was published in Amsterdam in 1936. It deals, in a way that is almost open, with Klaus's former lover and brother-in-law, Gustaf Gründgens, and his rise to power as an actor in Nazi Germany. Although it has its dramatic moments, some of it is very badly written. The narrative regularly gets carried away in its efforts to portray the Nazis as pure evil and the actor Hendrik Höfgen as ambitious, flawed, sexually perverse, a man ready to sell his soul while tempting others to do the same.

Some of the writing, in its flatness and exaggeration, would have made Thomas Mann wince. But one section of the book must have hurt him more than any number of threatening letters from Erika. Klaus, it seems to me, managed to include aspects of his father in the character of Höfgen. This is something that Mann in his diaries and his letters, as published in English, makes no mention of, and I can find no reference to it in the many biographies of Mann. Nonetheless, it seems clear that Klaus used a small part of his father in his attempt to dramatize political treachery for the sake of artistic success.

In *Mephisto*, Hendrik marries Barbara Bruckner, a version of Erika, whose father is also a version of Thomas Mann. Hendrik's new father-in-law was "a scholar and thinker who was not only one of the most eminent and talked about figures on the European literary scene but also one of the most influential in political circles." The actor's father-in-law is referred to throughout as "the privy councillor," or the "Geheimrat," a term used in the Mann family to describe not Thomas Mann, but Mann's own father-in-law, Alfred Pringsheim.

When Thomas Mann, an awkward, ambitious young man from the Baltic, married Katia Pringsheim, he was no less intimidated by the cultural sophistication and general social confidence of Katia's family than Hendrik Höfgen was by the family of Barbara Bruckner in *Mephisto*. (Golo remembers his father saying of Katia's family: "They have never liked me, nor I them.") In some passages, the novel seems to be merging the relationship between the provincial actor Gründgens and the Manns with the relationship between Thomas Mann and the Pringsheims. In that sense Thomas Mann appears hidden in the character of Höfgen, both of them marrying above their station, both later selling their soul, or refusing to speak out, for the sake of continued or greater fame as artists. Klaus, who wasn't generally given to subtlety, is subtle about this particular trick, but it wouldn't have escaped the attention of the old magician that his son, by using the word "Geheimrat" so often to describe Höfgen's father-in-law, was comparing his father to an artist who had famously sold his soul. Seven years later, Mann would begin his own book on the same subject, the magisterial *Doctor Faustus*.

In September 1936, Erika and Klaus moved from Europe to the United States, where Erika began an affair with a German doctor who was staying at her hotel. According to Sybille Bedford, she "went off women, she really became interested in men, she went off with people's husbands even." Klaus had an affair with an American dancer. *The Peppermill* was to be performed in New York with its European cast. Although the lyrics had been translated into English, some by Auden, the show was a disaster and soon taken off.

Very quickly Erika learned enough English to begin giving lectures all over the U.S. When Klaus's visa ran out he returned to Europe, staying with his parents in Switzerland, amazed to find that, without consulting him, his father had founded his own bimonthly journal for German émigrés and appointed an editor. Klaus wrote in his diary: "I perceive, again, very strongly and not without bitterness, Z.'s complete coldness to me . . . His universal lack of interest in people is here especially intensified." It's clear from Erika's letters that Klaus was taking a great deal of heroin.

In March 1937 the entire Mann family, including Heinrich, was granted Czechoslovak citizenship. Klaus could now travel to Budapest to seek treatment for his heroin addiction, treatment which did not fully work. Six months later he returned to the U.S. and to Erika, who took him with her on what became joint lecture tours. Their titles included "What Price Peace?," "What Does the Youth of Europe Believe in Today?" and "Our Father and His Work." They wrote two books together.

Soon, Thomas and Katia Mann arrived in America as well,

and, with their fourteen suitcases in tow, began to tour the country too. When Klaus published a new novel, his father wrote to say that he'd admired it, adding that when he first saw it he "secretly had the wicked intention" of not reading it through but "just looking into" it. Of the letters he received from his father about his work, Klaus noted in his diary: "He writes to complete strangers just as pleasantly. A mixture of highest intelligence, almost charitable courtesy – and ice coldness. This is especially accentuated when it concerns me." In 1939, Mann published *Lotte in Weimar*, in which Goethe's son is introduced as follows: "August is his son; and to the father's mind the boy's existence exhausted itself in that fact." He added: "To be the son of a great man is a high fortune, a considerable advantage. But it is likewise an oppressive burden, a permanent derogation of one's ego." The great man settled in Princeton, where he had Bruno Walter and Einstein for neighbours.

In 1938 Klaus and Erika reported on the Spanish Civil War which had broken out in 1936. Erika wrote *School for Barbarians*, a book on the Nazi education system; it sold 40,000 copies in the U.S. in the first three months after publication. Erika slowly became one of the most successful and highly paid women lecturers in the country. Both she and Klaus believed passionately that America should straightaway enter the war and were appalled by the attitude of Auden and Christopher Isherwood, who had left England and thus avoided active involvement in the war. In his diary, Klaus recognized in Auden "the cold charms" of Gustaf Gründgens, but he refused to be seduced by them. When he saw the ménage that Auden had established in Brooklyn with Carson McCullers, Gypsy Rose Lee, Benjamin Britten, Peter Pears, Chester Kallman, Paul Bowles and Jane Bowles, among others, he wrote in his diary: "What an epic one could write about this!" Soon Golo too moved in, having escaped from the Nazis by walking over the

Pyrenees with his Uncle Heinrich, Alma Mahler and Franz Werfel.

Isherwood, who was in the habit of thinking well of people, thought Klaus "without vanity or self-consciousness"; "his great charm," Isherwood said, "lay in this openness, this eager, unaffected approach." Others didn't share his view. Glenway Wescott called Klaus a "tragic twerp"; Janet Flanner thought he was pathetically dominated by Erika, who flew to Europe in 1940 to work as a war correspondent for the BBC, leaving Klaus in New York feeling "envy and anxiety" and resenting the fact that his sister had once again left him behind. He would continue to be supported financially by his parents. When a New York editor informed Auden and Kallman that he would soon be publishing Klaus's autobiography, they fell around laughing and said: "What will you call it? The Invisible Man? The Subordinate Klaus?"

Klaus's autobiography was called *The Turning Point*. It was an exercise in tact. He couldn't attack his father openly, since he was living off him financially and operating in the U.S. in his father's shadow, a shadow that was both protective and damaging. In his autobiography he took every opportunity to single out and praise his uncle Heinrich rather than his father, but was careful not to write about his father in the same wounded tone he used in his diaries. The account in the book of his father hollering from the window on seeing his son leaving home – "Good luck, my son! And come home when you are wretched and forlorn" – reads like pure mythology, or a sad joke. When he wrote to Klaus about the book, Mann told him he had absolutely no memory of ever saying that.

In Klaus's version of the early years in exile when his father would not denounce the regime, he exalted Heinrich for being "the first to receive the enviable distinction" of getting on Goebbels's blacklist. His uncle, he wrote, "had left Berlin soon after the Reichstag Fire and, once in France, lost no time in raising his voice to arraign and ridicule the brown canaille . . . Heinrich Mann – a man in his early sixties at the beginning of his exile – experienced something like a second youth." He himself, he wrote, was on Goebbels's second list and Erika on the third. When he came to write about *Die Sammlung*, he mentioned that it was produced under the sponsorship of "André Gide, Heinrich Mann and Aldous Huxley." There was no mention of his father.

"As for our father," he finally wrote, the Nazis, "still afraid of public opinion abroad," were more "reluctant" to place him on a blacklist: "At this point his works were not officially banned; although as far back as 1933, to ask openly for a book by Thomas Mann in a German bookstore was a risky thing to do. For his feelings towards Nazism were generally known, and were emphasized, furthermore, by his refusal to return to Munich." When Klaus mentioned "the inevitable clash" between his father and the Nazis, he neglected to say that it didn't take place until 1936. He described the immense comfort and ease of his father's early exile in Switzerland without any appearance of irony. By the time the book appeared, Thomas Mann had reinvented himself as the most vocal and serious opponent of the Nazis among the German exiles in the United States. It must have pleased him that Klaus had done nothing to damage his new position. He wrote him a bland and affectionate letter: "It is an unusually charming, kind, sensitive, clever and honestly personal book." The poet Muriel Rukeyser remembered Klaus frantically waiting for this letter, tearing it open when it came and reading it "in a moving, suspended moment of all the mixed feeling that can be found in the autobiography itself."

In these years Klaus, without Erika, grew increasingly unhappy and went on taking drugs and falling unsuitably in love. The FBI was on his case, having been told that both he and Erika were Communists. "When Fascism spread across Europe," Weiss writes, "the FBI expended considerable time and resources harassing two of the strongest and most dedicated advocates for liberal democracy, both of whom had great respect for the government of the United States." Erika and Klaus were guilty, it seemed, not only of "premature" anti-Fascism but of "having affairs together." It was reported that "many queer-looking people" could be seen going into Klaus's hotel room in New York, as indeed they could. Klaus remarked in his diary that he liked "porters, waiters, liftboys and so on, white or black. Almost all are agreeable to me. I could sleep with all of them." Sybille Bedford recalled that what attracted Klaus "were the professional louts."

During this period, Erika grew closer to her father but, as Weiss writes, "Klaus's estrangement from the Magician did not ameliorate with the reconciliation of their political differences; it was always about something deeper. The sacred bond the siblings shared since childhood, forged in resistance to Thomas Mann and all he represented, no longer could sustain itself with the same passionate intensity."

After Pearl Harbor, Klaus decided to join the U.S. Army. The FBI reported that his first physical examination revealed a "syphilitic condition" and "13 arsenical and 39 heavy metal injections." He was rejected a number of times, partly because of his homosexuality, and then finally accepted in December 1942. When he was posted to the Mediterranean, Erika remarked that for the first time since their childhood he was almost happy. His parents came to see him off. He wrote in his diary: "At our farewell, Z. embraced me, something that had never happened before."

Klaus arrived in Germany the day after the surrender. He had believed that "when the Dictator has vanished – and only then, will it again be possible . . . to live in Germany, without fear and without shame." He now knew that wasn't true. On 16 May 1945, he wrote to his father:

It would be a very grave mistake on your part to return to this country and play any kind of political role here. Not that I believe you were harbouring any projects or aspirations of this kind. But just in case any tempting proposition should ever be made to you . . . Conditions here are too sad. All your efforts to improve them would be hopelessly wasted. In the end you would be blamed for the country's well-deserved, inevitable misery. More likely than not, you would be assassinated.

When he revisited the shell of the family home in Munich, Klaus discovered that it had been used as a *Lebensborn* during the war, an Aryan knocking-shop, "a place where racially qualified young men and equally well-bred young women collaborated in the interest of the German nation . . . Many fine babies were begotten and born in this house." When he interviewed Richard Strauss for the army magazine *Stars and Stripes,* Strauss praised Hans Frank, who ran Auschwitz, since Frank, unlike Hitler, "really appreciated my music." Klaus met Heinrich's first wife, who had been released from Terezín, and their daughter, who had also been imprisoned. He didn't believe that ordinary Germans were ignorant of what happened in the concentration camps. He wrote that he felt "a stranger in my former fatherland."

Erika arrived in Germany four months after Klaus. She wrote: "The Germans, as you know, are hopeless. In their hearts, self-deception and dishonesty, arrogance and docility, shrewdness and stupidity are repulsively mingled and combined." Bedford said of her: "Erika could hate, and she hated the Germans. You see, Erika was a fairly violent character. At one point during the war, she propagated that every German should be castrated. And vengeance – Klaus wasn't like that at all. Erika was very unforgiving."

On her arrival in Munich, she registered a claim on the old family house, something that poor impractical Klaus had neglected to do. Her other task was to report on the Nüremberg Trials. She was the only one of the journalists allowed into the hotel where the Nazi leaders were being held. She let them know who she was. "To think that that woman has been in my room," Julius Streicher remarked. Goering had something more interesting to say. He explained that "had he been in charge of the 'Mann case,' he would have handled it differently . . . Surely a German of the stature of Thomas Mann could have been adapted to the Third Reich." Erika reported that "when a slight thunderstorm had frightened Göring into an equally slight heart attack, the creator of the Blitz was given a mattress for his cot, and breakfast in bed." When she visited Hans Frank and Ribbentrop, "the Butcher of Poland was reading the Bible to the ex-champagne salesman."

Erika and Klaus were increasingly at sea in the new Germany. Klaus began to work in films, collaborating briefly and painfully with Roberto Rossellini. Someone who worked with him in these years said: "He was a restless man. He had so many ideas and so much energy . . . I don't think he could sit still for two minutes. He had a cigarette perpetually in his mouth and was in constant movement. You could feel the vibrations of his energy."

It should have been possible for Klaus's books, especially *Mephisto* and *The Turning Point*, which had been published during his exile, to begin appearing in the new Germany. But the new Germany was strange. Gustaf Gründgens was back on the stage, as popular and successful as he had been when he had Goering to protect him. Weiss reports that having with difficulty secured a ticket for a sold-out performance, Klaus "was speechless to discover that Gründgens, stepping onto the stage during the first act, received a show-stopping standing ovation."

In response he wrote an article suggesting that Emmy Sonnemann, the actress who married Goering, should also have her career revived. "Perhaps someone gassed at Auschwitz," he wrote, "left behind some stage piece in which the esteemed woman could make her second debut. The good woman surely knew nothing about Auschwitz – and besides, what does art have to do with politics?" When the German edition of *The Turning Point* appeared in 1952, Gründgens demanded that sections of the book that damaged his reputation be removed. They were. *Mephisto* appeared in German in 1956 but only in the GDR: no West German publisher would touch it, even after Gründgens's suicide in 1963. Erika brought the case to the West German Supreme Court, which ruled in favour of suppressing the book, preserving Gründgens's posthumous reputation. After a long wait, a paperback version finally appeared in West Germany in 1981, as well as a film adaptation.

In 1946, as his ex-lover and current nemesis was being applauded on the stage, Klaus decided to return to America for an extended visit. Since he had nowhere else to go, he planned to make his way to Los Angeles, where his parents were installed in a large and splendid house in Pacific Palisades; but his father had been diagnosed with lung cancer and was being operated on in Chicago. Erika flew from Nuremberg to be with her father. She never again left his side. For the next nine years she was Mann's secretary and chief confidante. Just as she and Klaus had once been inseparable, now she and her father were never apart. Years later, Elisabeth Mann remembered:

She returned home, because she had exhausted her career, and so devoted herself to the work of her father . . . Erika was a very powerful personality, a very dominant, domineering personality, and I must say that this role that she played in the latter part of her life as manager of my father was not always very easy to take for my mother, because she had been used to doing all of that.

Among other tasks, Erika set about cutting the final manuscript of *Doctor Faustus* by forty pages; her father believed she had improved the book.

Klaus wrote to his mother suggesting that a cottage be found for him near his parents' home and since he could not drive, he would also need "an old Ford and a young driver . . . The driver must also be able to cook a bit and have a pleasant appearance." His mother replied immediately. "A house to rent and a car and a driver who can cook, who also was attractive! With a lot of luck, one can get a room from upwards of one hundred dollars . . . This is democracy!" Klaus arrived in Los Angeles at the end of July but was back in New York by the early autumn. He was once more in exile, this time from his family as well as his country. He had lost his sister to his father and had used up his mother's patience. In 1948 he said: "It is only the parts of my life in which she [Erika] shares that have substance and reality for me."

Klaus now moved between New York, Paris, Zurich, Vienna and Amsterdam. When he returned once more to Los Angeles, his parents asked him to leave after a month as other siblings and cousins were coming to stay. Klaus, with Erika's help, found a place nearby. Six days after moving in, he attempted suicide by slitting his wrists, taking pills and turning on the gas. He was hospitalized and the incident was reported in the press. His father didn't visit. Mann wrote to a friend: "My two sisters committed suicide, and Klaus has much of the elder sister in him. The impulse is present in him, and all the circumstances favour it – the one exception being that he has a parental home on which he can always rely." His mother, when she heard the news, is reported (by Elisabeth) to have snapped: "If he wanted to kill himself, why didn't he do it properly?" Erika wrote to a friend: "As you may have read, Klaus – my closest brother – tried to do away with himself which was not only a nasty shock but also involved a great deal of time-devouring trouble." On 1 January 1949 Klaus wrote in his diary: "I do not wish to survive this year." In April, in Cannes, he received a letter from a West German publisher to say that *Mephisto* couldn't appear "because Mr.

Gründgens plays a very important role here." The following month he succeeded in killing himself. He was forty-two.

Mann was in Stockholm with Katia and Erika when he heard the news. "My inward sympathy," he wrote in his diary, "with the mother's heart and with E. He should not have done this to them . . . The hurtful, ugly, cruel inconsideration and irresponsibility." He wrote to Heinrich: "His case is so very strange and painful, such skill, charm, cosmopolitanism, and in his heart a death-wish." He wrote to Hermann Hesse: "This interrupted life lies heavily on my mind and grieves me. My relationship with him was difficult and not free of guilt. My life put his in a shadow right from the beginning." He decided not to attend his son's funeral or interrupt his lecture tour. Of all the family, only Michael, the youngest sibling, on tour with the San Francisco Symphony, attended the funeral; he played a largo on his viola as the coffin was lowered into the ground.

Later, Elisabeth would say of Erika: "When Klaus died, she was totally, totally heartbroken – I mean that was unbearable for her, that loss. That hit her harder than anything else in her life." Erika returned with her parents to the U.S. and sought citizen-ship only to find that she was once more under investigation by the FBI. By 1950 there was even a move to deport her for being a Communist. Before it went any further, she decided to leave, tak-ing her parents with her. They had become close enough for her father to write in his diary about his concern for Erika: "she could so easily follow her brother. Certainly she does not want to live any longer than us." They sold the house in Pacific Palisades in June 1952 and moved to Switzerland. Thomas Mann died three years later at the age of eighty.

Erika fought with her other siblings; she and Elisabeth didn't speak for a decade. In 1961 her mother wrote to her brother: "What is ruining . . . my old age, is the more than unfriendly rela-tionship of all my children towards the good, fat, eldest." Erika was busy editing a three-volume edition of her father's letters, fighting the case for Klaus's book in the West German courts, and battling with her first husband after all these years. When two German newspapers insinuated that she had had an incestuous relationship with Klaus, she sued and won. She died in 1969 at the age of sixty-three, leaving some of her assets to Auden, whom she had not seen for years.

Her mother lived until 1980. Monika, whose husband drowned in front of her when their ship crossing the Atlantic was torpedoed in 1940, moved to Capri in 1953 and died in 1992. Golo, who returned to Germany in the late 1950s and became a historian, died in 1994. Michael committed suicide in 1977. This left Elisabeth, who lived until 2002. She devoted most of her life to the study and protection of the ocean. In her later years, she made herself available to interviewers and biographers. In a series of television drama-documentaries made for German television about the family, she appeared as a figure of calm and melancholy wisdom. ("When you get past the age of 30," she had told Golo, "you should stop blaming your parents for what you are.") There was a strange, dry, serene resignation about her appearance as she returned to the places where the Manns had lived, commenting to the camera on the damage that had been done with a sort of acceptance and a sense that nothing had escaped her.

# Borges: A Father in His Shadow

On 9 March 1951 Seepersad Naipaul wrote from Trinidad to his son Vidia, who was an undergraduate at Oxford: "I am beginning to believe I could have been a writer." A month later, Vidia, in a letter to the entire family, wrote: "I hope Pa does write, even five hundred words a day. He should begin a novel. He should realise that the society of the West Indies is a very interesting one – one of phoney sophistication." Soon, his father wrote again to say that he had in fact started to write five hundred words a day. "Let me see how well the resolve works out," he wrote. "Even now I have not settled the question whether I should work on an auto-biographical novel or whether I should exhume Gurudeva." *Gurudeva and Other Indian Tales* had been privately published in Port of Spain in 1943. It would be Seepersad Naipaul's only book. He died in 1953 at the age of forty-seven.

For writers and artists whose fathers dabbled in art and failed there seems always to be a peculiar intensity in their levels of ambition and determination. It is as though an artist such as Picasso, whose father was a failed painter, or William James, whose father was a failed essayist, or V. S. Naipaul, sought to compensate for his father's failure while at the same time using his talent as a way of killing the father off, showing his mother who was the real man in the household.

Jorge Luis Borges was in Majorca in 1919, writing his first poems as his father, Jorge Guillermo Borges, was working on his only novel, which, like Seepersad Naipaul's book, was printed privately. (Borges's mother later told Bioy Casares that she had spent her life with "dos locos," two madmen – her husband and her son.) The novel, called *El Caudillo*, published in 1921 when the author was forty-seven and his son twenty-two, was not a success. Seventeen years later, as his health was failing, Borges Senior suggested that his son rewrite the book, making clear that Jorge Luis, or Georgie as he was known in his family, had been consulted during its composition. "I put many metaphors in to please you," he told his son, asking him to "rewrite the novel in a straightforward way, with all the fine writing and purple patches left out."

The longest work of fiction Jorge Luis Borges ever produced was quite short: a mere fourteen pages. It was called "The Congress" and first published in 1971, although it had been on his mind for many years. Edwin Williamson, in his biography of Borges, writes about the parallels between the story and *El Caudillo*. Borges sought in his story, according to Williamson, not only to mirror the novel his father wrote but also "to transcend it . . . The basic structure and plot of the two works are identical: there is a powerful chieftain poised between civilisation and barbarism." There are many other close connections between the plots of the two stories.

Thus the literary legacy handed to Borges was clear: he would have to fulfil "the literary destiny" that his father "had been denied," as Williamson puts it. The ironies and absurdities of this were not lost on him. In the months after his father's death he wrote one of his great serious spoofs, "Pierre Menard, Author of Don Quixote," a meditation, using a straight face and no "fine writing" or "purple patches," on the idea of rewriting as an inspired enterprise, and on the concept of the writer as a force of culture imprisoned by language and time to such an extent that plagiarism becomes innovation, and reading itself a form of literary experiment.

It may also not have been lost on Borges, and it is not lost on the reader, that "The Congress" is not only a version of *El Caudillo* but a parody of Borges's earlier work, playing with all his old tricks, using a deadpan narrative, full of recondite facts and obscure references, to coax a shadow universe into pure existence. It was obviously written by someone who had read Borges. By 1971, however, Borges was clearly not himself. In "Borges and I," he wrote:

I must remain in Borges rather than in myself (if in fact I am a self), and yet I recognise myself less in his books than in many others, or in the rich strumming of a guitar. Some years ago I tried to get away from him: I went from suburban mythologies to playing games with time and infinity. But these are Borges's games now – I will have to think of something else.

With Borges it is always dangerous to infer that biographical material – his love life, his jobs or his relationship with friends or family – inspired the tone and content of certain works. Although there may be ample evidence for such a reading, especially in his poems, there is a real possibility that the books he read mattered much more to Borges than the events of his life. Six months before his father's death, Williamson points out, Borges wrote a book review for an Argentine magazine that is much more likely to have offered the inspiration for "Pierre Menard" than his father's vain request. The book was Paul Valéry's *Introduction à la poétique*. Williamson writes: "The same text, according to Borges, could mean different things to different readers in different periods, and he quoted a line from a poem by Cervantes to show that a reader in the 20th century would derive a different sense from the very same words." Borges wrote: "Time – a friend to Cervantes – has corrected the proofs for him."

While his father's example offered him a bookish future and literary ambitions, Borges's mother's legacy was more ambiguous and difficult and perhaps more powerful. She was acutely conscious of her family's history and status in Argentina. She was pure criollo, of Spanish descent born in South America, descended from the early settlers, men involved in the creation of an independent Argentina. Her grandfather led the cavalry charge at the battle of Junín in 1824, the second last battle in the liberation of South America. Later, after the battle of Ayacucho, he was promoted to the rank of colonel by Simón Bolívar. The heroic deeds done by members of her family made her proud, and she spoke of them constantly.

From his mother, Borges heard a great deal about old glories and fame that had faded, with the implication that he somehow could restore the family to its former level of importance. "As most of my people had been soldiers," he wrote, "and I knew I would never be, I felt ashamed, quite early, to be a bookish kind of person and not a man of action." Yet the presence of his ancestors' swords in the house and their lives as men of action obsessed him all his life. He wrote about knife fights and daggers and swords with a relish that only the truly sedentary can feel: "In a desk drawer, among rough drafts and letters, the dagger endlessly dreams its simple tiger's dream, and, grasping it, the hand comes alive because the metal comes alive, sensing in every touch the killer for whom it was wrought."

Borges's grandfather on his father's side was also a colonel who fought in battles. He married an Englishwoman, Fanny Haslam, leaving her a widow with two sons three years after their marriage, when he was shot in one of the many internal feuds that beset Argentine affairs. ("The bullet which shot dead Francisco Borges" is mentioned in "Things," one of Borges's best poems.) Fanny and her sons spoke English at home; Fanny ran the household as though they were in England. Borges was attached to his grandmother; her version of England was as influential as his mother's account of the family's former splendour. Fanny travelled to Europe with the Borges family and lived close to them in Buenos Aires until her death in 1935, at the age of ninety-three.

The Buenos Aires that Borges loved and celebrated was not the new, rich city teeming with immigrants from the south of Italy or from Galicia. It was the old city of the criollos that his mother had known, and the area around Palermo in the north of the city, down on its luck, where his father built a house beside Fanny Haslam's house and where Jorge Luis and his sister, Norah, were brought up. Close to Palermo was open countryside. A city both half imagined and half built ("Only one thing was missing – the street had no other side") replaced in Borges's imagination "the greedy streets / jostling with crowds and traffic." He and his sister did not play with children who were rough. Since his mother had contempt for the new rich of the city and no time for the new immigrants, it was easier to keep the children secluded.

Borges was taught to read Spanish by his mother and English by his grandmother. Later, an English tutor was employed. Once Borges could read he was free, even though he was sickly and solitary. "If I were asked to name the chief event in my life," he wrote, "I should say my father's library." He did not go to school until he was eleven. He must have been a strange sight, small, bookish, precocious, full of stories about heroic ancestors. He was bullied by other boys from the beginning until he was withdrawn from the school. "One of his recurrent nightmares as an adult," Williamson writes, "was of being tormented by dwarfs and little boys." Three years later he was sent to secondary school, but not for long. In 1913 his father decided to take the family to Europe the following year and educate the children in Geneva, where he could be treated by a famous doctor for an eye disease from which he suffered.

Thus, early in 1914, the Borges family rented out their property in Buenos Aires and began wandering in Europe. Like the James family, they would be dragged by a restless father from city to city, from hotel to rented quarters. As with William and Henry James, this life apart from his peers would be the making of

Borges as an artist, though it would mean that his life, when he later returned to Argentina, would be more complicated. Once more, school in Europe was a nightmare since he did not speak the same language as his classmates; once more, as his ability to read French improved, he found that the only comfort available was in books. He read Carlyle in English, and soon began to read philosophy in German. In 1917, when he was eighteen, he began a friendship with someone his own age, Maurice Abramowicz, who also loved books and poetry. It was the first of many such sustaining literary friendships.

The Borges family spent the war years in Switzerland; once the war was over they moved to Spain: first to Barcelona, then to Majorca, then to Seville and Madrid. Jorge Luis was writing poetry and allying himself with any young Spanish avant-garde writers he could find. The group with which he became involved in Seville and Madrid was called the Ultraísta movement. They were close in aims and style to the Imagists, and influenced by the work and personalities of Apollinaire and Marinetti. Borges loved staying up all night talking books and poetry, sitting in cafés and walking the streets. Madrid, where the family stayed for two months, was a perfect site for this; Borges got to know many of the leading young Spanish poets there. When he left Madrid to go back to Majorca with his family, he had young literary men in Madrid and in Geneva to write to regularly, sending new poems and letters of hope and despair about the work he was attempting. "I lack a goal," he wrote to Abramowicz, "or rather I have too many goals before me. I think I'm sunk, and won't be able to salvage more than two or three metaphors from the wreckage."

In 1921, after an absence of seven years, the family returned to Buenos Aires. Borges had very little formal education, no qualifications and no friends. He walked the streets of the Palermo district where he had grown up, and then began to explore other parts of the city, until the city itself became the subject of his first book of poems:

> *If things are void of substance*
> *And if this teeming Buenos Aires*
> *Is no more than a dream*
> *Made up by souls in a common act of magic,*
> *There is an instant*
> *When its existence is gravely endangered*
> *And that is the shuddering instant of daybreak.*

He was an exile in his own country. He wrote to a friend in Spain: "Don't abandon me in this exile of mine, which is over-run by arrivistes, by correct youths lacking any mental equipment, and by decorative young ladies." Once more, how-ever, he found a kindred spirit, a friend of his father's called Macedonio Fernández, who met with friends on a Saturday night in a café to discuss matters such as "the uses of metaphor or the inexistence of the self." In these first months in Buenos Aires, as his father promised and then postponed a return to Europe, Borges also began to write philosophical essays with titles like "The Nothingness of Personality" and "The Blue Sky Is Sky and Is Blue." Soon, he became involved in a number of literary magazines.

In July 1923 the Borges family, complete with Fanny Haslam, set sail for Europe again, spending a year wandering in England, France, Switzerland and the Iberian Peninsula. Borges renewed friendships in Madrid. Williamson in his biography is "virtually certain" that Borges met Lorca on this visit, but it is absolutely certain in any case that he read Lorca's work and paid real atten-tion to his efforts at blending folk poetry with the most modern techniques.

What Lorca was doing became for Borges and his friends in Argentina, as it would for writers in every country on the periphery, a working-out of a serious dilemma: whether to adopt a full European Modernist identity or to describe Argentina (or Trinidad, or Ireland) in all its colour and exotic variety to the world. If the second choice were to be taken in Argentina, there was a useful example: a long narrative poem, using a great deal of dialect, by José Hernández called *El Gaucho Martín Fierro*, the first part of which was published in 1872. The poem quickly became immensely popular, its six-line ballad-like stanzas glorifying the life of the Argentine pampas and the rough, brave cowboys who inhabited them. The poem was published in English in a translation by Walter Owen in 1935:

> *And on the spot like two mad bulls*
> *Into each other we tore;*
> *The man was quick, but a bit too rash,*
> *And a backhand slash soon settled his hash,*
> *And I left him grunting and thrashing about,*
> *With his tripes all over the floor.*

"The figure of the gaucho," Williamson writes, "thus came to embody the unresolved question of national identity, a question that would gnaw away at the Argentine conscience and would resurface periodically in a violent impulse to hold onto or to retrieve some vital essence that might be lost as Argentina acquired the trappings of a modern nation." Indeed, Hernández's impulse in writing the first part of the poem was to protest against Argentina turning its back on its heritage and becoming unduly modern and civilized.

In a lecture he gave in Buenos Aires in 1950 about gaucho literature, Borges very cleverly ducked the choice between Martín Fierro and a pure European example. He pointed out that the richness of gaucho literature in Argentina arose not from the gaucho's isolation but from the close relationship many of the gaucho writers had with the literary world of

Buenos Aires. "Gaucho poetry," he wrote, "is a perhaps unique fusion between the city spirit and rural forms." The following year, in a brilliant and wise lecture called "The Argentine Writer and Tradition," he returned to the subject, pointing out that *El Gaucho Martín Fierro* and other poems by Hernández's contemporaries did not come direct from an oral tradition, but were highly wrought literary artefacts. "I believe that Martín Fierro," he wrote, "is the most lasting work we Argentines have written; I also believe, with equal intensity, that we cannot take Martín Fierro to be, as has sometimes been said, our Bible, our canonical book." His argument was with critics who suggested that "the lexicon, techniques and subject-matter of gauchesco poetry should enlighten the contemporary writer, and are a point of departure and perhaps an archetype." He attacked the idea that "Argentine poetry must abound in Argentine differential traits and in Argentine local colour."

Borges admired *Martín Fierro*, then, for its self-conscious manipulation of language and for its hybrid nature. In 1924 he read Joyce's *Ulysses* and found a template for what he would view as the role of peripheral societies in the creation of literature. Of Irish writers he wrote:

The fact of feeling themselves to be Irish, to be different, was enough to enable them to make innovations in English culture. I believe that Argentines, and South Americans in general, are in an analogous situation; we can take on all the European subjects, take them on without superstition and with an irreverence that can have, and already has had, fortunate consequences.

This was written in 1951, when most of Borges's great work had been done, but as early as 1925 he was arguing the case for a new and strange cosmopolitanism that would also make a hero of the local: 'Already Buenos Aires, more than a city, is a country, and one must find the poetry and the music and the painting and the religion and the metaphysics that will do justice to its grandeur. That is the extent of my hope, which invites us all to be gods and to work towards its incarnation." Over the next few years, as he wrote a short biography of a minor poet of the city's suburbs, he would refine this view; he would come to see both his city and his country as places of estrangement and their legacy as thin; he would accept a need to create a universe in their stead and find a language precise enough to re-create the essential contours of that new world.

In 1951, to illustrate his point, he described his story "Death and the Compass," composed nine years earlier, as

a kind of nightmare, a nightmare in which elements of Buenos Aires appear, deformed by the horror of the nightmare; and in that story, when I think of the Paseo Colón, I call it Rue de Toulon, when I think of the *quintas* of Adrogué, I call them Triste-le-Roy; after the story was published my friends told me that at last they had found the flavour of the outskirts of Buenos Aires in my writing. Precisely because I had not abandoned myself to the dream, I was able to achieve, after so many years, what I once sought in vain.

In the early 1930s Borges began to consider what could be done in fiction. "He was proposing an aesthetics of radical mistrust," Williamson writes. "His basic contention was that fiction did not depend on the illusion of reality; what mattered ultimately was an author's ability to generate 'poetic faith' in his reader." Fiction, Borges believed, did not hold up a mirror to reality, instead it became "an autonomous sphere of corroborations, omens and monuments."

In 1931 the magazine *Sur* was launched by Victoria Ocampo, a member of one of the oldest and wealthiest families in Argentina, a woman "easily dictatorial and excessively bossy" in Borges's words. She would play a significant role in winning him fame as a writer. Borges continued to write essays and reviews and to take part in literary faction fighting. In 1933 he found his first real job, working on the literary supplement of a daily paper. Here he wrote a number of fictionalized biographies and some fables; he assembled them in his first book of fiction, *A Universal History of Infamy*, which was published in April 1935; by the end of the year it had sold thirty-seven copies. Borges had placed himself in what was for him a fortunate position of having no world to describe, except an invented one, and no audience to speak of, allowing him the luxury to address his fictions to one or two of his friends. The world could, if it pleased, listen in, but it would take time.

Bioy Casares, the reader who would matter most to Borges, came, like Ocampo, from the higher reaches of Argentine society. Ocampo introduced them in 1932, when Bioy was eighteen and Borges thirty-two. Borges's mother must have been pleased at his friendship with this scion of the cattle-ranching oligarchy whose father was a cabinet minister and whose family owned one of the most prominent dairy businesses in the country. Bioy was handsome, self-confident and well read. He would come to have what was perhaps the largest personal library in all of South America. He also owned an estate in the country where Borges spent some time in 1935. Both men loved recondite references, strange books, literary jokes. Bioy, like Borges, had no illusions about his fellow countrymen's interest in serious literature, but he had many other illusions and he sought now with his new friend to put them into print.

After Borges lost his job at the literary supplement, he began his career as a librarian in January 1938 in a working-class district on the other side of Buenos Aires. It was ignominious. There were so few books in the library that they did not need anyone to catalogue them; fifty people were doing a job that a third of them could have easily done. When Borges attempted to do some work, he was taken aside and told that he would ruin it for the rest of them. His colleagues had no interest in books. Borges did his day's work in an hour. The pay was miserable. In his "Autobiographical Essay," he wrote: "Sometimes in the evening, as I walked the ten blocks to the tramline, my eyes would be filled with tears." He kept sane by doing translations, including a selection of Kafka's stories. Soon after he started his work in the library his father died.

Over the next two years Borges published some of his best fiction. "Pierre Menard" appeared in *Sur* in May 1939, "Tlön, Uqbar, Orbis Tertius" a year later. In between, he wrote "The Library of Babel." In December 1940 *Sur* published "The Circular Ruins" and the following month "The Lottery in Babylon," and "A Survey of the Works of Herbert Quain" three months later. These were among the stories gathered into a book, *The Garden of Forking Paths*, which *Sur* published at the end of 1941. While the author's friends viewed this as a significant literary event, it failed to win any of the National Awards for Literature, the judges deeming it inappropriate to recommend to the Argentine people "an exotic and decadent work" that followed "certain deviant tendencies of contemporary English literature," hovering "between the tale of fantasy, a pretentious and recondite erudition, and detective fiction."

The eight stories that make up the sixty pages of *The Garden of Forking Paths* represent Borges's best work. For any biographer an exhumation and an autopsy of the years during which they were composed is a great challenge. It is hard to allow for the possibility that nothing, nothing at all, caused these to come into being. Borges did not keep diaries or write many letters; in interviews done years later he tended to be vague and misleading.

It is possible that certain things that happened in 1939 and 1940 mattered. His translating Kafka, for example; his having a magazine at his disposal with an imperious editor and an international circulation; his father's death; his dreadful job with seven or eight hours a day free to do nothing; his reading of Dante while travelling on the tram to and from work – or perhaps more importantly his claim to have done so; the outbreak of war and his deep opposition to the Nazi and Peronist regimes; his rejection by a woman with whom he had fallen in love; his need to amuse and impress Bioy Casares. Any biographer has to take these into account, and Williamson does so. He gives, however, an extraordinary emphasis in his book to Borges's relationship with a number of women, suggesting that these doomed and deeply unhappy relationships were fundamental to Borges's work.

Borges, it is true, spent much of his life hanging out with women who would neither sleep with him nor marry him. The advantage for any biographer is that if you throw a stone in Buenos Aires you are likely to hit one of these women or their many descendants, or indeed their volumes of memoir.

The story begins in Geneva where, it is said, Borges Senior asked his son, then aged nineteen, if he had ever slept with a woman. When Borges said no, his father arranged "to help the youth negotiate the usual rites of passage to manhood," as Williamson puts it, by giving him the address of a brothel and telling him that "a woman would be waiting there" at an appointed time. It was, of course, a disaster. Borges Junior was shocked at the idea that he was sharing a woman with his father. Afterwards, according to Williamson, the adolescent Borges was taken to see a doctor who recommended a change of climate and fresh air and exercise. Williamson's footnote for this points us to page 50 of María Esther Vázquez's *Borges: Esplendor y Derrota* (1996). Vázquez had known Borges well, but this is no excuse for her account of the aftermath of his visit to the brothel: "He had such a terrible crisis that he cried for three successive days; he did not eat nor sleep . . . he only cried." She goes on: "With the stoicism of a monk, this healthy young man seemed to give up the necessities of the body to find in literature the only source of satisfaction and enjoyment."

Even had Vázquez written that Borges cried for merely two days and then rose on the third, I would not believe a word of it. Nor do I believe the account in James Woodall's life of Borges, also published in 1996: "What happened is a matter for speculation. It seems probable that Georgie's virginity ended with the predictable fumbling and rush of any inexperienced teenage male, though he was especially horrified at the loss of physical self-possession at the moment of climax." Woodall points then to a reference to this disastrous sexual initiation in Borges's story "The Other," published in 1975. Borges, in the story, meets his double and tells him: "Nor have I forgotten a certain afternoon in a second-floor apartment on the Plaza Dubourg." His double corrects him: "Dufour." And he accepts the correction. Woodall quotes an earlier biographer who has, in his wisdom, pinpointed the place of assignation nominated by Borges Senior as the rue Général Dufour in Geneva.

It really is possible that all of this is rubbish, that, despite the breathless accounts by a number of his women friends who fell for the story, Borges's father never sent him to a brothel at all and that something much less dramatic – his first reading of Whitman, for example – happened on the Plaza, or rue, Dufour. Or else Borges put the name in for no reason, just as he briefly allowed in the same story American bank-notes to carry a date.

We do have real evidence, however, that Borges went to brothels in Majorca in 1921. His literary group used to meet in a brothel, or what innocent young men might have thought was a brothel. Borges wrote to the writer Guillermo de Torre, who would marry Norah in 1928, about "feeling up the breasts or thighs of the smiling, uncomprehending girls." And in a letter to Abramowicz, he wrote:

And then at roulette I enjoyed an unheard-of run of luck – at least for me – (60 pesetas with a capital of one peseta!) which allowed me to score three nights in a row at the brothel. A sumptuously filthy blonde, and a brunette we called "The Princess" on whose humanity I took off as if flying a plane or riding a horse.

He also wrote about his love for a prostitute called Luz: "I tell you, I really loved that Luz: she was so playful with me and behaved with such ingenuous indecency. She was like a cathedral and also like a bitch."

While it is possible that some of this is true, it reads more like boasting and is treated with caution by Williamson. Nonetheless, Borges himself, the arch-priest of pure invention trading as deep research, would surely have been appalled at the inability of Vázquez, Woodall, Williamson and many more who have not yet written their books to create at least the illusion of verisimilitude in their statements and assertions about his early sex life.

Williamson, however, follows every lead. Each intellectual woman who rejected Borges is given star treatment, and he cleverly finds clues in the poems and stories. Borges, during all this time, was living with his mother and going slowly blind. One evening, when he was out with one of his women friends, Estela Canto (who, in her book *Borges a contraluz*, would propagate the story of Borges and the brothel), Canto overheard him calling his mother on the telephone: "Yes, yes, Mother . . . Yes . . . from here we'll be going to the Ambassador . . . Yes, Mother. Estela Canto . . . Yes, Mother." He was forty-five years old. Williamson lists many of the other women with whom Borges was in love. For their names alone they deserve to be remembered: Norah Lange, Haydée Lange, Marta Mosquera Eastman, Susana Bombal, Esther Zemborain de Torres Duggan, Pippina Diehl de Moreno Hueyo, Beatriz Bibiloni Webster de Bullrich, Ema Risso Platero, Silvina Bullrich, Delia Ingenieros, to name but a few. Williamson's analysis of Borges's "single, involuntary criterion" in choosing these women is interesting. "He fell for women who would be unacceptable to Mother, either because they came from an inferior social class or because they did not meet the high standards of respectability required by Doña Leonor."

By the late 1950s, Borges was blind. Doña Leonor became, Williamson writes, "her son's secretary and business manager, his general guide and protector, and she had gathered about her a circle of well-bred ladies who fussed over Georgie and acted as an admiring chorus to his every success and distinction." One visitor remembered the maid asking Doña Leonor if she should pour some wine for Borges and the mother answering: "El niño no toma vino" ("niño here can mean both "boy" and "heir"). By this time Borges's work was winning attention in Europe, and he was being invited to lecture at universities in the United States. Some of the time his mother, now almost ninety, accompanied him.

Borges dreamed of marriage, of getting away from her. She helped him by suggesting a woman whom he had known years earlier, now widowed. She was called Elsa Astete. While Borges's mother liked her for her deference, nobody else did. She was not smart or high enough on the social scale for Bioy or his wife. Other friends of Borges thought her "frumpish, provincial and rather plain." They were married in 1967. The marriage was not a success.

Once more, Borges was luckier in his friendships than in his loves. In 1967, in the United States, he met the translator and writer Norman Thomas di Giovanni, then in his mid-thirties. Over the next few years, having moved to Buenos Aires, di Giovanni coordinated the translation of Borges's poetry into English, using some of the best contemporary poets and translators such as

Alastair Reid, Richard Wilbur and John Hollander. He also worked with Borges on translating his prose works into English, and coaxed him into producing new stories and a long autobiographical piece for the *New Yorker*. All of this is vividly described in *The Lesson of the Master: On Borges and His Work*, which di Giovanni published in 2003.

When Borges wanted to leave his wife, di Giovanni masterminded his departure. Since there was no divorce in Argentina in 1970, they had to move with care. Elsa had no clue that he was going to leave her. "That chill grey winter's morning," di Giovanni wrote,

I lay in wait for Borges in the doorway of the National Library, and the moment he arrived I leaped into his taxi and off we sped for the intown airport. Borges, a trembling leaf and utterly exhausted after a sleepless night, confessed that his greatest fear had been that he might blurt the whole thing out to Elsa at any moment.

Elsa was at home making *puchero*, a stew. She had asked Borges as he went out the door what he wanted for lunch. "What pained me most," she said in an interview in 1993, "was that when Borges asked for *puchero*, he already knew that he would not be coming back."

In the early years of the twenty-first century, Jorge Luis Borges and Bioy Casares joined Marcel Proust and Lillian Hellman to become a distinguished band of writers whose maids wrote books about them. Bioy's maid Jovina got in first; her book, *Los Bioy*, which is a wonderful account of half a century of service, appeared in 2002. It is clear that she felt affection for Bioy and his wife; despite her best intentions, however, she managed to portray them as capricious and mad and permanently horny, a wealthy pair of monsters, like two figures in an early Polanski film. Then in 2004 came Epifanía Uveda de Robledo, or Fanny, Borges's maid. She had revenge on her mind, for the slights inflicted on her by Borges's mother and the injuries, real or imaginary, inflicted by Maria Kodama, whom Borges married some months before his death. Fanny managed also in *El Señor Borges* to make her master seem like a saint and herself a reticent and faithful maid for whom one could, in all conscience, write a glowing reference.

In 1939 Bioy Casares married Silvina Ocampo, the sister of Victoria Ocampo. Silvina was twelve years older than he. Jovina came to work for them ten years later and stayed with them until the death of Bioy in 1999. Bioy loved women. He told Jovina: "I have a defect, Jovina, a great weakness. I love women so much that if a broomstick dressed up as a woman, I would follow that broomstick." Jovina realized that his marriage did not prevent him from broomsticking to his heart's content on a daily basis, usually in the afternoon: he played tennis in the morning, and in the evening wrote his books and had supper with his wife and Borges. When, after supper, he and Borges collaborated on their books, Jovina noticed that they roared with laughter.

Bioy made no bones about his affairs. One day, for example, he arrived home with a baby, who was thereafter brought up in his household as his daughter. Later, other fruits of his great sexual energy would emerge. Silvina believed that Jovina had powers and every time she sent one of her manuscripts or a manuscript by Bioy to the publishers she would make Jovina touch the pages to give them luck. Silvina depended on Jovina for the smallest things and demanded that her food be personally served by Jovina or she would not eat it. (Similarly, Borges's mother would ring for the maid in the middle of the night and explain that she merely wanted to see her.) When Bioy was in hospital he insisted that his meals be cooked and carried to the hospital by Jovina. He was, however, embarrassed at leaving the food the hospital provided, and suggested to Jovina that she could solve the problem by eating this food herself on her visits.

Jovina had to keep at bay the many women who wished to sleep with Bioy, including at times Elena, the wife of Octavio Paz, who had a long affair with him.

While Jovina wrote with relish and love and understanding of her employers' madnesses and foibles, Fanny, Borges's maid, wrote in some bitterness. Having worked for the family for more than thirty-five years, she was left homeless and almost penniless on Borges's death. Compared to the Bioys' household, where it was all go, Leonor Borges maintained a very respectable and stolid home life for herself and her son. The Borges apartment was tiny – the Bioys had twenty-two rooms – yet Fanny was forced to wear a uniform and cut her hair short; there was never a radio or a television in the apartment. Borges, she notes, was an obedient son. Every time he came home from somewhere he would go to his mother's bedroom and tell her what he had done. Then he would undress for bed and find Fanny and put out his hand and receive two sweets. He did this, according to Fanny, all his life.

Borges was much tortured, according to Fanny, by the possibility of winning the Nobel Prize. On the day of the announcement journalists would queue outside his door. This would happen year after year.

Fanny's book really comes into its own when Borges gets married. Borges the bachelor was dressed by Fanny every morning. "I dressed him entirely, including learning to make the knot of his tie. I put on his clothes, his socks, his shoes, his trousers, everything. Absolutely everything." The wife, however, told Fanny that every morning she opened a drawer and told Borges to dress himself. One day, as a result, he appeared with two odd shoes. The wife also forbade his old nightgown that went down to his ankles and made him wear pyjamas.

Fanny blames his mother for the wedding: "Doña Leonor was a good woman, but very authoritarian. It was the mother and the sister who arranged the wedding because he never said anything, never knew anything . . . They bought the furniture, they bought the apartment." The son, however, now sixty-eight years old, did not want to sleep with his new wife, and demanded that his old single bed be brought to the new apartment. On the wedding night his mother suggested that he and Elsa go to a hotel, but Borges wanted to sleep in his own bed and his mother had to accompany Elsa to the bus stop and send her home. In the morning when Fanny woke Borges she asked him how he had slept on his wedding night. He looked at her and smiled and said: "I dreamed all night that I was hanging out of a tram."

Maria Kodama, who features in the second half of Fanny's book, was born in 1937, the daughter of a German mother and a Japanese father. She appeared first in Borges's circle in the mid-1960s, attending his classes on Anglo-Saxon at the National Library in Buenos Aires. She gave off an aura of reticence, mystery and self-possession. Fanny remembered her coming to the Borges apartment with other students:

One day Maria stayed behind when the other students left and began to chat with Doña Leonor. Señor Borges's mother . . . asked her: "Are you in love with Georgie?" Kodama, perhaps a little surprised by the question, replied that no, she was in love with Borges's writing, but not with the man. When Maria had gone Doña Leonor said in a loud voice, but as though she were talking to herself: "That one with the yellow skin is going to end up with everything."

In 1971, after the break-up of his marriage, Borges travelled to Iceland, where he found Kodama waiting for him. It was here, it seems, that they became lovers. Back home, however, Borges returned to live with his mother, now ninety-five, and Fanny.

Leonor did not die until 1975, when she was ninety-nine. She was buried with the rest of her ancestors in the family vault in the Recoleta cemetery, where Borges himself would be expected to lie when his time came.

After his mother's death, Borges travelled with Kodama, but in Buenos Aires he did not let his sister or the maid or his closest friends know the truth of their relationship. Much that is cruel and unusual has been written about Kodama, but Williamson in his biography is not keen to add to these comments. He recognizes that for the last fifteen years of Borges's life, this was his closest and happiest relationship.

On 28 August 1979 Borges changed his will. Previously, he had left his estate to his sister and his two nephews; now, he left it to Kodama. He also left Fanny half of whatever money he had in his bank accounts, but later, in 1985, deleted this clause, leaving her very little. This obviously reflected his irritation at Fanny's disapproval of Kodama.

In the years between the death of his mother and his own death, Borges and Kodama seemed to be on a permanent book tour and appeared to derive nothing but pleasure from it. By the end of 1985, however, it was clear to Borges that he was dying. He wished to go back to Europe, but kept this a secret from many friends and from his sister. In the middle of December, he and Kodama arrived in Geneva. Kodama, in an interview in 1999, told Williamson:

He told me that we would be going to Italy and then we would stop over in Switzerland. I thought it was logical that he should wish to say his farewells, but when we arrived in Geneva, he said: "We're not going back, we're staying." It was clear to me that he had decided this beforehand, when he learned that he was going to die.

Works of genius come from strange sources. It is unimaginable that Borges or Bioy or Silvina Ocampo could have produced social realism in which domestic life would appear as a feature. All three created work that was playful, self-referential, that invented its own world partly because the world outside was not of much interest to them. It could be argued that Borges's fiction and poetry were essentially apolitical, that he was more interested in literature than life and that his work is all the better for this. But it is difficult for any writer in an unstable, emerging or peripheral country, no matter how enigmatic or strange the work, to remain outside politics.

It is also possible to argue that Borges's writing was indeed political, that he himself was a political activist all his life, that his lack of interest as an artist in the world outside the book arose from his and his mother's dislike of the dominant elements in Argentine society, that his style and his system developed not despite Argentine society but because of it.

Yet Borges's politics were not simple. In 1928, for example, he supported Hipólito Irigoyen of the Radical Party for the presidency, not merely because Borges's grandfather had been a friend of the party's founder, but because Irigoyen was more moderate in his nationalism and more open to democracy than his opponents. Borges wrote a manifesto in favour of Irigoyen, and signed a letter to the newspaper supporting him. Two years after Irigoyen's victory, when the military took over, Borges wrote to a friend in Brazil: "We have sacrificed Myth for the sake of realism . . . Now we have independence under martial law, a sycophantic press, the perpetual wrangling of the left-wingers, and the fiction that the former dotty administration was 'cruel and tyrannical.'"

The fact that his hero had been deserted by the people of Buenos Aires, who had ransacked Irigoyen's house, helped Borges to get over his idealization of the city. In 1931 he wrote a savage attack on his country in an essay, "Our Inabilities." He attacked the "pompous self-valorisation of the place our country occupies among the other nations" and "the unrestrainable delight in failure." Finally, he wrote, "a poverty of imagination defines our place in death." The old world of the criollo, so longed for by Borges's mother, could only be found, he said, in the northern provinces of Uruguay.

In 1934 Borges wrote the preface to a poem celebrating a failed armed uprising, which he called "a patriotic uprising," by militant members of the Radical Party. Yet, while some of his friends supported the reduction of Argentina's economic dependence on Britain, Borges understood that this would move them slowly towards a sort of Argentine nationalism bordering on fascism. His own views on what Argentina might become were outlined in 1928 and reiterated in a radio broadcast in 1936:

This is a confederacy without precedent: a generous adventure by men of different bloodlines whose aim is not to preserve their lineages but to forget those lineages in the end; these are bloodlines that seek the night. The criollo is one of the confederates. The criollo, who was responsible for creating the nation as such, has now chosen to be one among many.

In this speech, Borges wrote the death sentence for his family's sense of power and entitlement in Argentina.

As the 1930s went on and writers took sides, Borges moved sideways. There is no evidence that he even attended the PEN International Congress in Buenos Aires in September 1936, in which political division was the main feature. Instead, Borges and Bioy set up a magazine called *Destiempo*, whose title indicated, Bioy said, "our wish to have nothing to do with the superstitions of the age."

Borges felt a very deep attachment to an old and unsullied Argentina, but understood, as the 1930s went on, that such an attachment could lead easily to a native fascism. He wrote a number of trenchant attacks on Hitler's regime in Germany. He wrote in support of a cultural openness, an Argentine cosmopolitanism, but grew to believe, with some justification, that he and a few friends carried this banner alone. He ceased to believe in the city or its people, he believed that the pampas and the gauchos were sour jokes, he hated the government and he grew at times to distrust history, including his own. The way was open for him to write a fiction that would be distinguished by its pure determination to leave most things out.

The possibility that Borges would have a quiet life, writing his stories, seeing his women, pleasing and annoying his mother, supping with Bioy and working in the library, came to an end in February 1946 with the election of Perón, whom Borges had vehemently opposed. Borges's name was on a list of 2,000 state employees who, for one reason or another, were to be dismissed. In his "Autobiographical Essay," Borges wrote about what happened: "I was honoured with the news that I had been 'promoted' out of the library to the inspectorship of poultry and rabbits in the public markets." When he asked why, he was told (he claims): "You were on the side of the Allies – what do you expect?"

Williamson rightly deals with Borges's version of this story with suspicion. He argues convincingly that Perón himself would not have even known about such a low-level dismissal, that the job inspecting the "poultry and rabbits" was probably invented by Borges. He writes that Borges's being moved rather than completely dismissed was done as a favour to him, and that he was probably, in fact, appointed an inspector at the Department of Beekeeping: that is, apiculture rather than aviculture (poultry). But the latter job was too good a story even for the Peronist press, who gloated.

A crowded dinner was given in Borges's honour by his supporters. His speech against Perón was read out: "Dictatorships breed oppression; dictatorships breed servility; dictatorships breed cruelty; more loathsome still is the fact that they breed idiocy . . . Fighting these sad monotonies is one of the many duties of a writer. Need I remind readers of Martín Fierro . . . that individualism is an old Argentine virtue?" One of the younger writers at the dinner recalled that Borges at this time was regarded "as a sort of anti-Perón."

After a few months out of a job, Borges began to work as a teacher of literature, travelling through Argentina to give lectures:

At 47 I found a new and exciting life opening up for me. I travelled up and down Argentina and Uruguay, lecturing on Swedenborg, Blake, the Persian and Chinese mystics, Buddhism, gauchesco poetry, the Icelandic sagas, Heine, Dante, expressionism and Cervantes. Sometimes my mother or a friend accompanied me. Not only did I end up making far more money than at the library, but I enjoyed the work and felt that it justified me.

While Borges gave lectures, his mother, at the thought of Perón in the Casa Rosada, the president's house, went mad. "The Peronist threat to the constitution," Williamson writes, "brought out a latent, ancestral heroism in this formidable woman." In September 1948, at the age of seventy-two, she joined a demonstration against Perón. When the police came, a few ladies, including Doña Leonor and her daughter, stood their ground and were arrested. They were sentenced to thirty days in jail; Leonor, because of her age, was allowed to spend a month under house arrest, but Norah spent a month in jail in the company of prostitutes.

In 1950, when Perón had effectively made himself president for life, Borges agreed reluctantly to become president of the Argentine Society of Writers. "I tried to think as little as possible about politics," he wrote.

All the same, just as a person who has toothache thinks about that toothache the moment he wakes up, or a man who has been left by a woman thinks about her the moment he opens his eyes, I used to say to myself every morning, "That man is in the Casa Rosada," and I would feel upset, and in a way, guilty too, because I thought of the fact of not doing anything or doing so little – but what could I do?

"In every lecture I gave, I would always express my views against the government," Borges wrote. "Many distinguished men of letters did not dare set foot inside the doors of the Society of Writers." After the death of Eva Perón in 1952, when Borges refused to put up a portrait of Perón and his dead wife on the walls of the society's premises, the society was closed.

After the fall of Perón in 1955, Borges wrote: "I remember the joy we felt; I remember that at that moment no one thought about themselves: their only thought was that the patria had been saved." Within weeks, with the help of Victoria Ocampo, among others, he was appointed director of the National Library. Doña Leonor was delighted; the family was being restored to a position of importance.

The fall of Perón represented a problem for his opponents. It was clear that in any free election he would win, with considerable support from the trade unions and the city's poor. Nonetheless, he was a demagogue who behaved like a dictator. He was replaced by the military, themselves representatives of an old oligarchy. Borges supported the new regime wholeheartedly as they banned the Peronist party, including banners, symbols and music. When a further military coup, led by men who wished to allow free elections, was put down, the government, ignoring the sentences handed down by a military tribunal, executed thirty-two of the rebels by firing squad.

Elections were held, with Perón and his party banned. Perón ordered his supporters to return blank ballot papers and these numbered more than the votes for the legal parties. Borges and Bioy drew up a manifesto to support the government. Borges wrote that Argentina was rapidly recovering its health, "but there still remain many recalcitrant patients who refuse to get better and who resist revolutionary therapy. We shall have to persist with the treatment, increasing the dose of democracy for the more rebellious to see if they can be cured once and for all." Borges, for his support, was rewarded with the Chair of English and American Literature at the University of Buenos Aires. In his "Autobiographical Essay," he gives a funny, folksy version of the reason for his appointment: "Other candidates had sent in pains-taking lists of their translations, papers, lectures and other achievements. I limited myself to the following statement: 'Quite unwittingly, I have been qualifying myself for this position throughout my life.' My plain approach gained the day." This is rubbish. He got the job because of his support for the regime. His mother, who had conspired to get it for him, had thus further reason for joy.

Other writers, who were as anti-Peronist as Borges, were appalled by the new government and Borges's blanket support for it. These included Ernesto Sabato. Borges's predicament is put succinctly by Williamson: "How do you create a democracy when the largest sector of the electorate will elect a totalitarian leader who is ideologically opposed to liberal democracy?" In 1963, as Perón increased his influence, and new elections were called, Borges left the Radical Party and joined the Conserva-tives, believing them to have better anti-Peronist credentials. He allowed them to hold a reception to announce his membership, at which he made a speech.

The spectre of Perón continued to haunt Argentina. In 1973 his party, once more legalized, won the election, which paved the way for his return. Borges told an Italian newspaper that those who voted for Perón were "six million idiots." He was now too famous to be fired from his job and was told that he could remain without interference. He resigned, however, in October 1973. Nine months later, Perón died, to be replaced by his widow, Isabelita.

Borges had lost his arch-enemy. He had no one now to denounce except the people. "Our country," he said in 1975, "is going through a moral crisis. We have taken to worshipping luxury, money and other myths and dogmas. I think ours is a venal country." Around this time Naipaul came to Argentina to cast his cold eye on Borges and his country. He made many sweeping statements, including the following two marvellous sentences: "There is no history in Argentina. There are no archives; there are only graffiti, polemics and school lessons." Perón, Borges told Naipaul, "represented the scum of the earth."

"For the contemplation of his country's history," Naipaul wrote, "Borges substitutes ancestor worship." But in the second half of the 1970s, as the Peronists developed a terrorist army, a new breed of army general emerged in control of the country. The myth of a military splendour that had created Argentina, and the sense of glamorous lone knife-fighters, both of which had nourished Borges's work, became a pale parody of what was really happening in the streets of his city. "Perhaps, then," Naipaul wrote, "parallel with the vision of art, there has developed, in Borges, a subsidiary vision, however unacknowledged, of reality. And now, at any rate, the real world can no longer be denied."

The real world came to Borges in the guise of the young men who visited his apartment to read to him. Buenos Aires is now full of them. The best account of that experience is by Alberto Manguel in *A History of Reading* (1996) and *With Borges* (2004):

In that sitting-room, under a Piranesi engraving of circular Roman ruins, I read Kipling, Stevenson, Henry James, several entries of the Brockhaus German encyclopedia, verses of Marino, of Enrique Banchs, of Heine (but these last ones he knew by heart, so I would barely have begun my reading when his hesitant voice picked up and recited from memory; the hesitation was only in the cadence, not in the words themselves, which he remembered unerringly) . . . I was the driver, but the landscape, the unfurling space, belonged to the one being driven . . . Borges chose the book, Borges stopped me or asked me to continue, Borges interrupted to comment, Borges allowed the words to come to him. I was invisible.

Paul Theroux in *The Old Patagonian Express* (1979) remembered reading Kipling ballads to the blind old man, being stopped after every few stanzas as Borges exclaimed how beautiful they were, his favourite being "The Ballad of East and West." Evita, he told Theroux, was "a common prostitute," as the writer, taking a more benign view than Naipaul, went back to see him again and again.

He stayed up late, eager to talk, eager to be read to; and he was good company. By degrees, he turned me into Boswell . . . There was something of the charlatan in him – he had a way of speechifying, and I knew he was repeating something he had said a hundred times before. He had the beginnings of a stutter, but he calmed that with his hands. He was occasionally magisterial, but he could be the opposite, a kind of student, his face elfin with attentiveness, his fingers locked together. His face became aristocratic in repose, and when he bared his yellow teeth in the exaggerated grin he used to show pleasure – he laughed hard at his own jokes – his face came alight and he looked like a French actor who has realized that he has successfully stolen the show.

In 1976 Isabelita Perón's government was replaced by a military dictatorship, the most murderous regime in Argentine history. As in 1955, Borges was so pleased at the end of the Peronist regime that he was happy to support the new one. He had lunch with General Videla and thanked him "for what he had done for the patria, having saved it from chaos, from the abject state we were in, and, above all, from idiocy." This support was noted by Chile; Pinochet offered him an Order of Merit, which he accepted. He then agreed, against the advice of his friends, to visit Chile to accept an honorary doctorate. He attended a private dinner with Pinochet. He made a mad speech praising the sword of his ancestors and the sword that was "drawing the Argentine republic out of the quagmire." This would not have helped him to win the Nobel Prize for which he was heavily tipped that year.

Nor would his remarks on a visit to Spain in 1976 have done him much good. He called Videla's regime "a government of soldiers, of gentlemen, of decent people." He declared his admiration for what General Franco had done in Spain. He then, sounding like Salvador Dalí, made rude remarks about Lorca:

Neither he nor his poetry have ever interested me. I think he's a minor poet, a picturesque poet, a sort of professional Andalusian . . . The circumstances of his death were rather favourable to him; it's convenient for a poet to die in that fashion and, what's more, his death provided Antonio Machado with the opportunity to write a marvellous poem.

Like a good number of Argentines, Borges discovered the truth of what was happening when he was outside Argentina. In Spain in 1980, where he received the Cervantes Prize, the highest honour that can be given to a writer in the Spanish language, he indicated a change of heart about the regime. While he had refused to support the Mothers of the Plaza de Mayo, who were the first to protest openly about the disappearances, he soon began to relent. Later, in Argentina, he was visited by a woman from an old Buenos Aires family who told him that her daughter had disappeared. He told her "he lived a very insulated life because he was blind and could not read the newspapers," but that he believed her story. When she brought a friend whose daughter had also disappeared, Borges decided to sign a petition calling on the government to provide information on the fate of the disappeared. He persuaded Bioy to sign also. In a dispute between Argentina and Chile over islands in the Beagle Channel, he supported Chile. Nonetheless, Borges's new dislike of the regime was not unequivocal. Even by the end of 1981 he would say: "I think this government is a necessary evil because democracy would give us another Frondizi" – one of the leaders of the Radical Party in the 1950s – "or at worst another Perón."

Once the Falklands War was over – he had described it as "two bald men fighting over a comb" – he could no longer maintain the view that the military government was a necessary evil. He revised his position.

It is true we have had dictators . . . but they had popular support. These are gangsters. This is a country of madmen. No, this is a country of wise but desperate people in the hands of madmen . . . I believe our only hope is democracy. Our only way out is an election . . . If elections are held the Peronists will win . . . and if they aren't held we shall continue to be governed by people who are equally discredited.

In the end, when the election was won by Raúl Alfonsín of the Radical Party in 1983, Borges said: "We had emerged from a nightmare, and that collective act of faith was what could save us all."

For 1984 and 1985, however, Argentina was forced to relive the nightmare, first through the commission of inquiry into the disappearances chaired by Ernesto Sabato, which reported in December 1984, and then by the trial of the generals, with evidence given by the relatives of the disappeared and by those who were tortured. Borges attended this trial in July 1985 and heard evidence of torture. He expressed his horror to reporters afterwards and in an open letter to a newspaper.

It must have occurred to him that his own earlier support for the generals was well remembered. As Alfonsín's position slowly weakened in 1985, Borges realized that one or other of the parties he now hated – the Peronists or the military – would retake power in Argentina. On 16 October, in an interview with a Swiss journalist, he expressed the wish to become a Swiss citizen and to die in Switzerland. In the new will in which he disinherited Fanny, he also left his sister his share in the family tomb in the Recoleta cemetery, where his mother was buried.

His final journey to Europe with Maria Kodama would become controversial in Argentina. Fanny insisted he did not wish to leave: "Of one thing I am sure: Señor Borges did not want to go, but he did not have sufficient energy to oppose whoever brought him. He said to me in a half-broken voice: 'Fanny, I don't want to go, I don't want to go.'"

This, considering the evidence, seems unlikely. His going alone to Europe with Kodama knowing that he would not return to Argentina seems to have been a deliberate act. In a late poem, "The Web," he began:

> *Which of my cities will I die in?*
> *Geneva, where revelation came to me*
> *Through Virgil and Tacitus, certainly not from Calvin?*

After the Falklands War he had also written a poem, "The Confederates," in favour of Switzerland, praising its "tower of reason and firm faith" where different races and religions and languages had "resolved to forget their differences and accentuate their affinities." He made it the title poem of his last book of verse.

On 26 April, while in Geneva, Borges and Maria Kodama were married by proxy in Paraguay. He died in Geneva on 14 June. He is buried close to John Calvin in the Cimetière de Pleinpalais, also known as the Cemetery of the Kings, close to the old city in Geneva. It is a calm, unostentatious cemetery, with single graves

mostly of famous people, the very opposite in tone to the Recoleta in Buenos Aires in which baroque and gothic-windowed
family vaults do battle with the rococo and the overadorned.
Borges's gravestone was clearly designed by Kodama with references and images that mattered to them both in their relationship.
In death, his grave did not make him an Argentine hero, but
rather the husband of a woman he had loved for the last fifteen
years of his life. After Borges's death, Kodama did not make
many friends among his family and associates. Both Norah
Borges's sons and Fanny sought to have the revised will thrown
out, but they lost. Kodama runs Borges's estate.

In 1999 Kodama told Edwin Williamson that Borges was fully
aware of the political import of his dying in Geneva and his wishing to be buried there. "You see," Borges had told her, "I've
become a kind of myth, and whenever the issue arises of my
being buried over here, people may recall the book I have written, *The Confederates*, and they'll think about it, people will come
here and ask themselves: why? That will be my small contribution to changing the world."

In Buenos Aires, Norah Borges made a statement: "I have
heard through the newspapers that my brother has died in
Geneva, far from us and from many friends, of a terrible illness
that we did not know he had. I am surprised that his last wish was
to be buried there, he always wanted to be with his ancestors and
with our mother in the Recoleta."

While Kodama suggested that Borges's reasons for dying in
Geneva were essentially political and public, there were also private reasons. Borges spoke a great deal about his father in the last
weeks. His father had taken him to this city at the age of fifteen
in an effort to civilize him, to remove him from the world of his
ancestors to a place where the shadows were more complex and
rich, from a place, run by his mother, where battles were glori-
fied, to a place, run by his father, where poetry would matter and

becoming a writer could be a real vocation. His father, Borges had written, "was such a modest man that he would have liked being invisible." Now, in the weeks before his death, Borges wrote to the Spanish news agency EFE asking to be left alone: "I am a free man. I have decided to stay in Geneva, because I associate Geneva with the happiest days of my life . . . I think it strange that someone should not understand and respect this decision by a man who, like a certain character of Wells's, has resolved to be an invisible man."

# Hart Crane: Escape from Home

There are certain single volumes of American poetry, some of them first books or early books, that carry with them a special and spiritual power; they seem to arise from a mysterious impulse and to have been written from an enormous private or artistic need. The poems are full of a primal sense of voice, and the aura of the voice in the rhythms of the poem suggests a relentless desire not to make easy peace with the reader. If some of these poems have the tone of prayers, they are not prayers of comfort or of supplication as much as urgent laments or cries from the depths where the language has been held much against its will or has broken free, and now demands to be heard.

Such tones can be found in the very opening lines of the first poem in Brigit Pegeen Kelly's *Song* (1995):

> *Listen: there was a goat's head hanging by ropes in a tree.*
> *All night it hung there and sang. And those who heard it*
> *Felt a hurt in their hearts and thought they were hearing*
> *The song of a night bird.*

Or Louise Glück's *The Wild Iris* (1992):

> *At the end of my suffering*
> *there was a door.*
> *Hear me out: that which you call death*
> *I remember.*

Or the first lines of "Epistle," the first poem of Li-Young Lee's first book, *Rose* (1986):

*Of wisdom, splendid columns of light*
*waking sweet foreheads,*
*I know nothing*

*but what I've glimpsed in my most hopeful of daydreams.*
*Of a world without end,*
*amen,*

*I know nothing,*
*but what I sang of once with others,*
*all of us standing in the vaulted room.*

In "General Aims and Theories," written in 1925, Hart Crane tried to outline his sense of where this tone, so apparent in his own work, came from: "I am concerned," he wrote,

with the future of America, but not because I think that America has any so-called par value as a state or as a group of people . . . It is only because I feel persuaded that here are destined to be discovered certain as yet undefined spiritual qualities, perhaps a new hierarchy of faith not to be developed so completely elsewhere. And in this process I like to feel myself as a potential factor; certainly I must speak in its terms and what discoveries I may make are situated in its experience.

As is clear from his early letters, Crane as a reader set about preparing himself with enormous zeal and moral seriousness to become that "potential factor." Despite his provincial background and his problems with his parents, and then partly because of them, he found a tone and a poetic diction that matched a sensibility that was both visionary and deeply rooted in the real. In his poems he worked a gnarled, edgy sound against the singing line; he played a language dense with metaphor and suggestion against images and rhythms of pure soaring beauty. His syntax had something hard and glittering in it, utterly surprising. In his best poems he managed to make the rhythms – the hidden nervous system in the words and between the words – so interesting, intense and effortless that they command attention and emotional response despite their verbal density, basic difficulty and what Crane himself called "tangential slants, interwoven symbolisms."

Even though most of his poems were written when he was in his twenties – he was born in 1899 and committed suicide in 1932 – there is a definite sense from the few essays that Crane wrote and from the selection of his richly interesting correspondence now collected with his poems in a single volume that he had put considerable thought into his literary heritage and viewed his place in it with passionate sophistication. In 1926, in a letter to the editor of *Poetry*, Harriet Monroe, replying to her complaints about obscurity in his poem "At Melville's Tomb," Crane set down his defense of his poetry and offered one of his most detailed and useful explanations of what his lines actually meant, while making it clear that their meaning, while concrete and direct, was a dull business indeed compared to what we might call their force. The first stanza reads:

> *Often beneath the wave, wide from this ledge*
> *The dice of drowned men's bones he saw bequeath*
> *An embassy. Their numbers as he watched,*
> *Beat on the dusty shore and were obscured.*

"Take me for a hard-boiled unimaginative unpoetic reader, and tell me how *dice* can *bequeath an embassy* (or anything else)," Monroe wrote. Crane in his reply admitted that:

as a poet I may very possibly be more interested in the so-called illogical impingements of the connotations of words on the consciousness (and their combinations and interplay in metaphor on this basis) than I am interested in the preservation of their logically rigid significations at the cost of limiting my subject matter and perceptions involved in the poem.

In his next paragraph he emphasized, however, that there was nothing aleatory in his method. "This may sound," he wrote,

as though I merely fancied juggling words and images until I found something novel, or esoteric; but the process is much more predetermined and objectified than that. The nuances of feeling and observation in a poem may well call for certain liberties which you claim the poet has no right to take. I am simply making the claim that the poet does have that authority, and that to deny it is to limit the scope of the medium so considerably as to outlaw some of the richest genius of the past.

He then took Monroe through some lines of the poem, including "The dice of drowned men's bones he saw bequeath / An embassy." "Dice bequeath an embassy," he wrote,

in the first place, by being ground (in this connection only, of course) in little cubes from the bones of drowned men by the action of the sea, and are finally thrown up on the sand, having "numbers" but no identification. These being the bones of dead men who never completed their voyage, it seems legitimate to refer to them as the only surviving evidence of certain messages undelivered, mute evidence of certain things, experiences that the dead mariners might have had to deliver. Dice as a symbol of chance and circumstance is also implied.

Monroe had commented as well on the opening of the last stanza:

> *Compass, quadrant and sextant contrive*
> *No farther tides . . .*

"Nor do compass, quadrant and sextant," she wrote, "*contrive* tides, they merely record them, I believe."

"Hasn't it often occurred," Crane replied,

that instruments originally invented for record and computation have inadvertently so extended the concepts of the entity they were invented to measure (concepts of space, etc.) in the mind and imagination that employed them, that they may metaphorically be said to have extended the original boundaries of the entity measured?

In the same letter, he quoted from Blake and T. S. Eliot to show how the language of the poetry he wrote and admired did not simply ignore logic, it sought to find a logic deeply embedded in metaphor and suggestion. This poetry, he made clear, did not follow the lazy path dictated by the unconscious, or allow the outlandish or the merely associative to triumph, but was deliberate and exact, even though it belonged "to another order of experience than science." He worked towards both "great vividness and accuracy of statement," even if it might seem to some, including Monroe, that the vivid triumphed over the accurate.

Harold Hart Crane was born in Ohio, where his father owned a factory that made syrup, and later founded the Crane Chocolate Company, which manufactured candy. (His father invented the type of candy known as Life Savers.) The relationship between Crane's parents was often difficult, with many separations and reconciliations; Crane at the age of nine was sent to live with his maternal grandmother, Elizabeth Belden Hart, to whom he became very close. He shared a certain emotional instability with his mother, who joined the Christian Scientists. At sixteen he attempted suicide on the Isle of Pines off Cuba, a property owned by his mother's family.

From an early age Crane expressed his interest in becoming a poet. At seventeen, he published his first poem in a magazine. Entitled "C 33," it was about the trial and imprisonment of Oscar Wilde:

> *He has woven rose-vines*
> *About the empty heart of night,*
> *And vented his long mellowed wines*
> *Of dreaming on the desert white*
> *With searing sophistry.*
> *And he tented with far truths he would form*
> *The transient bosoms from the thorny tree.*
> *O Maternal! to enrich thy gold head*
> *And wavering shoulders with a new light shed*
> *From penitence, must needs bring pain,*
> *And with it song of minor, broken strain.*
> *But you who hear the lamp whisper through night*
> *Can trace paths tear-wet, and forget all blight.*

That same year, when he submitted poems to the magazine *Others* he was told by William Carlos Williams that they were "damn good stuff."

Part of the reason for Crane's supreme self-confidence and precocious ambition arose from the fact that his enthusiasm for writing was not watered down by much formal education. His reading became a way of escaping from the war between his parents. In his youth he found the poets he was looking for in the same way as rushing water will find a steep incline. He read Shakespeare, Drayton, Donne, Blake, Keats, Shelley, Coleridge, Whitman, Poe, Baudelaire, Rimbaud and Eliot with delight, and also the work of the Jacobean dramatists. And in the same years he could also list the poets whose work he disliked; they included Milton, Byron, Tennyson and Amy Lowell.

In 1917 his mother suggested that he drop the "Harold" when he published his poems: "In signing your name to your contributions & later to your books do you intend to ignore your mother's side of the house entirely . . . How would 'Hart Crane' be?" His father disapproved of his interest in becoming a writer: "Poetry is alright; your chosen vocation is alright, but when you are living in New York and spending $2 a week for tutoring [in French], out of an allowance of $25, it is not alright; it isn't as things should be."

In his late teens and early twenties Crane moved between New York and Cleveland, getting intermittent support, financial and emotional, from one or the other of his parents, and making literary friends, including Sherwood Anderson, whom he admired, and later Allen Tate, Waldo Frank and Eugene O'Neill, and meeting editors wherever he could. He had a number of homosexual love affairs. He read Dostoevsky with considerable interest, and "that delightful *Moby Dick*," and then a smuggled copy of James Joyce's *Ulysses*, writing to a friend: "He is the one above all others I should like to talk to." Eventually, having worked at odd jobs and published poems in magazines, he went to work for his father's company. But relations were difficult and Crane severed contact with his father for more than two years. He began working as an advertising copywriter the following year and held jobs in advertising agencies in Cleveland and New York between periods that he devoted to either writing or drinking or both.

Among poets and readers of poetry, Crane established a reputation as the most promising poet of his generation. In 1925, after his father refused to give him an allowance, the millionaire Otto Kahn gave him $2,000 to work on his long, ambitious poem *The Bridge*. In December 1926 his first book of poems, *White Buildings*, was published. His drinking increased, as did his erratic wandering and his constant difficulties with his parents. Like most young men of his age he wanted love from his mother and money from his father. Neither parent felt fully able to satisfy his needs, but by doing so sporadically, they seemed instead to magnify certain vulnerabilities in him.

In December 1928 Crane travelled to Europe, seeing Robert

Graves and Laura Riding in London and André Gide and Gertrude Stein in Paris. He continued working on *The Bridge*, which was published in a limited edition in Paris in 1930 and subsequently in a trade edition in New York. He moved to New York, where he wore out his welcome in a number of friends' houses, then back to Cleveland, and then travelled to Mexico in 1931. He was still drinking. On 27 April 1932, while returning to the United States from Mexico aboard the *Orizaba*, he jumped from the deck and drowned. His myth as the *poète maudit*, the doomed, wild, homosexual genius, America's Rimbaud, had begun; his very name was a warning to the young about the dangers and the delights of poetry. It was a myth that even the seriousness and the immense slow force of his poems and the studious tone of many of his letters would do little to dispel.

In April 1917 Crane wrote to his father of his great ambition: "I shall really without doubt be one of the foremost poets in America if I am enabled to devote enough time to my art." The poetry he intended to write was to be highly wrought and full of self-conscious and hard-won artistry. Although there are times in his work when a word or a phrase seems chosen at random, selected for its sound as much as its sense, his letters emphasize that he was not interested in a dream language or summoning his phrases at random from the well of the unconscious. In January 1921 he wrote to a friend about the Dadaist movement: "I cannot figure out just what Dadaism is beyond an insane jumble of the four winds, the six senses and plum pudding." And two weeks later he wrote to another friend: "There is little to be gained in any art, so far as I can see, except with much *conscious* effort." Later that year, he wrote again: "I admit to a slight leaning toward the esoteric, and am perhaps not to be taken seriously. I am fond of things of great fragility, and also and especially of the kind of poetry John Donne represents, a dark musky, brooding, speculative vintage, at once sensual and spiritual, and singing the beauty of experience rather than innocence."

The following year he wrote to Allen Tate: "Let us invent an idiom for the proper transposition of jazz into words! Something clean, sparkling, elusive!" In these letters from 1922, as he worked on his poem "For the Marriage of Faustus and Helen," he wrote to friends of the sheer effort each line took and the burden of symbolic meaning he was asking the words to carry. "What made the first part of my poem so good," he wrote, "was the extreme amount of time, work and thought put on it." In a letter to Waldo Frank in February 1923, he tried to indicate his intentions: "Part I starts out from the quotidian, rises to evocation, ecstasy and statement. The whole poem is a kind of fusion of our own time with the past. Almost every symbol of current significance is matched by a correlative, suggested or actually stated, 'of ancient days.'"

In an earlier letter, he made clear also that the second part of the poem was "a jazz roof garden description in amazing language."

> A thousand light shrugs balance us
> Through snarling hails of melody.
> White shadows slip across the floor
> Splayed like cards from a loose hand;
> Rhythmic ellipses lead into canters
> Until somewhere a rooster banters.

For anyone in those years writing poems that attempted to fuse deliberate and difficult structure with phrases filled with allusion and symbolic meaning, using rhythms that sought to seduce the reader with a mixture of the subtle and the strident, it was obvious that T. S. Eliot was an example to be welcomed and watched. Crane read *The Waste Land* as soon as it appeared. He was alert to the power of Eliot's influence and also to his own need both to absorb and to evade it. "There is no one writing in English who can command so much respect, to my mind, as Eliot," he wrote. "However, I take Eliot as a point of departure toward an almost complete reverse of direction . . . I feel that Eliot ignores certain spiritual events and possibilities as real and powerful now as, say, in the time of Blake."

The letters suggest that the poems Crane wrote came only with enormous concentration at times when he managed to make a densely packed music in his poetry that matched or impelled his complex aims in meaning and structure. His work did not come with the same effortless grace with which the poems of William Carlos Williams or Wallace Stevens, two poets whom he admired, seemed to come, and which allowed them to hold down jobs with ease and have what appeared, on the surface at least, a calm domestic life. The life Crane lived when he was not writing was troubled and messy, as his biographers have described.

For this reason, it is useful to have more than 500 pages of Crane's selected letters in the same volume as the poems that were published in his lifetime and the unpublished poems. The picture of the poet here is rather less alarming than the one that appears in the biographies. He seems at times almost dull, often thoughtful and responsible, and quite bookish. If his life in the letters is colourful, then the colour comes from the naked quality of Crane's ambition and the complex sensibility he exposed to his correspondents. His letters also throw real and sensuous light on the actual poems themselves as they were being written. Indeed, when he was not writing to his immediate family, Crane was writing almost exclusively to friends who were poets or who cared about poetry.

Early in 1923 he wrote to a friend about his plans for *The Bridge*:

I am too much interested in this *Bridge* thing lately to write letters, ads or anything. It is just beginning to take the least outline, – and the more outline the conception of the thing takes, – the more its final dif- ficulties appall me . . . Very roughly, it concerns a mystical synthesis of "America." History and fact, location, etc. all have to be transfigured into abstract form that would almost function independently of its subject matter . . . The marshalling of the forces . . . will take me months, at best; and I may have to give it up entirely before that; it may be too impossible an ambition. But if I do succeed, such a waving of banners, such ascent of towers, such dancing etc, will never before have been put down on paper!

Early the following year in New York, Crane met and fell in love with Emil Opffer, three years his senior, who worked in the mer- chant marine. Opffer found him lodgings at 110 Columbia Heights in Brooklyn in a house inhabited by Opffer's father, who was a newspaper editor, and other bohemians and artists. (John Dos Passos lived in the building for a while.) Crane wrote to his mother and grandmother about his new quarters: "Just imagine looking out your window directly on the East River with nothing inter- vening between your view of the statue of Liberty, way down the harbor, and the marvelous beauty of Brooklyn Bridge close above you on your right!" It was as though he had walked into his own poem. "I think," he wrote to Waldo Frank, "the sea has thrown itself upon me and been answered, at least in part, and I believe I am a little changed – not essentially, but changed and transubstan- tiated as anyone is who has asked a question and been answered." Again he wrote to his mother and grandmother about the view:

Look far to your left toward Staten Island and there is the statue of Liberty, with that remarkable lamp of hers that makes her seen for miles. And up to the right Brooklyn Bridge, the most superb piece of construction in the modern world, I'm sure, with strings of lights crossing it like glowing worms as the Ls and surface cars pass each other going and coming.

He confided to his mother about the poems he was writing:

There's no stopping for rest, however, when one is in the "current" of creation, so to speak, and so I've spent all of today at one or two stubborn lines. My work is becoming known for its formal perfection and hard glowing polish, but most of those qualities, I'm afraid, are due to a great deal of labor and patience on my part . . . Besides working on parts of my *Bridge* I'm engaged in writing a series of six sea poems called "Voyages" (they are also love poems) . . . I feel as though I were well arranged for a winter of rich work, reading and excitement – there simply isn't half time enough (that's my main complaint) for all that is offered.

In 1925 Crane moved home to Cleveland for a time and then to Patterson in upstate New York, where he shared a farmhouse with Allen Tate and Tate's wife Caroline Gordon before he fell out with them with much bitter correspondence and recrimination, some of which reads like high comedy. He desperately needed somewhere to work on his long poem before the money Otto Kahn had given him ran out. And just as his move to Brooklyn seemed to come as a piece of almost uncanny good fortune, allowing him to inhabit parts of the poem as he conceived of them, now he made another move that was to provide him with images, metaphors and suggestions fully matching the grandeur of his design. He had appealed to his mother to allow him to go to her property on the Isle of Pines, where he had not been since he was sixteen. She was at first uneasy about the idea, feeling, among other things, that he would disturb the housekeeper, but soon she relented. In early May 1926 Crane voyaged towards the scenes of some of the later sections of *The Bridge*.

Slowly, in what seemed like an undiscovered country waiting for its Columbus, he began to work, reading, planning his poem further, and then writing:

> *Here waves climb into dusk on gleaming mail;*
> *Invisible valves of the sea, – locks, tendons*
> *Crested and creeping, troughing corridors*
> *That fall back yawning to another plunge.*
> *Slowly the sun's red caravel drops light*
> *Once more behind us . . . It is morning there –*
> *O where our Indian emperies lie revealed,*
> *Yet lost, all, let this keel one instant yield!*

He worked on some of the earlier as well as the later sections, including "Atlantis." He wrote to a friend in New York: "I've been having a great time reading *Atlantis in America*, the last book out on the subject, and full of exciting suggestions. Putting it back for 40 or 50 thousand years, it's easy to believe that a continent existed in mid-Atlantic waters and that the Antilles and West Indies are but salient peaks of its surface."

In August 1926 he wrote to Waldo Frank: "I have never been able to live *completely* in my work before. Now it is to learn a great deal. To handle the beautiful skeins of this myth of America – to realize suddenly, as I seem to, how much of the past is living under only slightly altered forms, even in machinery and such-like, is extremely exciting."

He sent the sections of *The Bridge* as he finished them to editors and friends. On 22 July he sent Marianne Moore his poem "To Brooklyn Bridge" for *The Dial* (which she accepted); it would be the prologue for his long poem. Two days later he wrote to Waldo Frank: "That little prelude, by the way, I think to be almost the best thing I've ever written, something steady and uncompromising about it." Its last two stanzas read:

> *Under thy shadow by the piers I waited;*
> *Only in darkness is thy shadow clear.*
> *The City's fiery parcels all undone,*
> *Already snow submerges an iron year . . .*

> *O Sleepless as the river under thee,*
> *Vaulting the sea, the prairies' dreaming sod,*
> *Unto us lowliest sometime sweep, descend*
> *And of the curveship lend a myth to God.*

Crane was well aware that an epic poem could not be written in America in the 1920s. Such a poem would, he knew, because of its very ambition, be doomed to failure or something close to failure. This idea seemed, most of the time, to excite him. He was, it is important to remember, a poet in his twenties. At times he saw that the symbols would not carry the weight he gave them. "The bridge," he wrote to Waldo Frank in June 1926, "as a symbol today has no significance beyond an economical approach to shorter hours, quicker lunches, behaviorism and toothpicks."

But in other letters, including ones to Frank, and especially one written fifteen months later to his patron Otto Kahn that set out the grand design of the poem, he seemed to feel no doubt about the importance of his project. "*The Aeneid* was not written in two years," he wrote to Kahn, "nor in four, and in more than one sense I feel justified in comparing the historic and cultural scope of *The Bridge* to that great work. It is at least a symphony with an epic theme, and a work of considerable profundity and inspiration."

Like many young poets, he wrote home once his first book had appeared wondering what they would make of it. He wrote to his mother: "I'm very much amused at what you say about the interest in my book out there in Cleveland. Wait until they see it, and try to read it! I may be wrong, but I think they will eventually express considerable consternation."

His father was not impressed. As late as 1928, when *The Bridge* was almost finished, he suggested that his son learn a trade. But Crane was still adding to his store, discovering, for example,

Gerard Manley Hopkins early in 1928. "It is a revelation to me – of unrealized possibilities," he wrote to Yvor Winters, who seemed to admire his work, and with whom he had a fascinating correspondence until Winters reviewed *The Bridge* harshly, thus ending what had been a close literary friendship.

Crane seemed to derive energy and immense pleasure from travel. His letters from France and Mexico are filled with delight, even though it is clear that he was drinking a great deal in Mexico. It was there in 1932 that he broke rank, as he put it, with the "brotherhood," and began an affair with Peggy Cowley, who was in the midst of a divorce from Malcolm Cowley. "I think it has done me considerable good," he wrote. "The old beauty still claims me, however, and my eyes roam as much as ever. I doubt if I'll ever change very fundamentally."

Once *The Bridge* was finished and published, Crane continued working on a number of shorter poems, including "The Broken Tower."

> *The bell-rope that gathers God at dawn*
> *Dispatches me as though I dropped down the knell*
> *Of a spent day – to wander the cathedral lawn*
> *From pit to crucifix, feet chill on steps from hell.*

In Mexico he had been on a Guggenheim fellowship that ended on 31 March 1932, when he said to a friend, "I'm just plain Hart Crane again." He was unsure whether he wanted to remain in Mexico or return to the United States. The problem, as before, was money, and this problem now became more severe when he learned that his inheritance from his father's estate would be much less than he had expected, not enough to live on. His stepmother wrote to him on 12 April:

Nothing can be paid from the estate account to you in the way of your bequest . . . and there isn't any income from stocks to speak of. We are not making any money from our different businesses. The only thing we can do is to give you an allowance from my salary each month, and that I have made arrangements to do.

Crane was drinking wildly and behaving erratically but still spoke of plans for future work. It was clear because of the freedom he had won during his travels and his high ambition as a poet and also because of his constant drinking that he was in no state to go back to New York and work again in advertising, or make his living in any way. He spoke of suicide and, it was reported, made a number of wills. Eventually, it was decided that he and Peggy Cowley would sail back to the United States on the *Orizaba* from Veracruz. After a stop in Havana, it seems that Crane was badly beaten up on the ship in the early hours of 27 April. One of his fellow passengers, Gertrude Berg, saw that "he had a black eye and looked generally battered."

Close to noon that day he appeared on deck. "He walked to the railing," Berg remembered,

took off his coat, folded it neatly over the railing (not dropping it on deck), placed both hands on the railing, raised himself on his toes, and then dropped back again. We all fell silent and watched him, wondering what in the world he was up to. Then, suddenly, he vaulted over the railing and jumped into the sea . . . Just once I saw Crane, swimming strongly, but never again.

Although lifeboats were lowered, there were no further sightings of the poet. One of the most brilliant first acts in American literature had come to an end.

# Tennessee Williams and the Ghost of Rose

Although Henry James's sister, Alice, was five years his junior, they were the closest among the five James siblings. In her biography of Alice James, Jean Strouse has written:

Alice and Henry shared throughout their lives a deeper intellectual and spiritual kinship than either felt with any other member of the family. Within the family group the second son and only daughter were more isolated than any of the others . . . What bound Henry and Alice together was a . . . profound mutual understanding. Henry had withdrawn early from the competitive masculine fray to a safe inner world.

As a way of escape Henry James found his "safe inner world" through reading and writing; this was not available in the same way to Alice. Henry created a vast imaginative terrain that he inhabited with considerable determination, independence and strength of will; his only sister, on the other hand, became a reverse image of him – she was a weak patient, dependent on others, suffering from ailments not easy to name and impossible to cure. Henry James did not keep a personal diary and nowhere set down his dreams and fears, but it is clear from his letters about her, especially when she arrived in England in 1884 and after her death eight years later, that Alice's fate and her suffering preoccupied him a great deal while he also worked hard and managed a varied and busy social life.

Just as it is possible to read the character of Rosie Muniment, the witty invalid, in *The Princess Casamassima* as a version of Alice James, we can also read the children Miles and Flora in *The Turn of the Screw*, written three years after Alice's death, as versions of the two James siblings, Henry and Alice, who both lived unmarried and in exile in England, oddly abandoned and orphaned and, in certain ways, emotionally unprotected. In February 1895 James wrote in his notebook the idea of a

> possible little drama residing in the existence of a peculiar intense and interesting affection between a brother and a sister . . . I fancy the pair understanding each other too well – fatally well . . . [They] abound in the same sense, see with the same sensibilities and the same imagination, vibrate with the same nerves . . . Two lives, two beings, and one experience.

Although he never wrote this story, the notebook entry is fascinating for anyone interested in James's nonchalant masculinity and Alice's neurotic inertia, as it is for anyone looking at the richly complex emotional and creative life of Henry James and the diaries and letters of his sister, Alice.

In his *Memoirs*, Tennessee Williams, a writer both homosexual and hypochondriac who also devoted fierce energy to his work while his only sister suffered from a mysterious mental illness, wrote about his relationship to his sister, Rose:

> I may have inadvertently omitted a good deal of material about the unusually close relations between Rose and me. Some perceptive critic of the theatre made the observation that the true theme of my work is "incest." My sister and I had a close relationship, quite unsullied by any carnal knowledge . . . And yet our love was, and is, the deepest in our lives and was, perhaps, very pertinent to our withdrawal from extra-familial attachments.

Henry James and Tennessee Williams each marvelled at his sister's own prose style in diaries and letters. Alice's diary, James wrote, "is heroic in its individuality . . . and the beauty and eloquence with which she often expresses this, let alone the rich irony and humour, constitute . . . a new claim for the family renown. This last element – her style, her power to write – are indeed to me a delight."

Williams in his *Memoirs* quoted from Rose's letters: "I remember one that began with this phrase: 'Today the sun came up like a five-dollar gold piece!' Or another in which she wrote: 'Today we drove in town and I purchased Palmolive shampoo for my crowning glory.'"

In his two best early plays, Williams dramatized relations between siblings, one of them watchful, the other damaged and insecure; each contains a key moment in which the weaker sibling loses her moorings. In *The Glass Menagerie* (1944) Laura's brother writes poems, admires the work of D. H. Lawrence and works in a shoe warehouse, as Williams did, while Laura herself is, like Rose and indeed like Williams himself, immensely fragile and sexually insecure. (The mother in the play was, according to Williams's younger brother, so accurately based on their mother that she could have sued.) In the play, Laura is psychologically broken by the visit of one gentleman caller; in life, Rose's troubles began when she was abandoned by her ambitious boyfriend after her father had lost part of his ear in a fight at an all-night poker game, thus ruining his chance of further professional advancement. "Her heart broke, then," Williams wrote, "and it was after that that the mysterious stomach trouble began."

As he worked on *A Streetcar Named Desire*, which was produced in 1947, Williams was living in New Orleans with his boyfriend Pancho Rodriguez. In his notebook he wrote about the difference between them: "He is incapable of reason. Violence belongs to his nature as completely as it is abhorrent to mine." According to a friend, "Tennessee behaved very badly toward Pancho, and he did so by using Pancho for real-life scenes which he created – and then transformed them into moments of *A Streetcar Named Desire*." Thus Pancho, rough, less educated than Williams, became Stanley to Williams's Stella. The drama begins when Stella's unstable sister comes to New Orleans and has, eventually, to be taken away. Some of the most fruitful moments in Williams's work came when he found metaphors in drama for what had really happened to him and his sister, Rose.

Williams in his art thus gave shape to his life, or to the parts of it that really interested him. The other sources for his life that he left have to be read judiciously. His impressionistic book *Memoirs*, for example, which he wrote in 1975 at the age of sixty-four, in the words of his biographer Donald Spoto, "conceals more than it shares, misrepresents more than it documents, omits major events, confuses dates and . . . tells virtually nothing about the playwright's career." Williams's letters as source material are more useful, but they tended to be written to amuse and suit their recipients. Thus his notebooks, which he kept, mostly in diary form, between 1936 and 1958 and again briefly between 1979 and 1981, and which have been edited and annotated with fastidious care by Margaret Bradham Thornton, are the best guide we have to his life and his moods. About many aspects of him, this new volume is invaluable.

The entries we have begin when Williams was twenty-five and living with his family, struggling under considerable pressures to find a voice as a poet, short story writer and playwright. These pressures might explain the tone of self-obsession, self-pity and despair. The entries seem to have been written at night and he himself became alert to their morbid self-indulgence, quoting Nietzsche: "Do not let the evening be judge of the day." While he was trying to impress everyone in his creative work, in these pages he wished to impress no one and thus could be brutally honest about his own failings. It is interesting that when he found success and fame the tone did not change much, even when he had many lovers, enough money to travel and lots of friends and admirers. He still, when he came to write in his notebooks, felt at

times sorry for himself but at other times something more interesting and convincing, a huge unease about being in the world at
all, which nothing, no matter how thrilling, could lift or cure.

There is never a moment in his notebooks when he congratu-
lates himself on mastering the structure of a new play or creating
a new and memorable character or on that precise day writing a
speech that worked wonders. Only a few times did he write about
technical problems. (His observation that "the tragedy of a poet
writing drama is that when he writes well – from the dramatur-
gic technical pt. of view he is often writing badly" stands out in
this book.) He did not jot down ideas as they came to him, as
Henry James did, so we do not see in these pages the growth of
his most important plays from a single entry. Instead, Williams
noted what he was creating as a burden or a dull fact, including
scenes he was rewriting or demands from directors and producers. Often, on rereading work in progress, he noted its badness.
Precisely how his creative process operated he kept to himself.
Instead, he wrote about who had irritated him or pleased him
during the day, or how nervous he felt, how many pills he took or
how much alcohol he consumed, or how many lengths of the
pool he swam. He noted his fears and dreams.

It is strange how out of all of this mostly inchoate and random
writing, a sense of a personal vision emerges that would make its
way into the very core of Williams's main characters and scenes.
These entries capture an authentic voice, an artist alone and
deeply fearful and unusually selfish. Many of his most whining
entries were written on the very days when he was producing his
most glittering work. His whining was not a game or done for
effect; it seems, indeed, a rare example of whining both sincere
and heartfelt. Even when he was at his most successful, he could,
for example, write: "Today the dreaded occasion of reading over
the work and the (almost but never quite) expected fit of revulsion." Tennessee Williams meant business when he whined. And

thus somehow he managed to connect his own dark and obsessive complaints about his works and days, his own dread of life, to his characters and their fate. These notebooks, precisely because they were not intentionally created as raw material for work, now seem to be the rock on which his creations, sparkling and vivid versions of himself, were built.

In the early years he was coy about sex. In a diary entry for 1979 he disclosed: "Such was the Puritanism imposed by Edwina [his mother] that I did not masturbate till the age of Twenty-Six, then not with my hands but by rubbing my groin against my bed-sheets, while recalling the incredible grace and beauty of a boy-diver plunging naked from the high board in the swimming-pool of Washington U. in Saint Louis." The work he produced seemed almost part of a self-disgust, or a desperate need to overcome it, an aspect of pure frustration with himself and his circumstances. On 15 April 1936, for example, he wrote:

It's a horrible hot afternoon and I have that horrible oppressed feeling that hot weather gives me. This house frightens me again. I feel trapped – shut in. The radio is on – that awful ball-game – it will be going every afternoon now and hearing it makes me sick – I'm too tired to write – Can do nothing – I am disgusted with the story I wrote Saturday . . . It seems idiotic to me now . . . I wish I could write something decent – strong – but everything about me is weak – and silly – Terrible to feel like this.

The feeling of uselessness arose sometimes from his fears about his masculinity, the sense that he was a sissy, a guy without guts, as much as from his judgements on the badness of his work. Two weeks after the entry quoted above, he wrote: "I must remember that my ancestors fought the Indians! No, I must remember that I am a man – when all is said and done – and not a snivelling baby." And then on 8 May: "If only I could realize I am not 2 persons. I am only one. There is no sense in this division. An enemy inside myself! How absurd!" Later that year, it struck him about Shakespeare: "I bet he was a guy that had plenty of guts. No damn sissy." The following year, he wrote: "But if I were God I would feel a little bit sorry for Tom [Tennessee] Williams once in a while – he doesn't have a very gay easy time of it and he does have guts of a sort even though he is a stinking sissy!"

In the middle of all of this Williams was capable of what one presumes – it is hard to know – was irony, even self-mockery, when in April 1940 in New York he noticed the war: "Tonight Germany seized Denmark and war was declared by Norway – but infinitely more important is the fact that my play will be discussed and perhaps a decision rendered by the Theatre Guild."

As he moved away from home, Williams fell in love a number of times, first with a Canadian, Kip Kiernan, then with Pancho Rodriguez, and then Frank Merlo, with whom he lived for many years, but this did not prevent him from having many casual lovers, often one or two a day wherever he went. On 27 June 1941, he wrote: "I am fatigued, I am dull, I am bitter at heart. But I do not suffer much. I have diverted myself with the most extraordinary amount of sexual license I have ever indulged in."

This sexual licence, however, was accompanied by strange moments of unease about his sexuality and about homosexuality in general. When in 1941 a friend suggested that homosexuals should be exterminated at twenty-five "for the good of society," Williams wondered:

How many of us feel that way, I wonder? Bear this intolerable burden of guilt? To feel some humiliation and a great deal of sorrow at times is inevitable. But feeling guilty is foolish. I am a deeper and warmer and kinder man for my deviation. More conscious of need in others, and what power I have to express the human heart must be in large part due to this circumstance. Some day society will take perhaps the suitable action – but I do not believe that it will or should be extermination.

And sex itself much of the time, despite the energy he put into it, disappointed him. On 16 September 1941, he wrote, for example: "The cold and beautiful bodies of the young! They spread themselves out like a banquet table, you dine voraciously and afterwards it is like you had eaten nothing but air."

As he got older and began to travel, especially in Italy and Spain where he went every summer, he paid for sex, but this did not seem to make him happy either, especially afterwards. In Rome in July 1955 he wrote:

The most embarrassing of all relations is with a whore. At least, after the act, when you suffer the post-orgasmic withdrawal anyway, a good whore, in the sense of a really wise one, knows how to create an atmosphere that obviates this hazard but the one this afternoon, though divinely gifted in the practise of bed, made me feel very sheepish afterwards. I didn't know how to offer the money or how to say goodbye. It is because of my Puritanical feeling that it is wrong, wrong! – to use another being's body like this because of having need, on one hand, and cash on the other – Still – I owe more pleasure to this circumstance in life than anything else, I guess. Can I complain? Breast beating is twice as false as the love of any whore.

Because of his bad eyesight, Williams did not serve in the Second World War and it is an aspect of his honesty as well as his self-obsession that the war engaged him very little. In January 1942 he wrote:

I am frightened thinking of the changes or rather the increased vicissitudes the war may create in my life. I suppose if it did not affect me personally my feelings about it would be only abstractly regretful. Things have to impinge on my own life to matter to me very much. Is it that way with most people? Yes, I am sure that it is.

He had, as he said, a way of reducing or indeed elevating every-thing to the personal. In a letter to Elia Kazan about Nixon in August 1952, for example: "He looks like the gradeschool bully that used to wait for me behind a broken fence and twist my ear to make me say obscene things."

What impinged on Williams's life as much as his work, as is clear from these pages, was his family. His father appeared in the early entries as a threat and a nuisance, "a dormant volcano"; his younger brother Dakin hardly at all; his mother Edwina surpris-ingly little. But his maternal grandparents, whom he loved, were invoked regularly. His grandmother, also called Rose, was, he wrote in 1941, "a miracle of gentleness. A faded golden rose in fading sunlight. The finest thing in my life." And the fate of his sister, Rose, troubled him year after year, flitting through his waking life and his dreams. As he worked with fierce determina-tion on his plays, as he travelled the world like a maniac, as he sought new sexual partners, as he drank and took pills and went to parties, there was always the sense, made clear in many note-book entries, that he was in flight from what was done to his sister. He lived in the shadow of her suffering and there were times when he seemed to seek pleasure and experience enough for two of them.

Rose was sixteen months older than Williams; as children, they were very close. She saw her first psychiatrist when she was twenty-one. In 1937 she was diagnosed with dementia praecox, an early term for schizophrenia. In 1943 she underwent a pre-frontal lobotomy. In notes made in 1979 Williams wrote that his mother "approved for my sister to have one of the first pre-fron-tal lobotomies performed in the States because she was shocked by Rose's tastefully phrased but explicit disclosures of masturba-tion practised with Candles stolen from the Chapel, at All Saints in Vicksburg." Rose lived in institutions from 1943 for the rest of her life.

As Margaret Bradham Thornton makes clear in her copious annotations to these diaries – each right-hand page of Williams's entries is faced by a left-hand page of informative notes – Rose appeared in various guises in many of Williams's plays, poems and stories. Her life as it made its way into his imagination is central to his work.

In October 1936 Williams first noted a problem with Rose: "The house is wretched. Rose is on one of her neurotic sprees – fancies herself an invalid – talks in a silly dying-off way – trails around the house in negligees. Disgusting." Three years later, when the seriousness of her condition was fully clear, Williams wrote an emendation to this: "God forgive me for this!" In January 1937 Williams's mother wrote to her parents about Rose's breakdown and her "raving on the subject of 'sex' . . . and I was ashamed for Dakin and Tom to hear her the other night." The same day Williams wrote in his notebook: "Tragedy. I write that word knowing the full meaning of it. We have had no deaths in our family but slowly by degrees something was happening much uglier and more terrible than death. Now we are forced to see it, know it. The thought is an aching numbness – a horror!"

By May, when Rose had been moved to an institution, Williams's mother wrote to her parents once more: "Tom and I went out to see Rose Sunday . . . The visit made Tom ill so I can't take him to see her again. I can't have two of them there!" In September that year, having seen Rose, Williams wrote: "No, I haven't forgotten poor Rose – I beg whatever power there is to save her and spare her from suffering." The following year, he saw her again: "She is like a person half-asleep now – quiet, gentle and thank God – not in any way revolting like so many of the others – She sat with us in a bright sunny room full of flowers – said 'yes' to all our questions – looked puzzled, searching for something – sometimes her eyes filled with tears – (So did mine)."

In August 1939 Rose's medical report read: "Does no work.

Manifests delusion of persecution. Smiles and laughs when telling of person plotting to kill her. Talk free and irrelevant. Admits
auditory hallucinations. Quiet on the ward. Masturbates frequently. Also expresses various somatic delusions, all of which
she explains on a sexual basis. Memory for remote past is nil.
Appetite good. Well nourished."

Four months later when Williams had made another visit, he
wrote: "Visited Rose at sanitarium – horrible, horrible! Her talk
was so obscene – she laughed and spoke continual obscenities –
Mother insisted I go in, though I dreaded it and wanted to go out
and stay outside. We talked to the Doctor afterwards – a cold,
unsympathetic young man – he said her condition was so hopeless that we could only expect a progressive deterioration."

In March 1943, when Rose had a lobotomy, Williams wrote: "A
cord breaking. 1000 miles away. Rose. Her head cut open. A knife
thrust in her brain. Me. Here. Smoking. My father, mean as a
devil, snoring 1000 miles away."

Rose came to him in dreams in which his identity and hers
seemed confused. In December 1948, while crossing the Atlantic,
he noted:

Later I dreamed of my sister. Woke up. Then went to sleep and
dreamed of her again. At one point I was lying in her bed, the ivory-
colored bed: but it was not a dream of incest, although I am at a loss to
explain it. I was standing naked in a room. Heard footsteps. Jumped in
the bed to cover myself. Discovered it was my sister's bed. She entered
the room. Spoke to me angrily and pulled back the covers. I struggled
not to expose my nakedness. She turned away crossly while I got
hastily up from the bed. There I woke up.

Four years later in Spain he noted another dream: "I've dreamed
of my sister, seeing her in a cream colored lace dress which I had
forgotten. In the dream a lady who looked like my sister wore it
– then I had it on and then I was struggling to sit down between

two tables and was wedged so tightly between them I couldn't breathe."

In later years he saw more of his sister, writing in 1979 in Key West:

My sister Rose, the living presence of truth and faith in my life. If I go abroad to die, I must not leave her, afterwards, in the custody of her present companion, a tasteless woman whose idea of giving Rose a good time is to take her to the Masonic Lodge . . . Tonight she had dressed Rose for a party at Kate's in a livid green dress from Woolco's, as tasteless as possible and as unbecoming. I had said that Rose should have a green dress but I meant to buy it for her myself, in a pastel shade, such as lettuce.

Part of the reason for Williams's obsession with his sister was his feeling that he, too, could easily have followed her into a mental institution. "The shadow of what happened to Rose" haunted him in the years of his success and in subsequent years when the plays he wrote did not find large audiences or win much praise and he was addicted to various drugs and to alcohol. As early as his visit to her in 1939 he saw the danger for himself, as his mother had two years earlier. He wrote: "It was a horrible ordeal. Especially since I fear that end for myself." The artist Vassilis Voglis, a friend of Williams's, told his biographer Donald Spoto: "He was devoted to Rose, but in a way she was an extension of himself. He could have had the lobotomy. He felt the outsider, marred in some way. He really cared for her, and perhaps he never really cared for anyone else in his life, ever. And I think he knew it."

In 1973, speaking of his play *Out Cry*, he said:

I've had a great deal of experience with madness; I have been locked up. My sister was institutionalized for most of her adult life. Both my sister and I need a lot of taking care of . . . I'm a lonely person, lonelier than most people. I have a touch of schizophrenia in me and in order to avoid madness I have to work.

In his notebooks for 1957, Williams noted that he was "stealing a week between New York and the 'retreat' . . . at Stockbridge, assuming I do go there." He wrote to his mother:

I stayed only five minutes in the Institute. I took one look at the other patients and told Frank to carry my bags right back out to the car. I checked into the local hotel and stayed there over the weekend to make sure that this was not the place for me, then drove back to New York. I think the psychiatrist Dr. Kubie who is head of the analytic institute in New York, is right in thinking I need some therapy of that kind to relieve the tensions that I have been living under, but I think it's unnecessary for me to live in a house full of characters that appeared to be more disturbed than myself.

The following year, he wrote to Elia Kazan:

I had to defy my analyst to continue my work this past year. He said I was over-worked and must quit and "lie fallow" as he put it, for a year or so, and then resume work in what he declared would be a great new tide of creative power, which he apparently thought would come out of my analysis with him. I wanted to accept this instruction but without my work, I was unbearably lonely, my life unbearably empty.

In 1969, a period not covered in the notebooks, Williams was confined to a mental hospital in Saint Louis by his brother where he stayed for three dreadful months.

Williams managed in his best work to harness that shadow of madness that lay over him and that fell on his sister. He made it appear almost normal, an unsettled striving within the soul, a brave dreaming up of the more wondrous parts of the self. He made its roots seem common to us all. But then, as he must have seen it develop in Rose, he dramatized its growth into a sort of poisonous power that slowly overcame and undid his characters.

It is remarkable in the notebooks how little credit he gave himself for his own genius at handling and shaping this material, his skills at catching patterns of speech and building dramatic structure, his astonishing sympathy for powerless dreamers especially when they came dressed up and ready to kill or were full of hidden erotic hope. As his own power waned, he did not, as other dramatists did, spend time overseeing new productions of old work. It was part of his unresolved innocence, his own nature as a dreamer, that he went on writing, despite the fact that most of his work after *The Night of the Iguana* in 1961 seemed to fail; it had been a great struggle to start, and now, as the last miserable pages of his notebooks make clear, it was too much of a struggle to stop. He knew that the creation of his characters was what had justified his life. As he came close to the end he wrote: "Did I die by my own hand or was I destroyed slowly and brutally by a conspiratorial group? There is probably no clear cut answer . . . Perhaps I was never meant to exist at all, but if I hadn't, a number of my created beings would have been denied their passionate existence."

# John Cheever: New Ways to Make Your Family's Life a Misery

One of John Cheever's most famous stories is called "The Swimmer." It is set, like much of his fiction, in the lawned suburbs somewhere outside New York City, and it is filled, like most of his fiction, with despair. The hero, Neddy Merrill, the father of four daughters, is sitting by a neighbour's pool drinking gin when the idea comes to him that he might reach home by doing a lap of all of his neighbours' pools on the way. In the pages that follow he is both a mythical hero of the suburbs and a holy fool; he is both a legend in his own dreams and a ridiculous figure, a character whose reality is evoked by the close detail with which his world is described, but who is also a victim of his own imaginings. There is a realism in the way the detail and the characters are evoked that forces the reader to believe that this is actually happening – that Neddy is really swimming home, pool by pool – but there is also something else going on that makes us wonder if the story is a metaphor for something, or a parable. It ends with Neddy's arrival home to find his house dark and its doors locked. "He shouted, pounded on the door, tried to force it with his shoulder, and then, looking in at the windows, saw that the place was empty."

Cheever's journals for the months before he wrote the story included an entry that dealt with his increasing ambition and fame: "I dream that my face appears on a postage stamp." Soon afterwards, he wrote about something that might have prevented this actually happening: about a secret life that gave him creative energy and filled him with suburban shame. On the one hand, he wanted to be a happily married man and a devoted father, the man whom his friends and readers believed him to be. "It is my wife's body that I most wish to gentle, it is into her that I most wish to pour myself," he wrote. But, on the other hand, his thoughts had a habit of turning, as they did in that same diary entry, to his sexual interest in men, this time to a male figure he had seen by a swimming pool. "His soft gaze follows me, settles on me, and I have a deadly itchiness in my crotch." He thought about having sex in the shower with the young man; he contemplated "the murderous checks and balances of a flirtation." But then he realized that he was, in fact, a respectable married man with three children who dreamed of having his face on a stamp. "But then there are the spiritual facts: my high esteem for the world, the knowledge that it is not in me to lead a double life, my love of perseverance, a passionate wish to honour the vows I've made to my wife and children." Nonetheless, he was intrigued by the urge, which his creation Neddy Merrill would soon also feel,

to plunge into life, to race after our instincts, to upset the petty canons of decency and cleanliness, and yet if I made it in the shower I could not meet the smiles of the world . . . I have been in this country a hundred times before . . . Why should I be tempted to throw away the vast delights of love for a chance shot in a shower?

Thus "The Swimmer," read in tandem with Cheever's journals, becomes a version of the writer's dream and then his nightmare. His dream was that he should have "breached this contract years ago and run off with some healthy-minded beauty," his nightmare that he would come home to an empty house, that he would, because of instincts he barely understood and deeply despised, lose the domestic life he craved and the people he most loved. He wrote in his journals that he was locked into "the toleration of an intolerable marriage." Soon after his account of the man he had seen by the pool, he wrote of being with his younger son, Federico: "I have no freedom from him. Never having known the love of a father has forced me into a love so engulfing and passionate that there is no margin of choice."

He filled his journals with images of love for those around him and longing for domestic harmony, and then broke the harmony with images of despair, often caused by hangovers (he drank vast quantities, often starting in the morning), and of hate, usually for his wife (who for much of the time they were married did not speak to him, often with good reason). Few images of happiness or ease were allowed to stand. In 1963, for example, he registered a memory from childhood of being at the beach with his parents and his older brother, Fred, and then returning home.

We have our ice cream on the back lawn, read, play whist, wish on the evening star for a gold watch and chain, kiss one another goodnight, and go to bed. These seemed to be the beginnings of a world, these days all seemed like mornings, and if there was a single incident that could be used as a turning point it was, I suppose, when my father went out to play an early game of golf and found a dear friend and business associate on the edge of the third fairway hanging dead from a tree.

The tone in Cheever's journals was usually self-pitying and humourless. In the stories, however, he could turn domestic despair into comedy and then back again, often in a single phrase. Neddy in "The Swimmer," for example, Cheever wrote, "might have been compared to a summer's day, particularly the last hours of one." Or in "The Country Husband," as the children are bickering in their father's presence before their mother enters to announce that supper is ready in their nice suburban house, Cheever risks a phrase that makes you unsure whether to laugh or cry: "She strikes a match and lights the six candles in this vale of tears."

For Cheever, the house, the simple suburban house, was a sort of hell. Yet this was where he lived, and the idea of losing it, or being left alone in it, was a further depth of hell that he dreaded. In his journal for 1963 he brooded over this:

My grandfather is supposed to have died, alone, unknown, a stranger to his wife and his sons, in a furnished room on Charles Street. My own father spent two or three years in his late seventies alone at the farm in Hanover. The only heat was a fireplace; his only companion a halfwit who lived up the road. I lived as a young man in cold, ugly and forsaken places yearning for a house, a wife, the voices of my sons, and having all of this I find myself, when I am engorged with petulance, thinking that after all, after the Easter egg hunts and the merry singing at Christmas, after the loving and the surprises and the summer afternoons, after the laughter and the open fires, I will end up cold, alone, dishonoured, forgotten by my children, an old man approaching death without a companion.

Cheever had another problem besides his fear that his secret sexuality would be discovered and that he would lose the cocoon of domestic life that left him so blissfully unhappy. He was a snob. He believed that he was a Cheever and that this meant something, that he belonged in some way to American grandeur. Thus his social status in the suburbs mattered to him, as did material wealth and its trappings, even when he did not have them. The decline in fortune suffered by his parents and the drunken antics of his brother, their letting the family name down, filled him with as much shame as his own sexuality or his own drinking. In company he could be suave and charming, but the minute he was alone and putting pen to paper, this shame and its attendant dramas would make its way into his fiction and his journals in guises both comic and maudlin. He was aware, as were others, of his "cultivated accent" – his daughter, Susan, reported her friends asking if he was English or something – and noted that he should be careful with it. "When this gets into my prose, my prose is at its worst."

The first Cheever in America was Ezekiel, who was headmaster of the Boston Latin School from 1671 to 1708, and the author of a book on Latin that was the standard textbook in the United States for more than a century. On his mother's side, Cheever claimed to be descended from Sir Percy Devereaux, a mayor of Windsor: indeed, his mother kept a picture of Windsor Castle on her wall. But this was nonsense; he had no such ancestor. When Cheever's family wanted to mock him, they referred to him as the Lost Earl of Devereaux. His mother was a nurse; he gave some of her characteristics, such as her interest in organizing others, to Honora Wapshot in his first novel, *The Wapshot Chronicle*. Like Coverly Wapshot, Cheever blamed his mother for handing on some of her worst anxieties to him. His father was a shoe salesman.

In his early forties, after winning an O. Henry Award, Cheever went to see his mother. He reported the following exchange: "I read in the newspaper that you won a prize." "Yes, mother, I didn't tell you about it because it wasn't terribly important to me." "No, it wasn't to me either." In the Wapshot novels, everybody loves Coverly's older brother, Moses, but "everybody did not love Coverly." So, too, everyone loved Fred, John Cheever's older brother, who was born in 1905, but everybody did not love John, who was born in 1912. By the time his mother was pregnant with him, indeed, the marriage was under so much strain that Cheever's father invited an abortionist to dinner. As Blake Bailey writes in his biography: "It was a story that haunted Cheever the rest of his life . . . Not surprisingly, he saw fit to blame his mother for having the bad taste to tell him of the episode."

The family was affluent at first, living in a large house in Quincy, Massachusetts, but by the 1920s, as the Depression came to New England, Cheever's father's business failed and he began crying at the breakfast table. Fred was the strong one and excelled at sport whereas John was weak and prone to illness.

Fred defended him, however, punching an Irishman who said that his little brother looked like a girl when he skated. Cheever opened his story "The National Pastime": "To be an American and unable to play baseball is comparable to being a Polynesian and unable to swim." His uncle, when he saw him, said: "Well, I guess you could play tennis." Cheever covered his tracks by hating tennis all his life and developing an elaborate and conspicuous interest in sport, including baseball. "He flung himself into icy pools and skated with a masculine swagger," Bailey writes. While Fred was away at college, John also developed an interest in other pastimes, such as attending "a penis-measuring contest, followed by an orgy" and soon learning to masturbate with a boy called Fax Ogden. "Rainy days were best of all," Bailey writes, "as the two boys could stay in bed and practise, indefatigably, their favourite pastime." Cheever wrote in an unpublished memoir that "when one bed got gummed up we used to move to another."

Cheever was good at blaming people; so skilled did he become at it that he sometimes went as far as blaming himself. Since he never had a job or went out much, and mainly saw his family and his family only, he specialized in blaming them. He blamed his father and his brother for not playing ball with him when he was small. He blamed his father for losing his money, his brother for leaving home. He blamed his mother for many things, but principally for opening a gift shop to keep the family going and making a success of it. Once she opened the shop, Cheever wrote, "I was to think of her, not in any domestic or maternal role, but as a woman approaching a customer in a store and asking, bellicosely: 'Is there something I can do for you?'" The vulgarity of it all was an "abysmal humiliation" for him. When he read Freud, Cheever also discovered that his family was a "virtual paradigm for 'that chain of relationships' (weak father, dominant mother) 'that usually produces a male homosexual.'"

Thus they didn't just make him poor, they made him queer, and he spent the rest of his life resenting them.

Since home did not suit his tastes, Cheever invented an alternative and much grander home – the artists' retreat at Yaddo in upstate New York, where he first went when he was twenty-two. He seems to have enjoyed himself immensely there over the years. "It's the only place I've ever felt at home," he said. In 1977 he reminisced: "I have been sucked by Ned [Rorem] and others in almost every room and tried unsuccessfully to mount a young man on the bridge between the lakes." Soon, despite this, or because of it, he became a favourite of Mrs. Ames, who ran the place, and of the servants, who called him Lord Fauntleroy. ("Only dogs, servants and children know who the real aristocrats are," he liked to say.) One of his happiest memories was returning to Yaddo and overhearing the parlourmaid say: "Master John is back!"

Cheever's early stories deal with the nuclear family as a crucible of tension and betrayal; his families drink together and manage to cause each other nothing but pain. He became a master of the single, searing image of pure desolation in the midst of the trappings of good cheer and middle-class comfort. Because of his drinking habits and also because his talent seemed to focus best on the small moment of intense truth, he had real difficulty writing his first two novels. When he was forty, he gave 100 pages of a novel to the editor who had commissioned it to be told that they were worthless, that he should give up writing and look for another way of making a living. Although *The Wapshot Chronicle* (1957) and *The Wapshot Scandal* (1964) were well received and have their comic moments, there is something unfocused about the narratives and sketchy about the characters. As he came to the end of *The Wapshot Scandal* he wrote in his journal: "I cannot resolve the book because I have been irresolute about my own affairs."

This is an interesting understatement, but it was maybe as far as he could go. And it is a fascinating idea that his talent could thrive using the sharp system of the story, but he struggled so much with the novels simply because there were vast areas of himself that he could not use as a basis for a character dramatized over time. In his stories he could create a tragic, trapped individual in a single scene or moment; he had a deep knowledge of what that was like. In his two Wapshot novels, using broad strokes, he managed merely a comic family down on their luck.

The problem was partly his intense inhabiting of the domestic sphere and the suburban landscape, as though this were a way of shutting out the wider world, and partly his refusal even to recognize his own homosexuality as anything other than a dark hidden area of the self that could not be explored. "For Cheever it would always be one thing to have sex with a man," Bailey writes, "another to spend the night with him. The latter was a taboo he would rarely if ever violate until a ripe old age." In his journals he wrote: "If I followed my instincts I would be strangled by some hairy sailor in a public urinal. Every comely man, every bank clerk and delivery boy, was aimed at my life like a loaded pistol." One of his best friends in his twenties was Malcolm Cowley, through whom he had briefly met Hart Crane. (It was Cowley's wife who had been on the ship with Crane when he committed suicide in 1932.) A homosexual lifestyle, Cowley had warned Cheever, "could only end with drunkenness and ghastly suicide." As one of Cheever's colleagues in the Signal Corps in the Second World War remarked: "He wanted to be accepted as a New England gentleman and New England gentlemen aren't gay. Back then you have no idea of the opprobrium. Even in the Signal Corps, even in the film and theatre world, you were a second-class citizen if you were gay, and Cheever did not want to be that."

By the time he joined the Signal Corps, Cheever was married

and his wife was pregnant. In 1952, in one of the earliest entries in his journal, Cheever wrote:

I can remember walking around the streets of New York on a summer night some years ago. I cannot say that it was like the pain of living death; it never had that clear a meaning. But it was torment, crushing torment and frustration. I was caught under the weight of some great door. The feeling always was that if I could express myself erotically I should come alive.

Later, Mary Cheever would report that she knew that there was something wrong with the sexual aspects of her marriage. "I sensed that he wasn't entirely masculine." When asked if she discussed it with Cheever, she said: "Oh Lord, no. Oh Lord, no. He was terrified of it himself."

Cheever didn't like homosexuals. "Their funny clothes and their peculiar smells and airs and scraps of French" struck him as "an obscenity and a threat." Having struggled to remain monogamous (and heterosexual) for almost twenty years, he noticed a change coming. When he saw Gore Vidal on TV in the early 1960s he thought him "personable and intelligent" and then wrote: "I think that he is either not a fairy or that perhaps we have reached a point where men of this persuasion are not forced into attitudes of bitterness, rancour and despair." Soon afterwards, Cheever noted more men of his persuasion in a diner. "I think there is a fag beside me at the lunch counter," he wrote. "He drums his nails impatiently and who but a fag would do this?" He prayed for the surf to wash such people away. In 1960, nineteen years after his marriage, he spent a night with Calvin Kentfield, a writer he had met at Yaddo a decade earlier. He noted in his journal:

I spend the night with C., and what do I make of this? I seem unashamed, and yet I feel or apprehend the weight of social strictures, the threat of punishment. But I have acted only on my own instincts, tried, discreetly, to relieve my drunken loneliness, my troublesome hunger for sexual tenderness. Perhaps sin has to do with the incident, and I have had this sort of intercourse only three times in my adult life. I know my troubled nature and have tried to contain it along creative lines. It is not my choice that I am alone here and exposed to temptation, but I sincerely hope that this will not happen again. I trust that what I did was not wrong. I trust that I have harmed no one I love. The worst may be that I have put myself into a position where I may be forced to lie.

In 1964 Cheever invited the writer Paul Moor, who was a fan of his work, up to his hotel room in Berlin. "I think he was or may be a homosexual," he wrote to a friend about Moor. "This would account for the funny shoes and the tight pants and I thought his voice a note or two too deep." Later he wrote in a letter: "I would like to live in a world in which there are no homosexuals but I suppose Paradise is thronged with them." Cheever at this stage was fifty-two. Most of his observations about homosexuals are unusual perhaps in that he wrote them down and then did not want them destroyed after he died. But they were not unusual as ways for a married man who was gay to keep the world at arm's length by pretending, even if just as a brief respite, that other homosexuals were queer, while he just happened to like having sex with men. (Even in his late sixties Cheever barely tolerated this aspect of himself, and did not tolerate it at all in others. When an old friend confided that he, too, had had gay encounters, Cheever wrote in his journal: "I decided, before he had completed the sentence, that I would never see him again as a friend and I never did.")

Just as it is important to place Cheever's diaries and what would later become known as his self-loathing in its historical context, it might also help if we did the same with his drinking.

But even in the context of the time, he was drinking a lot. Bailey reports on his moods and phases as a drunk:

There was Cheever the antic, happy drunk, who one night in 1946 danced the "atomic waltz" with Howard Fast's wife, Betty, on his shoulders, until she put out a cigarette in his ear and he flung her to the floor. There was Cheever the mean drunk, whose dry wit would suddenly turn vicious at some vague point . . . And finally – more and more often – there was Cheever the bored and even boring drunk, pickled by the long day's drinking and wishing only for bed.

In the late 1950s, his brother Fred had to be hospitalized for "alcoholic malnutrition." "Alarmed that his brother's fate could prove to be his own," Bailey writes, "John pored over his journal and was appalled by the obviously 'progressive' nature of his disease." He looked up the telephone number of Alcoholics Anonymous. Later, he wrote in his journals: "Then, my hands shaking, I open the bar and drink the leftover whiskey, gin and vermouth, whatever I can lay my shaking hands on."

"My God, the suburbs!" Cheever wrote in 1960. "They encircled the city's boundaries like enemy territory and we thought of them as a loss of privacy, a cesspool of conformity and a life of indescribable dreariness in some split-level village where the place name appeared in *The New York Times* only when some bored housewife blew off her head with a shotgun." By this time he had been living in the suburbs for almost a decade, having moved in 1951 to Scarborough (with his wife, his daughter, Susan, born in 1943, and son Ben, born in 1948) and then in 1961 to a large house in Ossining, where he was to live for the rest of his life. His third child, Federico, was born in 1957 in Rome, during a family sojourn there paid for by MGM's purchase of the rights to one of his stories for $25,000.

Cheever's relationship with his children was very close and mostly difficult, partly because he had nothing much to do all day except lounge around looking at them in a state of half-inebriation and total dissatisfaction. Towards the end of his life, he told colleagues that once, after a row with his wife, he woke to find a message written in lipstick by his daughter on the bathroom mirror: "Dere daddy, don't leave us." When it was pointed out that such a scene occurs in his story "The Chimera," with the same misspelling, Cheever replied: "Everything I write is autobiographical." But this was not so. Like a lot of writers, everything he wrote had a basis in autobiography and another in wishful or dreamy thinking. His daughter later denied that the scene took place: "I know how to spell," Susan Cheever said, "and I think what we wanted was for him to leave us. One thing about my father was he was always there, you could not get rid of him. He worked at home, he ate at home, he drank at home. So 'don't leave us'? That was never the fear."

"Cheever," Bailey writes, "loved being a father in the abstract, but the everyday facts of the matter were often a letdown. He was dismayed by his oldest child, for one thing, as she continued to 'overthrow his preconceptions' by remaining, as he put it, 'a fat importunate girl.'" As she was growing up, her father was a nightmare. "I defied my father's fantasies," she wrote in her memoir, *Home before Dark*. "As an adolescent I was dumpy, plagued by acne, slumped over, and alternately shy and aggressive, and my lank straight brown hair was always in my eyes." When she invited boyfriends home, Cheever was not helpful. "He liked to invite my boyfriends off with him to go scything in the meadow or work on a felled tree with the chainsaw or clear some brush out behind the pine trees. I don't know what happened out there, but they always came back in a rage." With his older son, he was almost worse. Ben, Bailey writes, was

now old enough to be a considerable disappointment in his own right: as his father was at pains to remind him, he too needed to lose weight and do better in school and (especially) take an interest in sports like other boys . . . Cheever, a great reader of Freud, was not consoled by the news that homosexual tendencies are somewhat innate in all people; rather he became even more vigilant in cultivating a proper ethos for his older son. "Speak like a man!" he'd say, driven up the wall by the boy's high-pitched voice, not to mention his giggling ("You laugh like a woman!").

Cheever picked on one of his son's friends who he thought was effeminate. The boy, he wrote, "often stands with both hands on his hips in an attitude that I was told, when I was a boy, was the sign of a congenital queer . . . He is attached securely to my son and I do not like him."

Cheever's view of other writers was not sweet either. He wrote to a friend about John Updike: "I would go to considerable expense and inconvenience to avoid his company. I think his magnanimity specious and his work seems motivated by covetousness, exhibitionism and a stony heart." (Updike, when he read this remark in Cheever's published letters in 1994, returned the compliment, when he described his feelings about Cheever's drinking: "I felt badly because it was as though a natural resource was being wasted. Although the covetousness in me, and stony heart, kind of rejoiced to see one less writer to compete with.") In 1965 Cheever (who, unlike some of his fellow writers, was not boycotting the White House) managed to heckle Updike as he read a story at a reception there. "The arrogance of Updike goes back to the fact that he does not consider me a peer," he wrote in his journals, bitterly noting that Updike considered Salinger a peer.

Out of all this hate and resentment and foolishness, two figures escaped. One was Cheever's younger son, Federico, and the other was Saul Bellow. Cheever seems to have liked both of them; or both of them had worked out a way to evade the daily spite he directed at all others, including his editor at the *New*

*Yorker,* William Maxwell, who, he noted, bored him stiff. Federico got on with his father by not taking him seriously, by becoming his kid brother rather than his son, and then slowly becoming his father's protector. "More and more," Bailey writes, "Federico had become the father and John the wayward boy: the latter had to be told not to swim naked in other people's pools, not to use the chainsaw when drunk – on and on – while the former patiently absorbed the insults Cheever inflicted on whosoever presumed to look after him."

When Cheever met Bellow in the early 1950s he felt an instant rapport with him. "I do not have it in me to wish him bad luck: I do not have it in me to be his acolyte," he wrote. "I loved him," Bellow said in return, and added that Cheever had not tried Yankee condescension on him. "It fell to John to resolve these differences [of background]. He did it without the slightest difficulty, simply by putting human essences in first place."

When she read that Cheever said of Bellow, "we share not only our love of women but a fondness for the rain," Mary Cheever remarked: "They were both women haters." Certainly, most of the time, Cheever hated his wife. As the position of women in America began to change, and Mary Cheever developed independent views and ambitions, her husband's temper was not improved. "Educating an unintellectual woman," he remarked, "is like letting a rattlesnake into the house. She cannot add a column of figures or make a bed but she will lecture you on the inner symbolism of Camus while the dinner burns." His hatred for his wife disfigured some of his stories, including "An Educated American Woman" (1963) and "The Ocean" (1964). (He conceded that his depiction of "predatory women" was a "serious weakness" in his work.) "An Educated American Woman' is perhaps the best account we have of how frightened American men were by the possibility that their wives would be anything other than little homemakers.

Just as the position of women was changing in America, so, too, the prejudice against homosexuals was fading. While Cheever was threatened by the former, it was obvious that the latter would have a profound effect on him once he left his own house in Ossining and took a look at the world. In 1973, when he began teaching at the Iowa Writers' Workshop, he had T. C. Boyle, Ron Hansen and Allan Gurganus as students. Not only were these talented young writers, but one of them – Gurganus – was extremely handsome (as the photograph included in Bailey's biography makes abundantly clear) and, as Bailey puts it, "quite insouciantly gay." As Cheever admired Gurganus's work (and introduced him to Maxwell, who published one of his stories), he presumed that Gurganus would return the compliment by sleeping with him, despite the fact that he was almost fifteen years older than Gurganus's father. Some of his letters to Gurganus were playful, including the one where he asked (in return for the Maxwell introduction) for some favours. "All I expect is that you learn to cook, service me sexually from three to seven times a day, never interrupt me, contradict me or reflect in any way on the beauty of my prose, my intellect or my person. You must also play soccer, hockey and football." Gurganus let him know as sweetly as he could that while he liked him, he did not want to sleep with him. "How dare he refuse me in favour of some dim-witted major in decorative arts," Cheever wrote. He asked Gurganus to consider whether such figures "appreciate the excellence of your character and the fineness of your mind."

What Cheever was really looking for, as Gurganus put it, was "somebody who was literary, intelligent, attractive and manly, but gay on a technicality." Early in 1977, at the University of Utah, he met Max Zimmer, a PhD candidate in his early thirties, who had been brought up as a Mormon. As Cheever felt "a profound stirring of love" and came on to Max, Max felt "confusion and revulsion." That spring Cheever noted:

How cruel, unnatural and black is my love for Z. I seem to mean to prey on Z's youth, to drive Z into a tragic isolation, to deny Z any life at all. Love is to instruct, to show our beloved what we know of the sources of light, and this may be the declaration of a crafty and lecherous old man. I can only hope not.

In fact, he hoped not quite a lot of the time. And his hoping not was generally improved by sending Zimmer's work too to the *New Yorker*.

Since Cheever took the view that sexual stimulation could improve his eyesight, part of Max's function, once their affair began, was to offer the same comfort as a good pair of spectacles might have. (When driving at night, Cheever used to ask his wife to fondle his penis "to a bone.") "Whenever Max submitted a manuscript," Bailey writes, "Cheever would first insist that the young man help "clear [his] vision" with a handjob." Then (as Max noted in his journal) Cheever would "take my story upstairs and come back down with a remote look of consternation on his face and with criticisms so remote they only increase my confusion."

Max, who was confused, as they say, rather than actually gay, was uneasy and guilty in the Cheever household.

If he thought it was OK to parade me in front of Mary and his children, then I guess it was OK. The fact that I didn't feel OK doing it was my problem . . . Obviously it's what people in the East do, the way he takes it in stride. Sitting down at the dinner table with his family, an hour after I've given him a handjob and he still has stains in his corduroys from it, I guess this is OK here. It's tearing my guts out, but Ben's being nice to me, and Susie – who should take a fucking plate and bust it over my head – and poor Mary, you know.

In her memoir, Susan Cheever wrote about the view the family took of Max's presence.

He was often at the house in Ossining, and although this was not a comfortable situation for him, he treated my mother with a relaxed courtesy and respect. In fact, he treated her a lot better than my father did. I was always glad to see him. He was pleasant and funny, and when they were together my father seemed more accessible than he usually was.

In 1975, at the age of sixty-three, after a drunken term spent teaching at Boston University, Cheever stopped drinking. A year later, he finished his novel *Falconer*. Susan Cheever describes that year:

My father's certainty as a writer was never more apparent than during the year he was writing *Falconer* . . . Each chapter and scene seemed to stream from his imagination already written. These were the things he had been longing to say . . . *Falconer* is a novel about a man imprisoned for the murder of his brother. He is a heroin addict, and his marriage is a travesty of marriage vows. The center of the book is a tender homosexual love affair.

When the book was published, Cheever was on the cover of *Newsweek* with the caption: "A Great American Novel." The book was number one on the *New York Times* best-seller list for three weeks. In 1979 Cheever's collected *Stories* won a Pulitzer Prize and wide critical acclaim.

*Falconer* arose from the clash between the two most significant buildings in the town of Ossining: Cheever's suburban home, which was for him and his family often like a prison, and Sing Sing. In the early 1970s, when he had exhausted himself by drinking and had also exhausted himself writing slack stories on the subject of the deep despair and the minor travails inherent in American East Coast suburban life, Cheever was invited to teach at Sing Sing, where he befriended one of the prisoners. He saw a great deal of this man when he was released. "Almost every set piece in *Falconer*," Bailey writes, "almost every detail . . . appears somewhere in Cheever's journal entries about Sing Sing, based on information he'd extracted from inmates." The novel, which is short, has a relentlessness in tone, a gravity and seriousness, which is unlike anything else Cheever wrote. It is as though the book were not merely a strained metaphor for all the anguish Cheever felt and caused in his life, but an exploration and recognition of that anguish, presented in a style that was factual but also heightened and controlled and then filled with suffering. The style is risky in the way it allows bald statement to brush against an overall vision that is like something from the Psalms. The sense of violence, hatred, pain and deep alienation is offered raw; beside this, love, or something like love, comes as dark redemption or another form of power. In the middle somewhere are the grim ordinariness of prison life and some brilliant sex scenes. If you ignore the upbeat, cheesy ending, *Falconer* is the best Russian novel in the English language.

Cheever's journals for the months when he worked on his masterpiece are fascinating. He understood that even the smallest experience, such as a wait at an airport, can become something much larger in the imagination. "On the question of crypto-autobiography," he wrote,

and the fact that the greatness of fiction is not this, I am writing not from my experience as a teacher in prison but from my experience as a man. I have seen confinement in prison, but I have experienced confinement as a corporal in a line rifle company, as a stockade guard, as a traveller confined for 36 hours in the Leningrad airport during a blizzard, and for as long again in the Cairo airport during a strike. I have known emotional, sexual and financial confinements, and I have actually been confined to a dryout tank on 93rd Street for clinical alcoholics.

In the next entry, he ends with a remark that is one of the few endearing remarks in his journals and should be the motto of every writer alive: "All right, I want something beautiful, and it will be done by June."

Cheever enjoyed being famous and dry for the last few years of his life. Since there was something petulant and childish about him when he was a drunk, now merely the child remained. Susan wrote about these years, as he basked in late success.

Wealth and fame and love had an odd effect on my father . . . He went through a kind of adolescence of celebrity. At times he seemed to be his own number one groupie . . . In restaurants, he let head waiters know that he was someone important. Since this kind of behaviour was new to him, he wasn't particularly graceful about it.

Federico, whose remarks on his father are notable for their wisdom and general good humour, has the best line on his father's fame: "When you're a musician, people can ask you to play, and when you're a movie star, people can ask for your autograph, but what does it mean to be a famous writer? Well, you get to say pompous things. You get to talk about aesthetics and things like that. That's the goodies you get."

As he made an effort to repair the damage he had done to his family, Cheever was aware that his journals, 4,000 pages of them, lay in a drawer like a lovely toy time bomb. Two weeks before he died he phoned his son Ben: "What I wanted to tell you," he said, "is that your father has had his cock sucked by quite a few disreputable characters. I thought I'd tell you that, because sooner or later somebody's going to tell you and I'd just as soon it came from me." Ben wrote that he was "forgiving." "But mostly I was just bewildered, and I remember now that my reply came almost as a whisper: 'I don't mind, Daddy, if you don't mind.'" After his death, when Susan read the diaries, needing to flesh things out for her memoir, she was pretty surprised by the general tone and content, and "not only," as Bailey writes, "because of the gloomy, relentless sexual stuff." The *New Yorker*

was also able to write quiet and effective and emotionally charged sentences. The sixty-one words in the opening paragraph of *Go Tell It on the Mountain* have only one word – the first – with more than three syllables and forty-one words with only one syllable.

Everyone had always said that John would be a preacher when he grew up, just like his father. It had been said so often that John, without ever thinking about it, had come to believe it himself. Not until the morning of his fourteenth birthday did he really begin to think about it, and by then it was already too late.

This style seems closer to Hemingway than to jazz or James; it suggests that Baldwin was as comfortable with the tradition he inherited from a generation of writers most of whom were at the height of their fame as he was starting to write. No young writers ever wish to give too much credit to the writers who could have been their father. They prefer to pay homage to grandfathers or to painters or musicians or ballet dancers or acrobats. It is one way of killing your father, to pretend that he made no difference to you while watching his cadences like a hawk.

So, too, in Baldwin's short stories this plain opening style had not an ounce of James or of jazz. "The Rockpile" opens: "Across the street from their house, in an empty lot between two houses, stood the rockpile." "The Outing" opens: "Each summer the church gave an outing." "Sonny's Blues" opens: "I read about it in the paper, in the subway, on my way to work."

Between the publication of *Go Tell It on the Mountain* in 1953 and the volume of stories *Going to Meet the Man* in 1965, Baldwin wrote a piece for *The New York Times* that set about openly killing some of his literary fathers. In January 1962 he wrote:

Since World War II, certain names in recent American literature – Hemingway, Fitzgerald, Dos Passos, Faulkner – have acquired such

weight and become so sacrosanct that they have been used as touch-
stones to reveal the understandable, but lamentable, inadequacy of the
younger literary artists . . . Let one of us, the younger, attempt to create a restless, unhappy, free-wheeling heroine and we are immediately
informed that Hemingway or Fitzgerald did the same thing better –
infinitely better.

Having made clear, in grudging tone, his immense respect for
these writers, Baldwin proceeded to demolish them.

It is useful . . . to remember in the case of Hemingway that his reputation began to be unassailable at the very instant that his work began
that decline from which it never recovered – at about the time of *For
Whom the Bell Tolls*. Hindsight allows us to say that this boyish and
romantic and inflated book marks Hemingway's abdication from the
efforts to understand the many-sided evil that is in the world. This is
exactly the same thing as saying that he somehow gave up the effort to
become a great novelist.

Having also demolished Faulkner ("such indefensibly muddy
work as 'Intruder in the Dust' or 'Requiem for a Nun'") and "the
later development" of Dos Passos ("if one can call it that") and
Fitzgerald ("there is no longer anything to say about Fitzgerald"),
Baldwin considered the matter of America itself as a realm of
failed imaginations.

The previously mentioned giants have at least one thing in common:
their simplicity . . . It is the American way of looking on the world as
a place to be corrected, and in which innocence is inexplicably lost.
It is this almost inexpressible pain which lends such force to some of
the early Hemingway stories – including "The Killers" – and to the
marvelous fishing sequence in "The Sun Also Rises"; and it is also the
reason that Hemingway's heroines seem so peculiarly sexless and
manufactured.

Baldwin, in his attempt to establish a context for his own work, now invoked the spirit of Henry James by taking the unusual step of claiming James as a novelist who dealt with the matter of failed masculinity in America. In *The Ambassadors*, Baldwin wrote,

What is the moral dilemma of Lambert Strether if not that, at the midnight hour, he realizes that he has, somehow, failed his manhood: that the "masculine sensibility" as James puts it, has failed in him? . . . Strether's triumph is that he is able to realize this, even though he knows it is too late for him to act on it. And it is James' perception of this peculiar impossibility which makes him, until today, the greatest of our novelists. For the question which he raised, ricocheting it, so to speak, off the backs of his heroines, is the question which so torments us now. The question is this: How is an American to become a man? And this is precisely the same thing as asking: How is America to become a nation? By contrast with him, the giants who came to the fore between the two world wars merely lamented the necessity.

Baldwin understood the singular importance of the novel in America because he saw the dilemma his country faced as essentially an interior one, a poison that began in the individual spirit and only made its way then into politics. His political writing remains as raw and vivid as his fiction because he believed that social reform could not occur through legislation alone but through a reimagining of the private realm. Thus, for Baldwin, an examination of the individual soul as dramatized in fiction had immense power. It was, in the end, he saw, a matter of love, and he was not afraid to use the word. In his 1962 *New York Times* article he wrote:

The loneliness of the cities described in Dos Passos is greater now than it has ever been before; and these cities are more dangerous now than they were before, and their citizens are yet more unloved. And those panaceas and formulas which have so spectacularly failed Dos Passos have also failed this country, and the world. The trouble is deeper than we wish to think: the trouble is in us. And we will never remake those cities, or conquer our cruel and unbearable human isolation – we will never establish human communities – until we stare our ghastly failure in the face.

Before he began to publish fiction, Baldwin was a reviewer with attitude, a writer with a high sense of aesthetic grandeur, an Edmund Wilson with real poison in his pen. In the *New Leader* in December 1947, for example, the twenty-three-year-old Baldwin employed a triple negative to take a swipe at Erskine Caldwell's *The Sure Hand of God*: "Certainly there is nothing in the book which would not justify the suspicion that Mr. Caldwell was concerned with nothing more momentous than getting rid of some of the paper he had lying about the house, resurrecting several of the tired types on which he first made his reputation, and (incidentally) making a few dollars on the deal." Earlier that same year, he took on Maxim Gorky: "Gorky, not in the habit of describing intermediate colors, even when he suspected their existence, has in *Mother* written a Russian battle hymn which history has so summarily dated that we are almost unwilling to credit it with any reality." Gorky, he went on, "was the foremost exponent of the maxim that 'art is the weapon of the working class.' He is also, probably, the major example of the invalidity of such a doctrine. (It is rather like saying that art is the weapon of the American housewife.)"

Moving from Russia with careful, youthful deliberation and delight, Baldwin in August 1948 did something close to many serious novelists' hearts. He took on a popular writer much praised for his terse style and pace, in this case poor James M. Cain, author of *The Postman Always Rings Twice*. Baldwin considered Cain's body of work: "Not only did he have nothing to say," he wrote, but he drooled, so to speak, as he said it . . . He writes with the stolid, humorless assurance of the American self-made man. Rather a great deal has been written concerning his breathless staccato "pace," his terse, corner-of-the-mouth "style," his significance as a recorder of the seamier side of American life. This is nonsense: Mr. Cain writes fantasies and fantasies of the most unendurably mawkish and sentimental sort.

In January 1949 in an essay in *Commentary*, Baldwin formulated what would become his characteristic battle cry, which would so puzzle and irritate white liberals and reformers in the 1960s when they found they had reason to listen to him – the problem in America, he believed, lay in each individual American soul, black as much as white; and the black population was not seeking equality with a white world that had so significantly failed to understand itself, let alone those whom it had oppressed. "In a very real sense," he wrote in that essay,

the Negro problem has become anachronistic; we ourselves are the only problem, it is our hearts that we must search. It is neither a politic nor a popular thing to say, but a black man facing a white man becomes at once contemptuous and resentful when he finds himself looked upon as a moral problem for that white man's conscience.

In March 1950 Baldwin published a short story in *Commentary* called "Death of a Prophet," which he did not collect in *Going to Meet the Man*. It was, as far as I can make out, his second piece of published fiction. The first – also published in *Commentary*, in October 1948 – called "Previous Condition," was included in *Going to Meet the Man* and contained a few of the elements that went into *Another Country*. It is easy to see why Baldwin did not want to publish "Death of a Prophet" in a collection, as it too obviously contained the seeds of *Go Tell It on the Mountain*, being the story of a boy in Harlem whose father was a preacher. The subject of a father and his son, Baldwin knew, was an interesting one. In 1967, in a review in the *New York Review of Books*, he wrote: "The father–son relationship is one of the most crucial and dangerous on earth, and to pretend that it can be otherwise really amounts to an exceedingly dangerous heresy."

Although the story of the father and son told in "Death of a Prophet" and *Go Tell It on the Mountain* was, to a large extent, his own story, recounted also in some autobiographical essays, Baldwin understood that the tension between the generations of men was a quintessential American story. It was, he believed, not only what set America apart, but what disfigured his country – the shame, the lack of pride sons in a society moving onwards and upwards felt at their fathers.

Thus his work in his fiction, and even in a novel like *Another Country*, notable for the absence of fathers, dealt with a most public and pressing matter in the most private and personal way. In an essay in 1964 Baldwin formulated the theory of this:

And what happens to a person, however odd this may sound, also happens to a nation ... The Italian immigrant arriving from Italy, for example, or the sons of parents who were born in Sicily, makes a great point of not speaking Italian because he's going to become an American. And he can't bear his parents because they are backward. This may seem a trivial matter. But it is of the utmost importance when a father is despised by his son, and this is one of the facts of American life, and this is what we are really referring to, in oblique and terrible fashion, when we talk about upward mobility.

The writing in "Death of a Prophet" is high-toned, almost overwrought at times, but pitched with zeal and serious ambition and great tenderness. The story is what Baldwin himself called in a review in the *New Leader* in September 1947 "a study of human helplessness"; it sees the character of Johnnie, whose father is dying, and who has become a stranger in his father's eyes, not "in relation to oppression," as Baldwin put it in another piece on Gorky in 1947, but in relation to the character's own fear and inadequacy. Baldwin, even as he began, and despite his deep awareness of the relationship between the political and the personal, was determined that his characters should not be confined by a narrow political agenda; he sought to ensure that the behaviour and the failure of his characters should be seen first as particular and private and then only as part of some general malaise that took its bearings from the Fall of Man as much as the creation of slavery, and emphatically not from a predetermined role as black men oppressed by bad laws. He also wanted to follow the example of Robert Louis Stevenson, whose novels and stories he reviewed in January 1948; he wanted to write, as Baldwin put it, "superbly well" and know that this would be, as with Stevenson, "the most enduring delight." Baldwin wished to create and live as an American and as a man, and had much to say about the state of his nation and about its masculinity. (In April 1966 he wrote: "Much of the American confusion, if not most of it, is a direct result of the American effort to avoid dealing with the Negro as a man.") He was helped by his insistence that he did not belong to anyone's margin and his ability in the same moment to take possession of the margin when it suited his purpose. He relished the ambiguity of his position and was skilled at covering his tracks.

When it came to the matter of boxing, for example, a subject that would thrill many of his heterosexual colleagues, he claimed to know nothing. Instead, using the full force of his homosexuality, he wrote beautifully about Floyd Patterson and his fight with Sonny Liston in 1963, studying the state of the two men's souls and the intricacies of their auras with an erotic intensity. Of Patterson, he wrote:

And I think part of the resentment he arouses is due to the fact that he brings to what is thought of – quite erroneously – as a simple activity a terrible note of complexity. This is his personal style, a style which strongly suggests that most un-American of attributes, privacy, the will to privacy; and my own guess is that he is still relentlessly, painfully shy – he still lives gallantly with his scars, but not all of them have healed – and while he has found a way to master this, he has found no way to hide it; as, for example, another miraculously tough and tender man, Miles Davis, has managed to do.

Of Liston, Baldwin wrote:

He reminded me of big, black men I have known who acquired the reputation of being tough in order to conceal the fact that they weren't hard . . . Anyway, I liked him, liked him very much. He sat opposite me at the table, sideways, head down, waiting for the blow: for Liston knows, as only the inarticulately suffering can, just how inarticulate he is. But let me clarify that: I say suffering because it seems to me that he has suffered a great deal. It is in his face, in the silence of that face, and in the curiously distant light in his eyes – a light which rarely signals because there have been so few answering signals . . . I said, "I can't ask you any questions because everything's been asked. Perhaps I'm only here, really, to say that I wish you well" . . . I'm glad I said it because he looked at me then, really for the first time, and he talked to me for a little while.

But in those same years he also spoke and wrote as though he were a founding father, in an unassailable position in his country, one of its central voices. In *The New York Times* in 1959 he wrote:

I think that there is something suspicious about the way we cling to the concept of race, on both sides of the obsolescent racial fence. White men, when they have not entirely succumbed to their panic, wallow in their guilt, and call themselves, usually "liberals." Black men, when they have not drowned in their bitterness, wallow in their rage, and call themselves, usually "militant." Both camps have managed to evade the really hideous complexity of our situation on the social and personal level.

In the same year, in reply to a question about whether the 1950s as a decade "makes special demands on you as a writer," he adopted one of his best tones, lofty and idealistic and filled with candour, while remaining sharp and direct and challenging: "But finally for me the difficulty is to remain in touch with the private life. The private life, his own and that of others, is the writer's subject – his key and ours to his achievement." Henry James would have been proud of him.

(The pride worked both ways. In *Playboy* in 1964 Baldwin managed to commandeer James as a member of his tribe, as someone who did not, as the vast majority of Americans did, spend his life "in flight from death." He compared a passage from a letter James wrote to a friend who had lost her husband – "Sorrow wears and uses us but we wear and use it too, and it is blind. Whereas we, after a manner, see" – with these lines from Bessie Smith:

> *Good mornin', blues,*
> *Blues, how do you do?*
> *I'm doin' all right.*
> *Good mornin',*
> *How are you?*

Once more James would have been proud, although it should be added that in his lifetime or in the years after his death he and his followers were not ever fully aware that what he was really doing was singing the blues.)

In 1959 also, in a paper called "Mass Culture and the Creative Artist" given to a symposium, Baldwin concluded:

We are in the middle of an immense metamorphosis here, a metamorphosis which will, it is devoutly to be hoped, rob us of our myths and give us our history, which will destroy our attitudes and give us back our personalities. The mass culture, in the meantime, can only reflect our chaos: and perhaps we had better remember that this chaos contains life – and a great transforming energy.

He was, in these years, moving himself carefully to the centre of the debate, refusing a role, offered to him always, as spokesman for a minority, to be listened to only when that minority grew restive or dangerous or newsworthy.

During the 1960s, the voice Baldwin used in his journalism grew less ambiguous, however, more strident, especially when he was addressing a black audience. In a speech he gave to the Student Co-ordinating Committee in November 1963, after the Kennedy assassination, for example, he began:

Part of the price that Americans have paid for delusion, part of what we have done to ourselves, was given to us in Dallas, Texas. This happened in a civilized nation, the country which is the moral leader of the free world, when some lunatic blew off the President's head. Now, I want to suggest something, and I don't want to sound rude, but we all know that it has been many generations and it hasn't stopped yet that black men's heads have been blown off – and nobody cared. Because, as I said before, it wasn't happening to a person, it was happening to a "nigger."

Two years later, in an angry essay about black history, he saw no possibility of change, merely excuses for change.

In the meantime ladies and gentlemen, after a brief intermission – time out for one or two committee reports, time out for an antipoverty pep talk, time out to make a Vietnamese child an orphan and then lovingly raise him to love all our works, time out for a White House conference, time out to brief and augment the police forces, time out to buy some Negroes, jail some, club some, and kill some – after a brief intermission, ladies and gentlemen, the show begins again in the auction room. And you will hear the same old piano, playing the blues.

At other times, he seemed to be amusing himself by preaching to the white population, insisting that whites, in fact, were the group most in need of freedom from tyranny. In 1961 he wrote:

There is a great captive Negro population here, which is well publicized, and what is not known at all, is that there is a great captive white population here too. No one has pointed out yet with any force that if I am not a man here, you are not a man here. You cannot lynch me and keep me in ghettos without becoming something monstrous yourselves.

In *Playboy* in January 1964 he wrote: "What I'm much more concerned about is what white Americans have done to themselves; what has been done to me is irrelevant because there is nothing more you can do to me. But, in doing it, you've done something to yourself. In evading my humanity, you have done something to your own humanity."

In an essay called "The White Problem," also published in 1964, he sneered at the icons of white America, insisting that the difference between white and black in America was close to the difference between foolishness and seriousness, childhood and maturity:

In this country, for a dangerously long time, there have been two levels of experience. One, to put it cruelly, but, I think, quite truthfully, can be summed up in the images of Doris Day and Gary Cooper: two of the most grotesque appeals to innocence the world has ever seen. And the other, subterranean, indispensable, and denied, can be summed up in the tone and face of Ray Charles. And there never has been in this country any genuine confrontation between these two levels of experience.

In another essay from 1964, "Color and American Civilization," he had more fun at the expense of the neuroses suffered by his white brothers and sisters:

The white man's unadmitted – and apparently, to him, unspeakable – private fears and longings are projected onto the Negro. The only way he can be released from the Negro's tyrannical power over him is to consent, in effect, to become black himself, to become part of that suffering and dancing country that he now watches wistfully from the heights of his lonely power and, armed with spiritual traveler's checks, visits surreptitiously after dark . . . I cannot accept that proposition that the four-hundred-year travail of the American Negro should result merely in his attainment of the present level of American civilization. I am far from convinced that being released from the African witch doctor was worthwhile if I am now . . . expected to become dependent on the American psychiatrist. It is a bargain I refuse.

Five years later, writing in *The New York Times*, he was at his most eloquent, insisting once more that the black population's burden in the United States could not be changed by legislation but only by something more far-reaching in its implications – the total conversion of the white population, whose moral degeneration and distance from themselves he judged to be abject. "I will state flatly," he wrote,

that the bulk of this country's white population impresses me, and has so impressed me for a very long time, as being beyond any conceivable hope of moral rehabilitation. They have been white, if I may so put it, too long; they have been married to the lie of white supremacy too long; the effect on their personalities, their lives, their grasp of reality, has been as devastating as the lava which so memorably immobilized the citizens of Pompeii. They are unable to conceive that their version of reality, which they want me to accept, is an insult to my history and a parody of theirs, and an intolerable violation of myself.

In his fiction, Baldwin sought a new freedom, a freedom to create characters as he pleased. His black characters did not have to be filled with stoical virtue to be destroyed by white forces. His novel *Giovanni's Room* did not even have any black characters at all. Nor did his gay characters have their destiny worked out for them by history; he made them too interesting for that. In his journalism he sought to rewrite history before paying attention to politics. In an address to Harlem teachers in October 1963, he said:

What passes for identity in America is a series of myths about one's heroic ancestors. It's astounding to me, for example, that so many people really appear to believe that the country was founded by a band of heroes who wanted to be free. That happens not to be true. What happened was that some people left Europe because they couldn't stay there any longer and had to go some place else to make it. That's all. They were hungry, they were poor, they were convicts. Those who were making it in England, for example, did not get on the *Mayflower*. That's how the country was settled.

By 1979 his version of American history had become more alarmed. In an article for the *Los Angeles Times*, he wrote:

A very brutal thing must be said: The intentions of this melancholic country as concerns black people – and anyone who doubts me can ask any Indian – have always been genocidal. They needed us for labor and for sport. Now they can't get rid of us. We cannot be exiled and we cannot be accommodated. Something's got to give. The machinery of this country operates day in and day out, hour by hour, to keep the nigger in his place.

In that article he called the Civil Rights Movement "the latest slave rebellion."

Five years later in an article for *Essence*, he continued to muse on the idea of American history and genocide:

America became white – the people who, as they claim, "settled" the country became white – because of the necessity of denying the Black presence, and justifying the Black subjugation. No community can be based on such a principle – or, in other words, no community can be established on so genocidal a lie. White men – from Norway, for example, where they were *Norwegians* – became white by slaughtering the cattle, poisoning the wells, torching the houses, massacring Native Americans, raping Black women.

Reading his speeches and his journalism, it is, most of the time, easy to imagine, twenty years after his death, how he would respond to contemporary events. Hardly anything that has happened since 1987 would have surprised him. In 1979 he wrote: "If they couldn't deal with my father, how are they going to deal with the people in the streets of Tehran? I could have told them, if they had asked." It would be easy to put Baghdad or Basra in that sentence. In 1964 he wrote: "People who do not know who they are privately, accept, as we have accepted for nearly fifteen years, the fantastic disaster which we call American politics and which we call American foreign policy, and the incoherence of the one is an exact reflection of the incoherence of the other." It would be merely necessary now to change the dates. He would not have been surprised by the counting of votes in Florida; he would not have been shocked by Abu Ghraib; he would not have been shocked by New Orleans. He would have known each time what to say. On 9/11, however, it is harder to be sure of his response, except to suspect that the soaring pity he was capable of could have been matched by the calm eloquent wisdom that was, most of the time, his hallmark. But it is hard also not to remember what he told William Styron in 1960 when Styron and his friends asked him what was going to happen now. "Jimmy's face would become a mask of imperturbable certitude," Styron wrote. "'Baby, burn' he would say softly and glare back with vast glowering eyes, 'yes, baby, I mean *burn*. We will *burn your cities down.*'"

Reading his speeches and journalism now, there seems only one fresh hell that has happened in his country that he did not foresee and that would have shocked him deeply. And this is the huge and merciless increase in the prison population, especially of young black males. He saw the context for it, however, and made his own position very clear in his 1964 *Playboy* article:

The failure on our part to accept the reality of pain, of anguish, of ambiguity, of death, has turned us into a very peculiar and monstrous people. It means, for one thing, and it's very serious, that people who have had no experience have no compassion. People who have had no experience suppose that if a man is a thief, he is a thief; but, in fact, that isn't the most important thing about him. The most important thing about him is that he is a man and, furthermore, that if he's a thief or a murderer or whatever he is, *you* could also be and you would know this, anyone would know this who had really dared to live.

He did not see the full implications of this, and so in the same year he wrote something that seems naïve now, perhaps the only truly naïve observation he ever made: "There is a limit to the number of people any government can put in prison, and a rigid limit indeed to the practicality of such a course." And fifteen years later, in the *Los Angeles Times*, he ended his article on a note of pure optimism:

But black people hold the trump. When you try to slaughter people, you create people with nothing to lose. And if I have nothing to lose, what are you going to do to me? In truth, we have one thing to lose – our children. Yet we have never lost them, and there is no reason for us to do it now. We hold the trump. I say it: Patience and shuffle the cards.

The cards were shuffled all right; and the idea that there was a limit to the number of people any government can put in prison became a joker; the game included the possibility of "three strikes and you're out," with all the mindlessness and lack of compassion that that implied. At the end of 2005, there were close to 2.2 million prisoners in federal, state or local jails in the United States. Three thousand one hundred and forty-five black men out of every 100,000 lived as sentenced prisoners, compared to 471 white male sentenced prisoners per 100,000 white males; this compares to an estimated 3,000 out of every 100,000 members of the population of Russia who were in jail during Stalin's reign. As of 2006, seven million people in the United States were behind bars, on probation or on parole. The United States has 5 per cent of the world's population and 25 per cent of its prisoners, 737 per 100,000 compared to 100 in Australia and 59 in Norway and 37 in Japan and 29 in Iceland and India. England and Wales, with roughly the same crime rate as the United States, have 149 per 100,000 in prison. A report from the Justice Department estimated that 12 per cent of American black men in their twenties and early thirties are in jail now, compared to 1.6 per cent of white males of the same age group. The general prison numbers in the United States have doubled since 1990.

In his address to Harlem schoolteachers in 1963, Baldwin set the context for crime among young black men. He wrote about every street boy's relationship to the law.

If he is really cunning, really ruthless, really strong – and many of us are – he becomes a kind of criminal. He becomes a kind of criminal because that's the only way he can live. Harlem and every ghetto in this city – every ghetto in this country – is full of people who live outside the law. They wouldn't dream of calling a policeman . . . They have turned away from the country forever and totally. They live by their wits and really long to see the day when the entire structure comes down.

It seems sad, almost strange, reading his work now, even when its tone was calm and ambiguous and measured, but especially as he grew angry and strident, to realize that, in the twenty years after James Baldwin's death, brand-new structures made of concrete have gone up all over America with laws to match, and in those buildings much of the beauty he wrote about, and many of the dreams his friends had, lie incarcerated. Baldwin's legacy is to help us understand how something has happened that even he could not have imagined.

# Baldwin and Obama: Men Without Fathers

It seemed important, as both men set about making their marks on the world, for them to establish before anything else that their stories began when their fathers died and that they set out alone without a father's shadow or a father's permission. James Baldwin's *Notes of a Native Son*, published in 1955, begins: "On the 29th of July, in 1943, my father died." Baldwin was almost nineteen at the time. Barack Obama's *Dreams from My Father*, published in 1995, begins also with the death of his father: "A few months after my twenty-first birthday, a stranger called to give me the news."

Both men quickly then established their own actual distance from their fathers, which made their grief sharper and more lonely, but also emphasized to the reader that they had a right to speak with authority, to offer this version of themselves partly because they themselves, through force of will and a steely sense of character, had invented the voice they were now using, had not been trained by any other man to be the figure they had become. "I had not known my father very well," Baldwin wrote. "We got on badly, partly because we shared, in our different fashions, the vice of stubborn pride. When he was dead I realized that I had hardly ever spoken to him. When he had been dead a long time I began to wish I had."

Of his father, Barack Obama wrote: "At the time of his death, my father remained a myth to me, both more and less than a man. He had left Hawaii back in 1963, when I was only two years old, so that as a child I knew him only through the stories that my mother and grandparents told."

Both men then, using photographs and memories, commented on their fathers' blackness. In both cases it seemed important to state or suggest that the father was more black than the son. Baldwin wrote that there was something buried in his father that had lent him his "tremendous power and, even, a rather crushing charm. It had something to do with his blackness, I think – he was very black – with his blackness and his beauty."

When Obama was a child, he wrote, "my father looked nothing like the people around me in that he was black as pitch, my mother white as milk."

In both cases too, the writers sought to make clear that their fathers' pasts were not their own pasts, but the past as a different country, a country they did not share. "He was of the first generation of free men," Baldwin wrote. "He, along with thousands of other Negroes, came North after 1919 and I was part of that generation which had never seen the landscape of what Negroes sometimes call the Old Country." Obama's father was from a place even more distant: "He was an African, I would learn, a Kenyan of the Luo tribe, born on the shores of Lake Victoria in a place called Alego."

Although Obama mentions in passing in *Dreams from My Father* that he had read Baldwin when he was a young community activist in Chicago, there is no hint in the book that he modelled his own story in any way on Baldwin's work. In their versions of who they became in America and how, there are considerable similarities and shared moments not because Obama was using Baldwin as a template or an example, but because the same hurdles and similar circumstances and the same moments of truth actually occurred almost naturally for both of them.

Baldwin and Obama, although in different ways, experienced the church and intense religious feeling as key elements in their lives. They both travelled and discovered while abroad, almost as a shock, an essential American identity for themselves while in the company of non-Americans who were black. They both came to see, in a time of political division, some shared values with the other side. They both used eloquence with an exquisite, religious fervour.

As Northerners, they both were shocked by the South. They both had to face up to the anger, the rage, that lay within them, and everyone like them, as a way of taking the poison out of themselves. It is almost as though, in their search for power – Baldwin becoming the finest American prose stylist of his generation, Obama the President of the United States – they would both have to gain wisdom, both bitter and sweet, at the same fount, since no other fount was available. Their story is in some ways the same story because it could hardly have been otherwise.

In the essay "Notes of a Native Son," James Baldwin wrote about rage: "There is not a Negro alive who does not have this rage in his blood – one has the choice, merely, of living with it consciously or surrendering to it. As for me, this fever has recurred in me, and does, and will until the day I die." In his speech on race in March 2008, Barack Obama, in tones more measured, more patient, but no less urgent, dealt with the same issues as they were experienced more than fifty years after Baldwin's essay appeared:

That legacy of defeat was passed on to future generations – those young men and increasingly young women who we see standing on street corners or languishing in our prisons, without hope or prospects for the future. Even for those blacks who did make it, questions of race, and racism, continue to define their worldview in fundamental ways. For the men and women of Reverend Wright's generation, the memories of humiliation and doubt and fear have not gone away; nor has the anger and the bitterness of those years.

That anger may not get expressed in public, in front of white co-workers or white friends. But it does find voice in the barbershop or around the kitchen table. At times, that anger is exploited by politicians, to gin up votes along racial lines, or to make up for a politician's own failings.

In his first novel, *Go Tell It on the Mountain*, published in 1953, Baldwin wrote with remarkable eloquence about the power of prayer and preaching for an otherwise powerless community, the sense of time spent in church as a time filled with soaring possibilities in contrast to the bitter world outside. It was as though that very bitterness offered the congregation a unique insight into the suffering of Christ and made the congregation for that time of prayer and preaching a chosen people whose spiritual exaltation, in all its fiery rhetoric and colourful abandon, could never be experienced by white people.

Baldwin matched his novel with an essay, "Down at the Cross," published in 1962, where he wrote about his own conversion as an adolescent filled with doubts and fears and ambitions and a sharp sense of exclusion:

One moment I was on my feet, singing and clapping and, at the same time, working out in my head the plot of a play I was working on then; the next moment, with no transition, no sensation of falling, I was on my back, with the lights beating down into my face and all the vertical saints above me.

Baldwin emphasized that because black suffering had been transformed so secretly and so completely by black religious leaders into spiritual suffering, what happened in black churches would have to be fully understood, dramatized and explained before any solution would be possible. His first novel and his essay "Down at the Cross" sought to let white America into the secret that was Sunday for the black community:

The church was very exciting. It took a long time for me to disengage myself from this excitement, and on the blindest, most visceral level, I really never have, and never will. There is no music like that music, no dráma like the drama of the saints rejoicing, the sinners moaning, the tambourines racing, and all those voices coming together and crying holy unto the Lord. There is still, for me, no pathos quite like the pathos of those multicolored, worn, somehow triumphant and transfigured faces, speaking from the depths of a visible, tangible, continuing despair of the goodness of the Lord . . . Nothing that has happened to me since equals the power and the glory that I sometimes felt when, in the middle of a sermon, I knew that I was somehow, by some miracle, really carrying, as they say, "the Word" – when the church and I were one.

Out of oppression then came a freedom that only the church could offer and that gave the church a special, defining power for black communities, which was both beyond politics and deeply political, a power the Catholic Church in Poland and Ireland would also have. "Perhaps we were, all of us," Baldwin wrote, "bound together by the nature of our oppression, the specific and peculiar complex of risks we had to run; if so, within these limits we sometimes achieved with each other a freedom that was close to love."

In *Dreams from My Father*, Barack Obama described finding religion in Chicago, hearing about the history of the black church in America, the "history of slave religion . . . Africans who, newly landed on hostile shores, had sat circled around a fire mixing newfound myths with ancient rhythms, their songs becoming a vessel for those most radical of ideas – survival, and freedom, and hope." He described attending a sermon given by the Reverend Jeremiah Wright, pastor of Trinity United Church of Christ in Chicago:

People began to shout, to rise from their seats and clap and cry out, a forceful wind carrying the reverend's voice up into the rafters. As I watched and listened from my seat, I began to hear all the notes from the past three years swirl about me . . . The desire to let go, the desire to escape, the desire to give oneself up to a God that could somehow put a floor on despair.

The sermons heard in those churches preached not only about eternal life and the ethereal life of the soul, but about the sufferings of the soul on this earth, in this America, and the emotions to which this suffering gave rise, including despair and anger. In March 2008 Obama would try to explain that anger as one of the many essential parts of the religious services that black people had been attending all of their lives, the services that Baldwin had dramatized and described, and that the white majority had been excluded from. "The fact," Obama said,

that so many people are surprised to hear that anger in some of Reverend Wright's sermons simply reminds us of the old truism that the most segregated hour in American life occurs on Sunday morning. That anger is not always productive; indeed, all too often it distracts attention from solving real problems; it keeps us from squarely facing our own complicity in our condition, and prevents the African-American community from forging the alliances it needs to bring about real change. But the anger is real; it is powerful; and to simply wish it away, to condemn it without understanding its roots, only serves to widen the chasm of misunderstanding that exists between the races.

Obama's church was like the one that Baldwin described in *Go Tell It on the Mountain*, a place where "all the men seemed mighty," that "rocked with the Power of God," that offered the community a sort of nobility and unity and sense of transcendence not available elsewhere. "That has been my experience at Trinity," Obama said in March 2008.

Like other predominantly black churches across the country, Trinity embodies the black community in its entirety – the doctor and the welfare mom, the model student and the former gang-banger. Like other black churches, Trinity's services are full of raucous laughter and sometimes bawdy humor. They are full of dancing, clapping, screaming and shouting that may seem jarring to the untrained ear. The church contains in full the kindness and cruelty, the fierce intelligence and the shocking ignorance, the struggles and successes, the love and yes, the bitterness and bias that make up the black experience in America.

Baldwin was a child preacher, and that tone never left his system, just as it is part of the rhetoric he came to use later on. Since both men made clear that the church was not a place where arguments were held, but rather where souls were lifted up by grace as much as by language, where voices rose not in reason but in pure denial of reason for the sake of salvation, then to isolate some of Reverend Wright's views as expressed in his sermons and ask Obama to distance himself from them was to miss the point.

Had their ambitions been less focused and their personalities less complex, Baldwin and Obama could easily have become pastors, preachers, leaders of black churches. But for both of them there was a shadow, a sense of an elsewhere that would form them and make them, eventually, more interested in leading America itself, or as much of it as would follow, than merely leading their own race in America. Both of them would discover their essential Americanness outside America, Baldwin in France, the home of some of his literary ancestors, Obama in Kenya, the home of his father.

There is a peculiar intensity in the quality of their engagement with these foreign countries. Indeed, there are very few American writers born in the twentieth century whose level of involvement with another country equals Baldwin's with France; and it is impossible to think of another American politician who has been involved in the life of another country as Obama has been with Kenya.

Baldwin and Obama did not just observe these countries, finding out much about foreign morals, manners and social problems. What is crucial in both cases is that what they most fruitfully observed in the end was themselves. What they found within themselves changed them profoundly and made them different from everyone else around them; what they found gave these two fatherless men, already possessed of an eloquence that came from a source hidden from most Americans, a new power and a freedom and a sense of a destiny to fulfil.

Baldwin moved to Paris in November 1948 when he was twenty-four. "I left America," he wrote in 1959, "because I doubted my ability to survive the fury of the color problem here . . . I wanted to prevent myself from becoming *merely* a Negro; or, even, merely a Negro writer." In these years it occurred to him that while he was a stranger in Europe, he was not, as he had supposed, such a stranger in his own country. In one essay, describing life in a Swiss village, he wrote:

No road whatever will lead Americans back to the simplicity of this European village where white men still have the luxury of looking on me as a stranger. I am not, really, a stranger any longer for any American alive. One of the things that distinguishes Americans from other people is that no other people has ever been so deeply involved in the lives of black men, and vice versa.

In his introduction to *Nobody Knows My Name*, published in 1961, Baldwin wrote of his stay in France: "The question of who I was had at last become a personal question." In one of the essays in that book he described attending the Conference of Negro-African Writers and Artists in Paris in 1956 and finding an enormous gap between himself and the writers who had come from Africa and the Caribbean:

For what, at bottom, distinguished the Americans from the Negroes who surrounded us, men from Nigeria, Senegal, Barbados, Martinique

. . . was the banal and abruptly quite overwhelming fact that we had been born in a society which, in a way quite inconceivable for Africans, and no longer real for Europeans, was open, and, in a sense which has nothing to do with justice or injustice, was free. It was a society, in short, in which nothing was fixed and we had therefore been born to a greater number of possibilities, wretched as these possibilities seemed at the instant of our birth. Moreover, the land of our forefathers' exile had been made, by that travail, our home.

Baldwin summed up the result of his experience in France: "I found myself, willy-nilly, alchemized into an American the moment I touched French soil."

The realization that he was an American, albeit one who came into being through alchemy, had a profound impact on Baldwin not only as a political thinker and essayist, but as an artist. It allowed him to write two masterpieces – *Giovanni's Room* and *Another Country* – in which the souls of white people are examined with sympathy and tenderness; it allowed him to formulate a credo, as an artist who wrote also about black people, that their fate should not be predetermined by their colour but by the intimate spaces hidden in their souls. Our failure to love with due care became his subject; his genius was to spread that failure wide, make it an existential problem, almost a religious one. It also allowed him to realize that the history of black America belonged to whites as much as to blacks and that the "black-white experience [in America] may prove of indispensable value to us in the world we face today. This world is white no longer, and it will never be white again."

Thus when William Styron published *The Confessions of Nat Turner* in 1967 and was attacked by African-American critics for stealing the voice of a slave for his fiction, he was defended by Baldwin: "He has begun the common history – *ours*." Later, Baldwin told the *Paris Review*: "I admired him for confronting it, and the result . . . He writes out of reasons similar to mine – about something that hurt him and frightened him."

Although there are moments in Baldwin's speeches and writings that are angrier and more sectarian than the main body of his writing, his work seems astonishingly wise and for-giving, constantly ready to include the other side, insisting that the complex fate of being an American involved America in its both rich and hidden diversity and its both gnarled and noble history. It appears that such wisdom and sense of forgiveness came from how he lived, from his walking the streets of Euro-pean cities knowing that he was not at home and slowly realizing where home was. Home, oddly enough, was the United States.

On his first trip to Kenya, before he went to Harvard Law School, Barack Obama, who was twenty-seven, sensed his father's ghostly presence in the streets of Nairobi:

I see him in the schoolboys who run past us, their lean, black legs mov-ing like piston rods between blue shorts and oversized shoes. I hear him in the laughter of the pair of university students who sip sweet creamed tea and eat samosas in a dimly lit teahouse. I smell him in the cigarette smoke of the businessman who covers one ear and shouts into a pay phone; in the sweat of a day laborer who loads gravel into a wheelbarrow, his face and bare chest covered with dust. The Old Man's here, I think, although he doesn't say anything to me. He's here, asking me to understand.

In these chapters of his autobiography, as Obama attempted to understand his Kenyan heritage, there is a sharp feeling that this was an interlude in the life of an earnest American, at times a form of tourism, at other times a serious effort to resolve the most complex matters of identity and selfhood. There is a moment when he sat by the graves of his ancestors and wept:

When my tears were finally spent, I felt a calmness wash over me. I felt the circle finally close . . . I saw that my life in America – the black life, the white life, the sense of abandonment I'd felt as a boy, the frustration and hope I'd witnessed in Chicago – all of it was connected with this small plot of earth an ocean away, connected by more than the accident of a name or the color of my skin. The pain I felt was my father's pain. My questions were my brothers' questions. Their struggle, my birthright.

This passage displays the difference between Baldwin's sensibility and that of Obama. Whereas Baldwin sought to make distinctions, Obama always wants to make connections; his urge is to close circles even when they don't need to be closed or the closure is too neat to be fully trusted. Whereas Baldwin longed to disturb the peace, create untidy truths, Obama was slowly becoming a politician.

Despite his best effort to reconcile his own life at home with that of his Kenyan father, the chapters about Kenya in *Dreams from My Father* show Obama puzzled and ill at ease. Later, in his book *The Audacity of Hope*, he moved closer to the truth when he described his wife's admission on a flight back from Kenya to Chicago that "she was looking forward to getting home. 'I never realized just how American I was,' she said. She hadn't realized just how free she was – or how much she cherished that freedom."

Just as Obama, in his increasing urge to inspire, a necessary aspect of his calling perhaps, often seeks a rhetoric free of bitterness and high on healing, Baldwin, in his urge to speak difficult truths, to tell white people what they least wished to hear, sometimes moved towards a tone that was almost shrill. In his great good humour, however, he would perhaps enjoy more than anyone else reading this passage now from an essay written by him in 1965:

I remember when the ex-Attorney General, Mr. Robert Kennedy, said it was conceivable that in 40 years in America we might have a Negro

President. That sounded like a very emancipated statement to white people. They were not in Harlem when this statement was first heard. They did not hear the laughter and bitterness and scorn with which this statement was greeted . . . We were here for 400 years and now he tells us that maybe in 40 years, if you are good, we may let you become President.

Obama, running for President forty-three years later, just three years too late to fulfill what Robert Kennedy saw as conceivable, and Baldwin saw as far too late, ends *Dreams from My Father* with the phrase, "I felt like the luckiest man alive." Later, when he won his first election to the U.S. Senate, he wrote: "Still, there was no point in denying my almost spooky good fortune. I was an out-lier, a freak; to political insiders, my victory proved nothing."

Similarly, Baldwin in 1985 wrote about his own unique position and attitude in the formative years in Greenwich Village: "there were very few black people in the Village in those years, and of that handful, I was decidedly the most improbable." More than twenty years earlier he had written: "To become a Negro man, let alone a Negro artist, one had to make oneself up as one went along . . . My revenge, I decided very early, would be to achieve a power which outlasts kingdoms."

Both men set about establishing their authority by exploring themselves and how they came to make it up as they went along, as much as by exploring the world around them. In Obama's own mixed background he saw America; out of his own success, he saw hope and a new set of values. Out of his own childhood Baldwin produced a number of enduring literary masterpieces and out of his efforts to make sense of his own complex, playful personality and his own unique place in history he produced some of the best essays written in the twentieth century. Reading these essays and Obama's speeches, especially the ones that are filled with inspiration but short on policy, one is struck by the connection between them, two men remaking the world against all the odds in their own likeness, not afraid to ask, when faced with the future of America as represented by its children, using Baldwin's wonderful phrase, questions that are alien to most politicians: "What will happen to all that beauty?"

# Bibliography

Bailey, Blake. *Cheever: A Life* (London, 2009).

Bair, Deirdre. *Samuel Beckett* (London, 1978).

Baldwin, James. *Collected Essays* (New York, 1998).

———. *Early Novels and Stories* (New York, 1998).

———. *The Cross of Redemption: Uncollected Writings* (New York, 2010).

Barry, Sebastian. *Hinterland* (London, 2002).

———. *The Pinkening Boy: New Poems* (Dublin, 2004).

Butler, Marilyn. *Jane Austen and the War of Ideas* (Oxford, 1998).

Carolan, Stuart. *Defender of the Faith* (London, 2004).

Carpenter, Andrew (ed.). *My Uncle John: Edward Stephens's Life of J. M. Synge* (Oxford, 1994).

Carr, Marina. *Plays 2* (London, 2009).

Cheever, John. *Collected Stories and Other Writings* John Cheever (New York, 2009).

———. *Complete Novels* (New York, 2009).

Christiansen, Rupert. *The Complete Books of Aunts* (London, 2006).

Crane, Hart. *Complete Poems and Selected Letters* (New York, 2006).

Cronin, Anthony. *Samuel Beckett: The Last Modernist* (London, 1997).

Di Giovanni, Norman Thomas. *The Lesson of the Master: On Borges and His Work* (New York, 2004).

Doyle, Roddy. *Rory & Ita* (London, 2002).

Ellmann, Richard. *Yeats: The Man and the Masks* (London, 1988).

Fehsenfeld, Martha Dow, and Lois More Overbeck (eds.). *The Letters of Samuel Beckett: Volume I, 1929–1940* (Cambridge, 2009).

Foster, R. F. *W. B. Yeats, A Life I: The Apprentice Mage* (Oxford, 1997).

———. *W. B. Yeats: A Life II: The Arch-Poet* (Oxford, 2003).

Greene, David H. and Edward M. Stephens. *J. M. Synge 1877–1909* (London, 1959).

Grene, Nicholas (ed.). *Interpreting Synge: Essays from the Synge Summer School 1991–2000* (Dublin, 2000).

Hamilton, Hugo. *The Speckled People* (London, 2003).

Iglesias, Jovina, and Silvia Renee Arias. *Los Bioy* (Barcelona, 2003).

Kiberd, Declan. *Synge and the Irish Language* (London, 1979).

Knowlson, James. *Samuel Beckett: Damned to Fame* (London, 1996).

Kurzke, Hermann. *Thomas Mann: Life as a Work of Art* (Princeton, 2002).

Lee, J. J. *Ireland 1912–1985: Politics and Society* (London, 1989).

MacGreevy, Thomas. *Jack B. Yeats* (Dublin, 1945).

Maddox, Brenda. *George's Ghosts* (London, 1999).

Manguel, Alberto. *A History of Reading* (London, 1997).

Manguel, Alberto. *With Borges* (London, 2006).

Mann, Klaus. *Mephisto* (London, 1995).

———. *The Turning Point* (London, 1987).

Mann, Thomas. *Diaries 1918–1939* (New York, 1982).

María Esther Vázquez. *Borges: Esplendor y Derrota* (Barcelona, 1999).

McCormack, W. J. *Fool of the Family: A Life of J. M. Synge* (London, 2000).

Murphy, Gerald. *Take Me Away* (London, 2004).

Murphy, William M. *Family Secrets: William Butler Yeats and his Relatives* (Dublin, 1995).

———. *Prodigal Father: A Biography of John Butler Yeats* (Cornell, 1979).

Naipaul, V. S. *Letters Between a Father and Son* (London, 1999).

———. *The Return of Eva Perón* (London, 1980).

Obama, Barack. *Dreams from My Father* (New York, 2007).

Perry, Ruth. *Novel Relations: The Transformation of Kinship in English Literature and Culture 1748–1818* (Cambridge, 2004).

Saddlemyer, Ann (ed.). *Letters to Molly: John Millington Synge to Maire O'Neill 1906–1909* (Harvard, 1971).

Saddlemyer, Ann. *Becoming George: The Life of Mrs. W. B. Yeats* (Oxford, 2002).

Sampson, Denis. *Brian Moore: The Chameleon Novelist* (London, 1998).

Tanner, Tony. *Jane Austen* (London, 1986).

Theroux, Paul. *The Old Patagonian Express* (London, 1979).

Tomalin, Claire. *Jane Austen: A Biography* (London, 1997).

Trilling, Lionel. *The Moral Obligation to be Intelligent* (Chicago, 2008).

Uveda de Robledo, Epifanía, and Alejandro Vaccaro. *El Señor Borges* (Barcelona, 2005).

Weiss, Andrea. *In the Shadow of the Magic Mountain* (Chicago, 2008).

Williams, Tennessee. *Memoirs* (London, 2007).

———. *Notebooks* (ed. Margaret Bradham Thornton, Yale, 2006).

Williamson, Edwin. *Borges: A Life* (London, 2004).

especially to Mary Kay Wilmers and Daniel Soar at the *London Review of Books*; to Robert Silvers, and the late Barbara Epstein, at the *New York Review of Books*; and to Brendan Barrington at the *Dublin Review*. Also thanks to Angela Rohan for her work as an editor on the manuscript; and to Mary Mount, Ben Brusey and Keith Taylor at Penguin in London; to Nan Graham, Susan Moldow and Paul Whitlatch at Scribner in New York; and to Ellen Seligman at McClelland and Stewart in Toronto; also to my agent Peter Straus, and to Aidan Dunne, Catriona Crowe, Peggy O'Brien, Joseph Bartholomeo, Christina Hunt Mahony, Jonathan Allison, Cora Kaplan, Bill Schwartz, Lilian Chambers and Garry Hynes. I am especially grateful to the late Professor William Murphy for his kindness and encouragement when I worked on the letters of John Butler Yeats, which he had so painstakingly assembled, and which are kept in the Special Collections in the Library of Union College in Schenectady.

# Acknowledgements

"Jane Austen, Henry James and the Death of the Moth( given as the Troy Lecture at the University of Massachu Amherst in December 2010 and a version of it later publi the *London Review of Books*; "W. B. Yeats: New Ways to Ki Father" was first given as a lecture at the Yeats Summer Scl Sligo in 2004 and subsequently published in the *Dublin F* "Willie and George" was first published in the *London Rev Books*; "New Ways to Kill Your Mother: Synge and his Fa was first published in *Synge: A Celebration*, edited by Colm T "Beckett Meets His Afflicted Mother" and "Brian Moore: C Ireland Have I Come, Great Hatred, Little Room" were first lished in the *London Review of Books*; "Sebastian B; Fatherland" was first published in *Out of History: Essays o Writings of Sebastian Barry*, edited by Christina Hunt Mah "Roddy Doyle and Hugo Hamilton: The Dialect of the T was first published in the *New York Review of Books*; "The Mann: New Ways to Spoil Your Children" and "Borges: A Fa in his Shadow" were first published in the *London Review of B* "Hart Crane: Escape from Home" and "Tennessee Williams the Ghost of Rose" were first published in the *New York Revie Books*; "John Cheever: New Ways to Make Your Family's Li Misery" was first published in the *London Review of Books*; "B win and 'the American Confusion'" was given as a lectur( Queen Mary University of London in June 2007 and later p lished in the *Dublin Review*; "Baldwin and Obama: Men With Fathers" was first published in the *New York Review of Books*.

I am grateful to the editors who published these piece

# Index

Abbey Theatre, Dublin 44, 62, 65, 69, 75, 98–9, 114, 163
  J. M. Synge and 97; his plays for 97, 98–9, 106–7
Abramowicz, Maurice 217, 226
Aldington, Richard 72, 116
Alfonsín, Raúl 242, 243
Allgood, Molly 105, 106, 109
  J. M. Synge and 105, 106, 107–8, 109–10; correspondence with 80–81, 98–9, 105, 106, 108–9; Ann Saddlemyer: *Letters to Molly*, ed. by 80–81
André Deutsch (publisher) 138, 144
Astete, Elsa (wife (I) of Juan Luis Borges) 227, 228, 230–31
Athill, Diana 138, 143, 144
Auden, W. H. 197, 202
  as Erika Mann's husband (II) 196, 197, 201, 211
Austen, Jane 2–12, 14–15, 16
  as an aunt 4, 16
  on aunts 4, 14–16; in *Mansfield Park* 6–12, 15; in *Pride and Prejudice* 4–6, 12, 13, 16
  Marilyn Butler on 6
  on families 9–10, 11; in *Mansfield Park* 9–10
  her family 3, 4–5, 6
  Henry James on 14
  *Mansfield Park* 6–12, 17; Tony Tanner on 7, 8; Claire Tomalin on 7, 8; Lionel Trilling on 7–8, 11, 25
  on mothers/motherhood: in *Mansfield Park* 10–11, 16; in *Pride and Prejudice* 4, 9, 16
  *Pride and Prejudice* 3, 4–6, 9, 12, 13, 16, 23

Bailey, Blake, on John Cheever 280, 283, 286, 287–8, 289, 291, 293, 294
Bair, Deirdre, on Samuel Beckett 127, 128
Baldwin, James 296–315, 317–18, 327–8
  on American novelists 299–303
  *Another Country* 296–7, 298, 304, 324
  on boxing 305–6
  character 297, 307
  "Color and American Civilization" 310
  "Death of a Prophet" 303–5
  "Down at the Cross" 319
  on fathers 304–5, 316–17
  *Giovanni's Room* 311, 324
  *Go Tell It on the Mountain* 299, 304, 319, 321
  *Going to Meet the Man* 299, 303
  on Maxim Gorky 302, 305
  as homosexual 305–6
  on Henry James 297, 301, 307
  "Mass Culture and the Creative Artist" 307–8
  *Nobody Knows My Name* 323–4
  *Notes of a Native Son* 297, 316
  "Notes of a Native Son" (essay) 318
  "The Outing" 299
  in Paris 322, 323–5
  "Previous Condition" 303
  on prison/prisoners 313–15
  prose style 297–9, 311
  on race 306–7, 308–15, 318, 323, 325, 326–7
  religious beliefs 317, 319–20, 321, 322
  "The Rockpile" 299
  on Robert Louis Stevenson 305
  William Styron and 312–13, 324–5
  "The White Problem" 309
Banville, John 149, 172

Barry, Sebastian 156–65
  on fathers/fatherhood, in *Hinterland*
    157–65
  on Irish political life, in *Hinterland* 157, 158,
    159, 161, 162–5; Jocelyn Clarke on 163–4
  *The Pinkening Boy* 160
  "The Trousers" 160–6 1, 163
Beckett, Cissie *see* Sinclair, Cissie
Beckett, Frank (brother of Samuel
    Beckett) 113, 123, 124, 125, 130
Beckett, May (mother of Samuel Beckett)
    113, 121, 123
  mother/son relationship with Samuel
    Beckett 123–5, 130
Beckett, Samuel
  *All That Fall* 180
  art/artists, interest in 111, 112, 115, 121–3
  Deirdre Bair on 127, 128
  character 112, 119–22, 126
  *Company* 118
  his correspondence 111–35; *see also*
    individual correspondents
  Anthony Cronin on 126
  Suzanne Deschevaux-Dumesnil and
    132–3
  "Ding-Dong" 122
  *Dream of Fair to Middling Women* 132
  his drinking 123
  *Endgame* 125
  in France 123, 133; in Second World War
    133; in Paris 117, 124, 130, 131, 132;
    stabbing attack on, 1938 124, 132; as a
    teacher 117
  in Germany 121, 122–3; in Hamburg
    120, 123
  health 120, 124, 127; stabbing of, in
    Paris, 1928 124, 132; in psychoanalysis
    123–4
  on Ireland 117–18
  on James Joyce 131–2; work on proofs
    of *Finnegans Wake* 131
  James Knowlson on 127, 128, 130
  "Love and Lethe" 122
  Thomas MacGreevy and 111, 115, 116;
    correspondence with 111, 113, 116,
    118–19, 121–5, 127–9, 131–2, 133
  *More Pricks than Kicks* 122, 125, 129

  mother/son relationship with May
    Beckett 123–5, 130
  *Murphy* 114, 120
  on Proust 116, 119, 120
  his publishers 114, 119, 120
  religious beliefs 114–15, 129–30
  Sinclair/Gogarty libel action and 129–30
  "The Smeraldina's Billet Doux" 126–8
  *Whoroscope* 129
  as a writer 114–15, 121, 127–8, 130–31; on
    his writing difficulties 119–21
  Jack Yeats and 111, 112–13, 114, 115
Beckett, William Frank (father of Samuel
    Beckett) 117, 118, 125
  death 118–19, 123
Beckett family 125, 127
Bedford, Sybille 201, 205, 206
Bell, Vanessa 33, 41
Bellow, Saul, John Cheever and 288, 289
Bermann Fischer (publisher) 198
Best, Richard 101
Bioy Casares, Adolfo 222, 224, 227, 228,
    229–30, 232–3
  *Los Bioy*, his maid's book on 228–30
  *Destiempo*, journal published with Jorge
    Luis Borges 234
  political beliefs 238, 242
  death 229
Bioy Casares, Silvina (née Ocampo) 227,
    228–9, 232–3
Bolger, Ita *see* Doyle, Ita
Bolger, Jim (grandfather of Roddy Doyle)
    166, 167, 168
Bolger, Una 166, 167
Borges, Fanny (née Haslam) (grandmother
    of Jorge Luis Borges) 215, 216, 218
Borges, Jorge Guillermo (father of Jorge
    Luis Borges) 212–13
  *El Caudillo* 213–14
  father/son relationship with Jorge Luis
    Borges 213, 214, 224, 225, 244–5
  death 212, 213, 214, 223–4
Borges, Jorge Luis (Georgie) 212–45
  "The Argentine Writer and Tradition"
    220
  Elsa Astete, marriage (I) to 227, 228,
    230–31

"Autobiographical Essay" 223, 235, 238
his blindness 226, 227, 239–40
"The Blue Sky . . ." 218
"Borges and I" 214
Estela Canto on: *Borges a contraluz* 226
character 214, 216, 217, 227
"The Circular Ruins" 223
*The Confederates* 243, 244
"The Congress" 213–14
correspondence 217, 218, 226
"Death and the Compass" 221
*Destiempo*, journal published with Bioy
Casares 234
Norman Thomas di Giovanni on: *The
Lesson of the Master* . . . 238
father/son relationship with Jorge
Guillermo Borges 213, 214, 224, 225,
244–5
*The Garden of Forking Paths* 223
on gaucho (Argentinian) literature
219–21
Kafka, translations of 223–4
Maria Kodama and 229, 231–2, 243–4;
proxy marriage (II) to 243
as a librarian 222–3, 224, 235
"The Library of Babel" 223
literature: lectures on 236–7; love of
216, 217, 220, 222, 233
Lorca and 218, 241
"The Lottery in Babylon" 223
Alberto Manguel on 239–40
mother/son relationship with Leonor
Borges 226, 227, 231
"The Nothingness of Personality" 218
"The Other" 225
"Our Inabilities" 233–4
"Pierre Menard, Author of Don
Quixote" 213, 214, 225
political beliefs 233–43, 244
prose style 214, 217, 233, 236
*El Señor Borges*, his maid's book 228–9,
230, 232
in Spain 217; Madrid 217–18, 241
"A Survey of the Works of Herbert
Quain" 223
in Switzerland 216, 217; Geneva 232–3,
243–5

Paul Theroux on, in *The Old Patagonian
Express* 240
"Things" 215
"Tlön, Uqbar, Orbis Tertius" 223
*A Universal History of Infancy* 222
Paul Valéry: *Introduction à la poétique*,
review of 214
María Esther Vázquez on: *Borges:
Esplendor y Derrota* 224–6
"The Web" 243
his will 232, 244
Edwin Williamson on 213, 214, 216, 218,
224, 226, 227, 232, 235, 236, 238, 244
James Woodall on 225, 226
women, relationships with 224–7; in
brothels 224–6
death 230, 243–4
Borges, Leonor (mother of Jorge Luis
Borges) 212–13, 214, 215, 216, 222, 230, 236
Argentinian heritage 214–15
mother/son relationship with Jorge
Luis Borges 226, 227, 231
death 232
Borges, Norah (sister of Jorge Luis Borges)
216, 226, 232, 236, 244
Borges family 214–15, 244
Borgese, Giuseppe Antonio 185
Bowles, Paul and Jane 202
Brecht, Bertolt 188
Brennan, Robert 166, 167, 171
Butler, Marilyn, on Jane Austen 6

Cain, James M., James Baldwin on 302–3
Caldwell, Erskine: *The Sure Hand of God*,
James Baldwin on 302
Calthrop, Rosie 100–101, 102
Canto, Estela, on Jorge Luis Borges: *Borges
a contraluz* 226
Carolan, Stuart: *Defender of the Faith* 156–7
Carpenter, Andrew: *My Uncle John* 80
Carr, Marina: *On Raftery's Hill* 156, 157, 158–9
Cheever, Ben (son of John Cheever) 286,
287–8, 294
Cheever, Federico (son of John Cheever)
277–8, 286, 294
father/son relationship with John
Cheever 288–9

# Index

Cheever, Fred (brother of John Cheever) 278, 280–81
Cheever, John 276–95
    Blake Bailey on 280, 283, 286, 287–8, 289, 291, 293, 294
    Saul Bellow and 288, 289
    character 276–7, 278, 281; as a snob 279, 281, 282, 283
    "The Chimera" 287
    correspondence 285, 288, 290
    "The Country Husband" 278
    diaries 276–9, 282, 284–6, 288, 293–5
    his drinking 278, 285–6, 288, 292, 294
    "An Educated American Woman" 289
    *Falconer* 292–3
    on families 282–3
    as a father 286–7, 288–9
    as homosexual 277, 279, 281–2, 283, 284–5, 290–95
    "The National Pastime" 281
    "The Ocean" 289
    his Pulitzer Prize 292
    in Second World War in Signal Corps 283–4
    sexual life 276–7; *see also* as homosexual *above*
    in Sing Sing as a teacher 292–3
    *Stories* 292
    "The Swimmer" 276, 277, 278
    on John Updike 288
    *The Wapshot Chronicles* 280, 282
    *The Wapshot Scandal* 282
    death 294
Cheever, Mary (wife of John Cheever) 277, 278, 283–4, 286, 287, 289, 291, 295
Cheever, Susan (daughter of John Cheever) 279, 286, 287
    *Home before Dark* 287, 291–2, 294
Christiansen, Rupert: *The Complete Book of Aunts* 25
Clarke, Austin 120, 168
Clarke, Jocelyn 163–4
Coall, Talbot 84
Collins, Michael 79
Cowley, Peggy and Malcolm 260, 261, 283
Craig, George 126

Crane, [Harold] Hart 247–61, 283
    "At Melville's Tomb" 248–50
    *The Bridge* 252, 253, 255–6, 257–9, 260
    "The Broken Tower" 260
    "C33" 250–51
    character 251, 255, 261
    correspondence 247, 248, 253–4, 255–8, 260–61
    his drinking 252, 253, 260, 261
    T. S. Eliot and 250, 254–5
    financial position 252, 257, 259, 260
    "For the Marriage of Faustus and Helen" 254
    "General Aims and Theories" 247
    as homosexual 252, 256, 260
    Otto Kahn as his patron 252, 257, 259
    Harriet Monroe on 248–50
    Emil Opffer, homosexual affair with 256
    as a poet 247–8, 250, 252, 253–4, 255
    suicide attempt 250
    Allen Tate and 252, 254, 257
    "To Brooklyn Bridge" 258–9
    as a traveller 252–3, 260, 261
    *White Buildings* 252
    death by suicide 248, 253, 261
Crane family 247, 250, 251–2, 253, 256–7, 259, 260–61
Cronin, Anthony, on Samuel Beckett 126

de Torre, Guillermo 225
de Valera, Eamon 73, 75, 166, 168
Dennis, Patrick: *Genius* 296
Deschevaux-Dumesnil, Suzanne 132–3
di Giovanni, Norman Thomas 227–8
    on Jorge Luis Borges: *The Lesson of the Master . . .* 228
Didion, Joan 148
Doherty, Mark: *Trad* 157
Doyle, Arthur Conan, on the occult 54–5
Doyle, Gretta 166
Doyle, Ita (née Bolger) (mother of Roddy Doyle) 166–7, 168, 169–70, 173–4
Doyle, Roddy 166–74, 178, 180–81
    *The Commitments* 171
    on Dublin 171–2; in *A Star Called Henry* 172

on the Irish, in *Rory & Ita* 180–81
*Paddy Clarke Ha Ha Ha* 171
*Rory & Ita* ed. by 166–7, 168, 169–70, 172, 180–81
*The Snapper* 171
*The Van* 171
on the Virgin Mary 170
*The Woman Who Walked into Doors* 171
*Your Granny's a Hunger Striker* (unpublished) 170–71
Doyle, Rory (father of Roddy Doyle) 167, 168, 169–70, 171, 173–4, 178
on Fianna Fáil 172–3
Doyle, Seamus 166, 167, 168
Drury, Allen: *A Shade of Difference* 296
Duffy, Gavan 168
Dunne, John Gregory 148

Eisenstein, Sergei 121
Eliot, George 12–13, 27
Eliot, T. S. 116
Hart Crane and 250, 254–5
*The Waste Land* 254
Ellmann, Richard
Iseult Gonne and 73
George Yeats and 59, 60, 74, 76
*Yeats: The Man and the Masks* 33–4, 52

Foster, Roy
"Good Behaviour . . ." 92
on J. M. Synge 92, 97
on W. B. Yeats 53–4, 92, 97
Frank, Waldo, Hart Crane and 252; correspondence with 254, 256, 258–9
Friel, Brian 150, 151
on colonialism, in *Translations* 151
*Faith Healer* 150–51
Brian Moore and 150; correspondence with 147, 150–51; *The Lonely Passion of Judith Hearne*, screenplay for 150, 151

Glück, Louise: *The Wild Iris* 246
Gogarty, Oliver St. John
*As I Was Going Down Sackville Street* 129
Harry Sinclair's libel action against 128–30

Gogarty, Mrs. Oliver St. John 65, 73
Gonne, Iseult 63
Richard Ellmann and 73
Francis Stuart, marriage to 70
George Yeats and 62–3
W. B, Yeats and 52, 56, 57, 58, 60, 62, 63, 65–6, 70, 73
Gonne, Maud 52
imprisonment 63; release from 63–4
mental state 64
Ann Saddlemyer on 63, 64
J. M. Synge and 94
George Yeats and 57, 59–60, 63–4
W. B. Yeats and 52, 56, 57, 59–60, 62, 63–4, 65–6; at his death 75
Gorky, Maxim, James Baldwin on 302, 305
Greene, David, on J. M. Synge 80
Greene, Graham, Brian Moore and 153
Gregory, Augusta, Lady 92
character 64–5
*Cuchulain of Muirthemne*, review by J. M. Synge 102–3
health 71
*Home Ruin* (published anonymously) 88
Irish (Gaelic) language, interest in 88
as an Irish nationalist 88–9
J. M. Synge and 92, 96–7, 98–9, 102, 103, 105
George Yeats and 57, 64–5, 66
W. B. Yeats and 36, 39, 42, 44, 62, 64, 65, 71, 98–9; correspondence with 52–3, 56, 59, 67, 109
Grene, Nicholas, on J. M. Synge 81, 84, 88, 90, 92
Gründgens, Gustaf
Klaus Mann and 186, 190, 207–9
Klaus Mann on, in *Mephisto* 199

Hamilton, Hugo 174, 175
*Dublin Where the Palm Trees Grow* 174
on his father, in *The Speckled People* 174, 175, 181–2
on Irish (Gaelic) language 175, 176, 179, 181–2
"Nazi Christmas" 174–5
Hauptmann, Gerhart 72

Haughey, Charles J. 157, 158, 159, 161, 162–5
depicted in Sebastian Barry: *The Hinterland* 163–4
Heaney, Seamus 150
Hernández, José
Jorge Luis Borges on 220
*El Gaucho Martín Fierro* 219
Higgins, Aidan: *Langrishe, Go Down* 136
Hollander, John 228
Hopkins, Gerard Manley 259–60
Hyde-Lees, George *see* Yeats, George

James, Alice (sister of Henry James) 36, 54, 262–3
brother/sister relationship with Henry James 262–4
Jean Strouse on 262
James, Henry
on aunts 14–15; in *The Ambassadors* 22–3; in *The Golden Bowl* 23–4; in *The Portrait of a Lady* 15, 18, 22; in *The Turn of the Screw* 23; in *Washington Square* 15, 17–18; in *The Wings of the Dove* 24–5
on Jane Austen 14
autobiography 37, 39
James Baldwin on 297, 301, 307
brother/sister relationship with Alice James 262–4
character 14, 15–16, 262, 263
correspondence 39, 40, 262, 307
on families 54; in *The Wings of the Dove* 1
father/son relationship with Henry James (Senior) 35, 36, 38, 40
*The Golden Bowl* 23–4; William James on 39
on marriage, in *The Portrait of a Lady* 28–9
on mothers/motherhood: in *The Spoils of Poynton* 16; in *What Maisie Knew* 16
notebooks 263, 266
*The Portrait of a Lady* 15, 18–22, 28–9, 38
*The Princess Casamassima* 262
prose style 16, 40, 297
Jean Strouse on 262
*The Turn of the Screw* 23, 35, 262–3
Edith Wharton and 36–7

John Butler Yeats on 37
W. B. Yeats and 36–7
James, Henry (Senior) (father of Henry James) 34–5
character 36, 50
father/son relationship with Henry James 35, 36, 38, 40; with William James 36, 212
writings 35–6; collection edited by William James 38, 40
death 38
James, William (brother of Henry James)
as an artist 36, 40
father/son relationship with Henry James (Senior) 36, 212; as editor of his father's work 38, 40
on *The Golden Bowl* 39
Henry James, correspondence with 39, 40
*Pragmatism* 55
Jeffares, Norman: *Selected Poems of W. B. Yeats* 59
Joyce, James ("Shem") 66–7, 111, 112, 125, 131
on aunts, in *A Portrait of the Artist . . .* 13–14
Samuel Beckett on 131–2
"Clay" 134
"The Dead" 176
*The Dubliners* 134
*Finnegans Wake*, Samuel Beckett's work on proofs of 131
on Irish (Gaelic) language, in *A Portrait of the Artist . . .* 179–80
Thomas MacGreevy and 116
*A Portrait of the Artist . . .* 13–14, 176, 179–80
*Ulysses* 172, 220, 252
Joyce, Lucia 132
Joyce, Nora 116, 132

Kafka, Franz, Jorge Luis Borges' translations of 223–4
Kahn, Otto, as Hart Crane's patron 259
Kaun, Axel, Samuel Beckett, correspondence with 130–31
Keane, John B: *The Field* 145–6

Kelly, Brigit Pegeen: *Song* 246
Kiberd, Declan: *Synge and the Irish
    Language* 93–4
Knowlson, James, on Samuel Beckett 127,
    128, 130
Kodama, Maria
    Jorge Luis Borges and 229, 231–2, 243–4;
    proxy marriage to 243
Kurzke, Hermann, on Thomas Mann 196

Lee, J. J., on Irish (Gaelic) language 176–7,
    180, 181
Lee, Li-Young: "Epistle" 246
Lorca, Federico García 218–19, 241

McGahern, John 149
    *The Barracks* 136
    *Getting Through*, review by Brian Moore
        145
    *The Leavetaking* 146
    *The Pornographer* 146
MacGreevy, Thomas 69–71, 72, 76, 115–17
    Samuel Beckett and 111, 115, 116;
        correspondence with 111, 113, 116,
        118–19, 121–5, 127–9, 131–2, 133
    T. S. Eliot and 116
    "Exile" 116
    as homosexual 69, 116–17
    James Joyce and 116
    Jack Yeats, his essay on 111, 113, 116;
        their correspondence 111–13
MacKaye, Percy 43, 49
MacNeice, Louis: *Springboard: Poems
    1941–1944* 78
Maddox, Brenda, on *George Yeats: George's
    Ghosts* 55, 66, 67, 72
Manguel, Alberto, on Jorge Luis Borges, in
    *A History of Reading* and *With Borges*
    239–40
Mann, Elisabeth (daughter of Thomas
    Mann) 185, 196, 211
    Giuseppe Antonio Borgese, marriage to
        185
    father/daughter relationship with
        Thomas Mann 186
    on Erika Mann 198–9, 208
    death 211

Mann, Erika (daughter of Thomas Mann)
    185, 191–2
    in America 186, 191, 201, 202, 210; FBI
        investigation of 205, 210; lecture
        tours in 201
    W. H. Auden, marriage (II) to 196, 197,
        201, 211
    at the BBC 203
    Sybille Bedford on 201, 206
Mann, Erika
    character 193–4, 206
    correspondence 201
    father/daughter relationship with
        Thomas Mann 193–4, 198–9, 205, 208,
        210–11
    German citizenship, loss of 196–7
    Gustaf Gründgens and 190; marriage
        (I) to 186, 191
    as a lesbian 185, 190
    Elisabeth Mann on 198–9, 208
    Katia Mann and 199
    Klaus Mann, possible incest with 186,
        191, 193, 204–5, 211
    *The Peppermill*, her cabaret: in Munich
        192, 194; New York 201; Zurich 198
    political beliefs 192, 193, 202
    in post-war Germany 206–7; at
        Nüremberg Trials 207
    *School for Barbarians* 202
    in Switzerland 193, 198, 210–11
    Bruno Walter and 185
    Pamela Wedekind and 190
    as a writer 187–8
    death 211
Mann, Golo (son of Thomas Mann) 185,
    186, 193, 195
    on his family 187, 200
    as homosexual 185
    death 211
Mann, Heinrich (brother of Thomas
    Mann) 33, 185, 196, 197, 201, 206
    Klaus Mann on 203–4
    Thomas Mann and 194–6, 210
Mann, Katia (née Pringsheim) (wife of
    Thomas Mann) 185, 186, 200
    on her children 210–11
    correspondence 193

Mann, Katia – *cont.*
  Erika Mann and 199
  mother/son relationship with Klaus
    Mann 209
  Klaus Pringsheim, possible incest with
    185–6
  death 211
Mann, Klaus ("Eissi") (son of Thomas
    Mann) 185, 191–2
  in America 186, 191, 201, 203, 208, 209;
    FBI investigation of 204–5; in U.S.
    Army 205
  *Anja and Esther* 190–91
  W. H. Auden and 202
  autobiography: *The Turning Point*
    203–4, 207, 208
  Sybille Bedford on 205
  Bertolt Brecht on 188
  character 188, 193, 198, 207
  correspondence 205–6
  diaries 189–90, 194, 198, 202, 209
  as a drug addict 198, 201
  father/son relationship with Thomas
    Mann 186, 187–8, 197–8, 199, 201, 202,
    203–4, 205–6, 210; Klaus Mann on, in
    *Mephisto* 200–201
  Gustaf Gründgens and 186, 190, 207–9;
    Klaus Mann on, in *Mephisto* 199
  as homosexual 185, 186, 190, 204–5, 208
  Erika Mann, possible incest with 186,
    191, 193, 204–5, 211
  on Heinrich Mann 203–4
  *Mephisto* 199–200, 207, 208, 209–10
  mother/son relationship with Katia
    Mann 209
  political beliefs 194
  in post-war Germany 205–6, 207–8
  prose style 187–8, 190–91, 199, 200
  *Die Sammlung*, journal published by
    194, 196, 197–8, 199
  *The Siblings* 186
  in Switzerland 201
  *The Volcano* 186
  death by suicide 185, 189–90, 198, 209–10
Mann, Thomas 33, 185–211
  in America as an exile 187, 188–9, 193,
    201–3

*Buddenbrooks* 41, 188, 189
  character 188, 189
  correspondence 197, 198, 202, 211
  death, obsession with 188, 189
  *Death in Venice* 189
  diaries 186, 187, 193
  *Doctor Faustus* 189, 201, 208
  as a father 185, 186, 187, 188
  father/daughter relationship; with
    Elisabeth Mann 186; with Erika
    Mann 193–4, 198–9, 205, 208, 210–11
  father/son relationship with Klaus
    Mann 186, 187–8, 197–8, 199, 201, 202,
    203–4, 205–6, 210; Klaus Mann on, in
    *Mephisto* 200–201
  as a German 187, 188, 189, 194–7, 204;
    stripped of his German citizenship
    199
  in Hitler's Germany 123, 199
  as homosexual 185, 188–9
  on incest 185–6; in *The Blood of the
    Walsungs* 186; in *Disorder and Early
    Sorrow* 186; in *The Holy Sinner* 186; in
    *Joseph and His Brothers* 186
  *Joseph and His Brothers* 186, 193
  Hermann Kurzke on 196
  *Lotte in Weimer* 202
  *The Magic Mountain* 54, 187, 188, 189, 195
  Heinrich Mann and 194–6, 210
  Michael Marr on, in *Bluebeard's Chamber*
    189
  his Nobel Prize 187
  his publisher 198
  *Reflections of a Nonpolitical Man* 195
  in Switzerland 193, 198, 201, 210–11
  death 210
Mann family 185, 210–11
  gerontophilia among 185
  incest among 185–6
  Jewish background 191, 192
  suicide among 185, 209, 211
  Andrea Weiss on: *In the Shadow of the
    Magic Mountain* 185–6, 191, 207
Manning, Mary, Samuel Beckett, corre-
    spondence with 120, 122
Marr, Michael, on Thomas Mann, in
    *Bluebeard's Chamber* 189

Matheson, Cherrie, J. M. Synge and 91, 96,
101, 103
Monroe, Harriet, on Hart Crane 248–50
Moore, Dr. and Mrs. (parents of Brian
Moore) 138–9, 140–41, 143
father/son relationship with Brian
Moore 139, 140–41
Moore, Brian 134–55
*An Answer from Limbo* 136–8, 143–4, 148,
149; Brian Moore on 148
Diana Athill and 143, 144; correspond-
ence with 138
*Black Robe* 149–50, 151–3
in Canada 134, 135, 142–3, 152–3
*Catholics* 149; his opinion of 149–50
character 139, 143, 145, 150, 154
on colonialism, in *Black Robe* 151–3
*The Colour of Blood* 141, 153
correspondence 125, 138, 143, 147, 149
*The Emperor of Ice-Cream* 136–8, 139–41,
144, 146
father/son relationship with Dr. Moore
139, 140–41
*The Feast of Lupercal* 136–8, 146
Brian Friel and 150; correspondence
with 147, 150–51; *The Lonely Passion
. . .*, screenplay for 150, 151
*The Great Victorian Collection* 150
Graham Greene and 153
*I Am Mary Dunne* 146–7, 150
*Lies of Silence* 148
*The Lonely Passion of Judith Hearne*
134–6, 138, 142–3, 146, 149, 150, 151;
Brian Friel's screenplay for 150
*The Luck of Ginger Coffey* 136–8
John McGahern: *Getting Through*,
review of 145
on men, in *The Lonely Passion . . .* 134–5
on mothers/motherhood, in *An Answer
from Limbo* 148, 149
*No Other Life* 154
novels 144–5, 146, 153; pseudonymous
thrillers 142; *see also* individual titles
political beliefs 139–40
prose style 143, 146, 148, 154
his publisher 135, 138, 144
religion, rejection of 135, 139

Jean Russell and 144–50, 164
Denis Sampson on 138, 139, 145, 149–50,
153
in Second World War 141–2
on Second World War, in *The Emperor
of Ice-Cream* 140–41
*The Statement* 141
*The Temptation of Eileen Hughes* 147
*Torn Curtain*, screenplay for 144
on women: in *I Am Mary Dunne* 146–7,
150; *The Lonely Passion . . .* 134–6; *The
Doctor's Wife* 147–8
Moore, Jacqueline (Jackie) (née Sorois)
(wife of Brian Moore) 143–4
Frank Russell, affair with 144
Moore, Michael (son of Brian Moore) 142,
144
Morrell, Ottoline 68
Murphy, Gerald: *Take Me Away* 157
Murphy, Tom: *A Whistle in the Dark*
145–6
Murphy, William M. 38, 66

Naipaul, Seepersad 212
*Gurudeva and Other Indian Tales* 212
Naipaul, V. S (Vidia) 212, 239

O'Casey, Sean 65, 92, 114
Obama, Barack 317–18, 327–8
*The Audacity of Hope* 326
*Dreams from My Father* 316, 317, 320,
325–6, 327
on his father 316–17, 325
Kenya and 322–3, 325–6
on race 318–19, 321, 325–6
religious beliefs 317, 320–22
Ocampo, Silvina *see* Bioy Casares, Silvina
Ocampo, Victoria 221, 237

Pearse, Patrick 168, 170
Perón, Juan 235–9
Perugino: *Pietá*, Samuel Beckett on 121–2,
123
Pound, Dorothy (née Shakespear) 55, 56,
72
George Yeats, correspondence with
65

Pound, Ezra 53, 54, 63, 67, 72
  George Yeats and 76–7
Poussin, Nicolas 116, 122
Pringsheim, Alfred 186, 200
Pringsheim, Klaus 185–6
Proust, Marcel, Samuel Beckett on 116,
  119, 120

Quinn, John 37, 41
  correspondence 53, 57–8, 63, 64, 66, 67–81
  on John Butler Yeats 37–8
  W. B. Yeats and 49; their correspondence 66, 67–81

Reid, Alastair 228
Robinson, Lennox 69, 70, 72, 74, 76
Russell, Frank and Jean 144–5, 150, 154

Saddlemyer, Ann
  on Maud Gonne 63, 64
  *Letters to Molly* 80–81
  on George Yeats 59, 69, 70, 74, 75
  on W. B. Yeats 54, 58, 65, 71
Sampson, Denis, on Brian Moore 138, 139,
  145, 149–50, 153
Sassoon, Siegfried 72
Shakespear, Olivia 56, 60, 72, 73, 74
Sinclair, Boss (William) 125, 126, 127, 128
Sinclair, Cissie (née Beckett) (aunt of
  Samuel Beckett) 115, 125–6, 127–8
Sinclair, Harry 128–30
Spoto, Donald, on Tennessee Williams
  265, 273
Stephens, Annie (née Synge) (sister of J. M.
  Synge, mother of Edward Stephens)
  79, 84
Stephens, Edward (nephew of J. M. Synge)
  79, 80, 84, 100
  J. M. Synge, his biography of 79–80, 81,
  82, 83, 89, 91, 96, 100, 103, 104, 105; on
  his death 109–10; on Kathleen Synge
  82, 83, 95
  J. M. Synge's papers, as custodian of 79,
  80
  death 79, 80
Stephens, Lilo (wife of Edward Stephens)
  78–9

J. M. Synge: *My Wallet of Photographs*
  ed. by 79
J. M. Synge's papers, as custodian of
  80–81
Strouse, Jean, on Henry and Alice James 262
Styron, William, James Baldwin and 312–13
Synge, Annie *see* Stephens, Annie
Synge, Jane (sister of John Hatch Synge)
  (Aunt Jane) 84, 87, 88
Synge, John Hatch (father of J. M. Synge)
  81, 82, 87; death 82
Synge, J. M. (John Millington) 44, 45, 49,
  78–110
  birth 82
  Abbey Theatre, Dublin and 97; his
  plays for 97, 98–9, 106–7
  Molly Allgood and 105, 107–8, 109–10;
  correspondence with 80–81, 98–9,
  105, 106, 108–9; purchased by Edward
  Stephens 81; Ann Saddlemyer:
  *Letters to Molly* ed. by 80–81
  in Aran Islands 96–7, 99, 100, 101, 103,
  109; autobiographical essay 83, 85
  Rosie Calthrop and 100–101, 102
  Andrew Carpenter on: *My Uncle John* 80
  character 79–80, 81, 85, 92, 97–8, 99–100
  on County Wicklow 89–90, 92
  *Deirdre* 108
  Roy Foster on 92, 97
  Maud Gonne and 94
  David Greene on 80
  Nicholas Grene on 81, 84, 88, 90, 92
  Lady Gregory and 92, 96–7, 98–9, 102,
  103, 105; his review of her *Cuchulain
  of Muirthemne* 102–3
  his health 82, 85, 94–5, 102, 104, 105–6,
  107, 108
  *In the Shadow of the Glen* 92, 97, 103, 104;
  reviews of 104, 105, 109
  as an Irish nationalist 86, 87, 88–90, 93,
  94
  Declan Kiberd on: *Synge and the Irish
  Language* 93–4
  in Koblenz 90, 91, 108
  W. J. McCormack on: *Fool of the Family*
  87, 89
  Cherrie Matheson and 91, 96, 101, 103

mother/son relationship with Kathleen
Synge 84, 85–6, 87, 91, 94–5, 100–101,
102, 104, 105–6, 107–8
as a musician 86, 90
*My Wallet of Photographs* ed. Lilo
Stephens 79
papers/mss 79, 80, 81; deposited in
Trinity College, Dublin 81
in Paris 91, 93, 94, 95, 96, 100, 102, 103–4
*The Playboy of the Western World* 91, 97,
98–9, 101, 106; reviews of 107
as a playwright 79, 90, 98–9; see also
individual plays
religion, his rejection of 84, 85, 87
*Riders to the Sea* 97, 101, 103; reviews of
104–5
Edward Stephens's biography of 79–80,
81, 82, 83, 89, 91, 95, 96, 100, 103, 104,
105, 109–10
Samuel Synge on 82
*The Tinker's Wedding* 97, 103
at Trinity College, Dublin 85, 87–8
*The Well of Saints* 97, 105
*When the Moon Has Set* 102
W. B. Yeats and 92–4, 97–9, 103
death, from Hodgkin's disease 79, 94,
108–10; Lady Gregory on 98; Edward
Stephens on 109–10
Synge, Kathleen (née Traill) (mother of
J. M. Synge) 81, 82, 83–4, 107
Molly Allgood and 106
Synge, Kathleen
mother/son relationship with J. M.
Synge 84, 85–6, 87, 91, 94–5, 100–101,
102, 104, 105–6, 107–8
religious beliefs 83, 84, 85, 89, 95, 106
Edward Stephens on 82, 83, 95
Robert Synge, correspondence with
107–8
Samuel Synge, correspondence with
99, 100–101, 102
death 108
Synge, Robert (brother of J. M. Synge) 81,
86–7, 90, 95
on J. M. Synge's death 109
Kathleen Synge, correspondence with
107–8

Synge, Samuel (Sam) (brother of J. M.
Synge) 84
character 87
*Letters to my Daughter* 82
as a medical missionary in China 81, 82,
87
on J. M. Synge 82
Kathleen Synge, correspondence with
99, 100–101, 102
Synge family 78–110
property owned by 81, 82–3, 84
religious views 81, 82, 84; as Plymouth
Brethren 83
J. M. Synge's plays, their attitude to 79,
105

Tate, Allen, Hart Crane and 253, 254, 257
Thornton, Margaret Bradham, Tennessee
Williams's notebooks/diaries ed. by
265–75
Tóibín family 78–9, 166, 167, 173
Trollope, Anthony 25

Updike, John, John Cheever and 288

Valéry, Paul: *Introduction à la poétique*,
review by Jorge Luis Borges 214
Vázquez, Mariá Esther, on Jorge Luis
Borges: *Borges: Esplendor y Derrota*
224–5, 226

Wedekind, Pamela 190, 191
Weiss, Andrea, on the Mann family: *In the
Shadow of the Magic Mountain* 185–6,
191, 207
Wharton, Edith 24, 36–7
Wilbur, Richard 228
Williams, Dakin (brother of Tennessee
Williams) 270, 271, 274
Williams, Edwina (mother of Tennessee
Williams) 267, 270, 271, 273
Williams, Rose (sister of Tennessee
Williams) 270
brother/sister relationship with
Tennessee Williams 263–4, 265,
270–75; their correspondence 264
mental state 270, 271–2, 273, 274

Williams, Tennessee 263–75
  brother/sister relationship with Rose
    Williams 263–5, 270–75; their
    correspondence 264
  character 265–7, 268, 269–70, 275
  correspondence 264, 265, 270, 274
  diaries/notebooks 265–75
  *The Glass Menagerie* 264
  as homosexual 263, 265, 267–9
  *Memoirs* 263, 264, 265
  mental health 273–5
  *The Night of the Iguana* 275
  *Out Cry* 273–4
  Donald Spoto on 265, 273
  *A Streetcar Named Desire* 264–5

Yeats, Anne (daughter of W. B. Yeats) 62,
    63, 64, 66, 68, 71, 72, 74, 77
Yeats, George (née Hyde-Lees) (Mrs. W. B.
    Yeats) 52, 53, 116
  character 52, 55, 57, 62, 64–5, 72–3, 74, 75
  her drinking 69, 74
  Richard Ellmann and 59, 60, 74, 76 her
    family 55–6; her mother 56, 57,
    69–70
  Mrs. Oliver Gogarty, correspondence
    with 73–4
  Iseult Gonne and 62–3
  Maud Gonne and 57, 59–60, 63–4
  Lady Gregory and 57, 64–5, 66
  health 63, 64, 74
  houses/homes 52, 53, 63, 65–6, 73;
    Ballylee tower (Thoor Ballylee)
    66–8, 70–77; decline of 71–2
  intellectual abilities 55, 56
  Thomas MacGreevy and 69–71, 72, 76
  Brenda Maddox on: *George's Ghosts* 54,
    66, 67, 72
  Ottoline Morrell, correspondence with
    68
  the occult, interest in 53, 55–6, 57, 60, 64;
    her fake automatic writing 58–9, 60
  the Pound family and 54, 65; Ezra
    Pound and 76–7
  Lennox Robinson and 69, 70, 72
  Ann Saddlemyer on 59, 69, 70, 74, 75
  J. M. Synge and 92–4, 97–9, 103

John Butler Yeats on 64
  W. B. Yeats, marriage to 52–77; his
    feelings for her 58–60, 71–2, 73; at his
    death and burial 52, 75–6
  death 52, 76, 77
Yeats, Jack Butler (brother of W. B. Yeats)
    33, 36
  as an artist 111, 112; his subjects/style
    113–14
  Samuel Beckett and 111, 112–13, 114, 115
  Thomas MacGreevy's essay on 111, 113,
    116; their correspondence 111–13 as a
    playwright 41, 114
Yeats, John Butler (father of W. B. Yeats)
    34–5, 62
  as an artist 41
  character 34, 36, 41, 50–51
  father/son relationship with W. B. Yeats
    35, 36, 38–9, 40–51
  on Henry James 37
  William M. Murphy on 66
  John Quinn on 37–8
  as a writer 41, 42–8, 49–50
  on George Yeats 64
  W. B. Yeats, correspondence with 35, 37,
    38–40, 41–51, 66
  death 38
Yeats, Lily (sister of W. B. Yeats) 36, 62, 64,
    70
Yeats, Lolly (sister of W. B. Yeats) 62, 70
Yeats, Michael (son of W. B. Yeats) 62, 67,
    68, 72, 74
Yeats, W. B. (William Butler)
  Abbey Theatre, Dublin and 97
  American tour, 1920 67
  biographies of 76; see also individual
    authors
  character 41, 50–51, 53–4
  *The Countess Cathleen* 42
  Crazy Jane poems 73
  Richard Ellmann on: *Yeats: The Man and
    the Masks* 33–4, 52
  father/son relationship with John
    Butler Yeats 35, 36, 38–9, 40–51
  Roy Foster on 53–4, 92, 97
  "Four Years" (autobiographical essay)
    39, 52

## About the Author

Colm Tóibín is the author of six novels, including *The Master* and *Brooklyn*, and two volumes of short stories. His non-fiction includes *Lady Gregory's Toothbrush* and *Love in a Dark Time: Gay Lives from Wilde to Almodóvar*. He is a contributing editor at the *London Review of Books* and has been visiting writer at Stanford, Princeton, the University of Texas at Austin and Manchester University. He is currently Mellon Professor in the Humanities in the Department of English and Comparative Literature at Columbia University.

in France 75, 93, 94
"The Gift of Harun Al-Rashid" 61–2
Iseult Gonne and 52, 56, 57, 58, 60, 62, 63, 65–6, 70, 73
Maud Gonne and 52, 56, 57, 59–60, 62, 63–4, 65–6; at his death 75
Lady Gregory and 36, 39, 42, 44, 62, 64, 65, 71, 98–9; correspondence with 52–3, 56, 59, 67, 109
health 56, 58, 59, 60, 72, 73–4
*The Hour Glass* 36
houses/homes 52, 53, 63, 65–6, 73; Ballylee tower (Thoor Ballylee) 66–8, 70–77; decline of 71–2
George Hyde-Lees, marriage to 52–77; his feelings for her 58–60, 71–2, 73; his death and burial and 52, 75–6
Henry James and 36–7
Virginia Moore on: *The Unicorn . . .* 58–9
his Nobel Prize 68

the occult, interest in 36, 55–6, 59, 60–61
"Owen Aherne and His Dancers" 58
his papers/letters 52, 53
as a playwright 41–2, 44, 46–7, 49–50; *see also* individual plays
*The Pot of Broth* 98
John Quinn and 49; correspondence with 66, 67–8
religious beliefs 114
Ann Saddlemyer on 54, 58, 65, 71
"The Second Coming" 35
*Selected Poems . . .* ed. Norman Jeffares 59
sexual activities 56, 73–5; his vasectomy 73
Olivia Shakespear and 56, 60, 72, 73
J. M. Synge and 92–4, 97–9, 103
*The Tower* 71
*A Vision* 53, 61
John Butler Yeats, correspondence with 35, 37, 38–40, 41–51, 66
death/burial 52, 72, 75–6